Notable Women of Arkansas

Notable Women of Arkansas

From Hillary to Hattie, 100 Names to Know

Nancy Hendricks

BUTLER CENTER BOOKS

BUTLER CENTER BOOKS

The Butler Center for Arkansas Studies
Central Arkansas Library System
100 Rock Street
Little Rock, Arkansas 72201

www.butlercenter.org

First edition: March 2016
ISBN 978-1-935106-91-3

Manager: Rod Lorenzen
Book & cover design: Mike Keckhaver
Copyeditor: Ali Welky

Names: Hendricks, Nancy, author.
Title: Notable women of Arkansas:
from Hattie to Hillary, 100 names to know / Nancy Hendricks.
Description: Little Rock: Butler Center Books, a division of the Butler Center for Arkansas Studies at the Central Arkansas Library System, 2016. | Includes bibliographical references and index. | Description based on print version record and CIP data provided by publisher; resource not viewed.
Identifiers: LCCN 2016000895 (print) | LCCN 2015049816 (ebook) | ISBN 9781935106920 (e-book) | ISBN 9781935106913 (hardback) | ISBN 9781935106951 (paperback)
Subjects: LCSH: Women--Arkansas--Biography. | Arkansas--Biography. | BISAC: HISTORY / United States / State & Local / South (AL, AR, FL, GA, KY, LA, MS, NC, SC, TN, VA, WV).
Classification: LCC CT3262.A8 (print) | LCC CT3262.A8 H46 2016 (ebook) | DDC 920.7209767--dc23
LC record available at http://lccn.loc.gov/2016000895

Butler Center Books, the publishing division of the Butler Center for Arkansas Studies, was made possible by the generosity of Dora Johnson Ragsdale and John G. Ragsdale Jr.

Printed in the United States of America

This book is printed on archival-quality paper that meets requirements of the American National Standard for Information Sciences, Permanence of Paper, Printed Library Materials, ANSI Z39.48-1984.

Table of Contents

Acknowledgements

THIS VOLUME OWES MUCH to that wonderful resource, the online Encyclopedia of Arkansas History & Culture (www.encyclopediaofarkansas.net), launched nearly a decade ago as a project of the Butler Center for Arkansas Studies at the Central Arkansas Library System. The EOA is a free, fascinating, and authoritative source of information about the rich history and culture of Arkansas. Many of the entries in this book first appeared there (some written by myself) and have been adapted with the kind permission of the EOA staff. Many of the women included in this book currently have entries on the EOA, while others soon will. Sincere gratitude is offered to the Encyclopedia of Arkansas, its staff, its authors, and its supporters.

The author also thanks the staff of the Butler Center for Arkansas Studies and Butler Center Books—especially Butler Center manager David Stricklin, Butler Center Books manager Rod Lorenzen, Mike Keckhaver for his beautiful design work, and Ali Welky for diligent copyediting and proofreading—for supporting and encouraging this book spotlighting 100 notable women who have called Arkansas home. Many thanks to Stephanie Bayless, Mark Christ, Michael Dougan, and Rex Nelson for perusing the manuscript and offering their much appreciated comments for the back cover. All four are highly regarded historians, and their prestige is surpassed only by their kindness.

Finally, much appreciation is offered to the 100 inspiring individuals included in this book who made their mark on the world. We are proud to call them *Notable Women of Arkansas.*

—nh

Introduction

ARKANSAS IS POPULATED BY MODEST PEOPLE, some say. Arkansans usually do not boast about themselves or their accomplishments. It is also said that women do not often brag about themselves or their achievements. It might therefore be concluded that Arkansas women would be the humblest of the humble.

Yet they have everything to boast about. Their accomplishments, though often hidden under the proverbial "bushel basket," are world class. In this volume, you will meet one hundred women who have shone in the national spotlight, representing a diverse array of people whose only link to each other is that they have a connection with Arkansas.

Some were born in Arkansas, some were raised in Arkansas, some worked in Arkansas, and some chose Arkansas late in life. We have to go into the past to find some, while others live in the present. Over the years, these women have blazed trails in athletics, civil rights, literature, politics, science, show business, and the arts. They made headlines in their own time, or they may be poised to make history. They portrayed remarkable women of the past in plays or films, or became noteworthy in their own right. They faced off against such foes as the male-dominated publishing world and the Creature from the Black Lagoon.

Outlaws, Outcasts, and the Oscars

Some of these women were born in poverty while others came from unimaginable wealth. They have been outlaws and outcasts. They have been recognized with Oscars and the National Book Award. One was the first person from Arkansas ever to win Broadway's Tony Award. One Arkansas woman was single-handedly nominated for the Pulitzer Prize, the Tony Award, and three Grammys.

One raised a future statesman while using a newspaper to communicate her ideas, and one edited a newspaper while communicating with the supernatural. These women sang of wanting to be a cowboy's sweetheart and told tales from the South. Some are actresses who were nominated for the Academy Award, and some were portrayed by Academy Award–winning actresses.

You'll meet an Arkansas woman whose name is literally carved in stone with the names of Shakespeare and Mark Twain. You'll meet a presidential candidate whose initials are not HRC. You'll meet beauty queens on the runway and a runaway beauty queen. And you'll meet a trailblazing African American actress who, if she'd been born thirty years later, might have had a career like Halle Berry's. They are all Arkansas women with an impressive legacy.

Saddle Shoes to Combat Boots

It is important to remember that the women presented here are all individuals, each with her own backstory: family and childhood, loves and losses, dreams and fears, illusions and disillusionment, hopes for the future and ghosts from the past.

This is especially true of the girls who were part of the group called the "Little Rock Nine" during the 1957 desegregation crisis at Little Rock Central High School. But there were nine separate stories of those young people, including the six African American girls who were fourteen, fifteen, and sixteen years old at the time, facing unimaginable ordeals every day. Most of the women of the Little Rock Nine have said that one of their biggest concerns as teenage girls was what to wear on their first day of school at Central. When that day was over, some put those dresses away, never to be seen again. They speak of their excitement about the chance to meet new people at Central. They did—in the form of loud, angry, spitting, cursing mobs.

Their gallant young faces were seen around the world, but it is important to remember that they were still teenagers. As one of the group said, fifteen-year-olds usually just want to be loved and accepted. Instead, she notes, each day these young women shined their saddle shoes and went into combat.

An average day might include being spat on, cursed at, or pushed down. A bad day included an acid attack. While they were part of a group, each one ultimately had to face Central High—and her own fears—alone. Each one of the six young girls in the "Nine" is a unique individual with her own name. Each one has a story. And each one went on to live a full, productive life beyond 1957. You will read about each of the girls they were then, and the women they became.

Arkansas Women on the National Stage

For reasons of space, the women included here had to be limited to one hundred. So there were guidelines. Each prospective entry had to have a connection to Arkansas—born in Arkansas, raised in Arkansas, or a resident of Arkansas at some point in life. Each individual had to have made her mark nationally and/or internationally. Many others have made tremendous statewide contributions but could not be included in this particular volume, such as the poets laureate of Arkansas as well as the state's first female elected officials and jurists.

Arkansas women have made their marks nationally in all sorts of ways—in the arts, athletics, philanthropy, politics, publishing, religion, science, and show business. Even within individual fields, they represent a wide section of diversity: writers of everything from children's books to horror tales, musicians in genres from country to opera to avant-garde. These one hundred women reflect the diversity of the state.

The Name Game

If one of your favorites is not listed in the table of contents, check the index for a cross-reference, because there is always the matter of women changing their names upon marriage. Throughout their lives, most men retain the name they were born with. On the other hand, women may have a family name at birth, then they might marry and possibly re-marry after divorce or widowhood, with each transition usually bringing a name change. History records at least one woman, married to a governor of Arkansas, who declined to change her name upon marriage, at her peril.

In the chronological flow of each entry, the name used will be the name by which the woman was known at that point in her life.

Arkansas Women in Fact and Fiction

What is an "Arkansas woman"? Perhaps a place to start is how Arkansas women have been portrayed to the world as fictional characters. Certainly they have been denigrated by outsiders as comical, ignorant hillbillies. Even a presumed "insider," no less than an Arkansas legislator, said publicly in 1963, "When one of our women starts poking around in something she doesn't know anything about…we get her pregnant and keep her barefoot." By the way, he was re-elected.

Perhaps he might have learned something just by looking at three of the most noteworthy Arkansas women in fiction, represented over the years in both books and movies. What can Nellie Forbush, Lorelei Lee, and Mattie Ross tell us about Arkansas women in fact instead of fiction?

Mid-South to South Pacific

Ensign Nellie Forbush of Little Rock first appears in the Pulitzer Prize–winning book, *Tales of the South Pacific*, written in 1947 by a Pennsylvanian, James A. Michener. It was based on his experiences in the U.S. Navy while stationed in the Pacific Theater of operations during World War II. The stories were based on actual incidents he had observed, including prejudice against Pacific Islanders who were considered racially inferior by some of the American military personnel from the South. Nellie Forbush then became a main character in the Rodgers and Hammerstein musical based on Michener's novel. *South Pacific* opened on Broadway in 1949 and went on to become known worldwide in the 1958 movie of the same name.

Spunky Nellie Forbush calls herself a "cockeyed optimist." As an adventuresome navy nurse in World War II, she wants to see the world, but she is stunned by what she sees there as well as by her own reactions to it. She is forced to confront her ingrained racial prejudices, those that have been "carefully taught." Ultimately, through love and compassion, she grows to overcome them. Michener made the character a young Arkansas woman, perhaps as a symbol of the potential for someone raised a certain way to be transformed both by an independent nature and a wider world view. Incidentally, the movie version of *South Pacific*, dealing with racial prejudice, was being filmed in 1957—the same time as the racial crisis in Little Rock.

Diamond Girl

Lorelei Lee, who says she is "just a little girl from Little Rock," first appears in the 1925 bestseller *Gentlemen Prefer Blondes: The Intimate Diary of a Professional Lady*. It was written by Anita Loos, a Californian who settled in New York. Loos's novel also inspired a Broadway musical that opened in 1949, the same year as *South Pacific*. The stage version of *Gentlemen Prefer Blondes* starred Carol Channing, who crooned "I'm Just a Little Girl from Little Rock" and introduced the song that expressed Lorelei's philosophy of life: "Diamonds Are a Girl's Best Friend."

About two hours from Little Rock, at Arkansas's Crater of Diamonds State Park in Murfreesboro, visitors can dig their own diamonds out of the ground. Lorelei had other ideas. Though born into poverty and lacking formal education, she leaves Arkansas to embark on a quest for the kind of wealth and security that, at the time, only men bearing diamonds could provide.

In 1953, when the play was made into a movie, Lorelei Lee was famously portrayed by Marilyn Monroe in the film that made her a star. Little Rock's little girl "from the wrong side of the tracks" has become inextricably linked to Monroe, with her true-life persona eerily similar to Lorelei's. When another character says he thought she was dumb, Lorelei/Marilyn replies, "I can be smart when it's important, but most men don't like it." The line was suggested by Monroe herself.

Like Nellie Forbush, Lorelei Lee was raised to be a Southern girl of the "steel magnolia" variety, outwardly sweet and submissive but possessing an inner strength and iron will. Humor is also a characteristic trait of Lorelei Lee, easing the impression that she is simply a cold-hearted, cynical gold-digger. And then there is her tenacity. Though she starts out poor and uneducated from a low economic class, Lorelei is ultimately able to confidently enter the upper tiers of European society as a citizen of the world. In her expanded world view, she is similar to her fictional fellow Arkansan, Nellie Forbush. With humor and a good nature, along with single-mindedness of purpose, Lorelei Lee, the "little girl from Little Rock," is dealt a Hollywood happy ending.

InteGRITy

It is impossible to think of single-mindedness without considering Mattie Ross of *True Grit*. Once again, this fictitious Arkansas woman appears first in a book and later in movies. Mattie Ross is the fourteen-year-old heroine of the 1968 novel by Charles Portis as well as the 1969 movie and the remake in 2010. Of the writers who created the three fictional Arkansas characters discussed here, only Portis, born in El Dorado, is an Arkansas author. He chose a young woman from his home state as an iconic figure.

Amid colorful characters such as Rooster Cogburn in both the book and the films, Mattie Ross is the story's heart and soul. She hails from Dardanelle, Arkansas, about seventy-five miles northwest of Little Rock. In 1875 frontier Arkansas, the determined Mattie sets off on a perilous journey to avenge her father's murder. She is kidnapped, falls into a snake pit, and loses her arm, but she ultimately prevails. She is a person with what she calls "grit"—firmness of character, indomitable spirit, courage, tenacity, honor, strength, and determination.

Mattie Ross makes life choices that were unconventional for her place and time, becoming an independent woman who did not worry about what others might think. She never marries, but she cares for family above all else. She is tough but not bitter. She says, "I have left off crying, and giggling as well." She is witty and smart, daring and self-reliant. In her fourteen years, she has come to understand one thing: "You must pay for everything in this world, one way and another."

The traits of intelligence, optimism, courage, tenacity, character, and strength define Arkansas women, whether real people or fictional characters like Nellie Forbush, Lorelei Lee, and Mattie Ross. In short: InteGRITy. In this volume, you will meet a hundred women who have it.

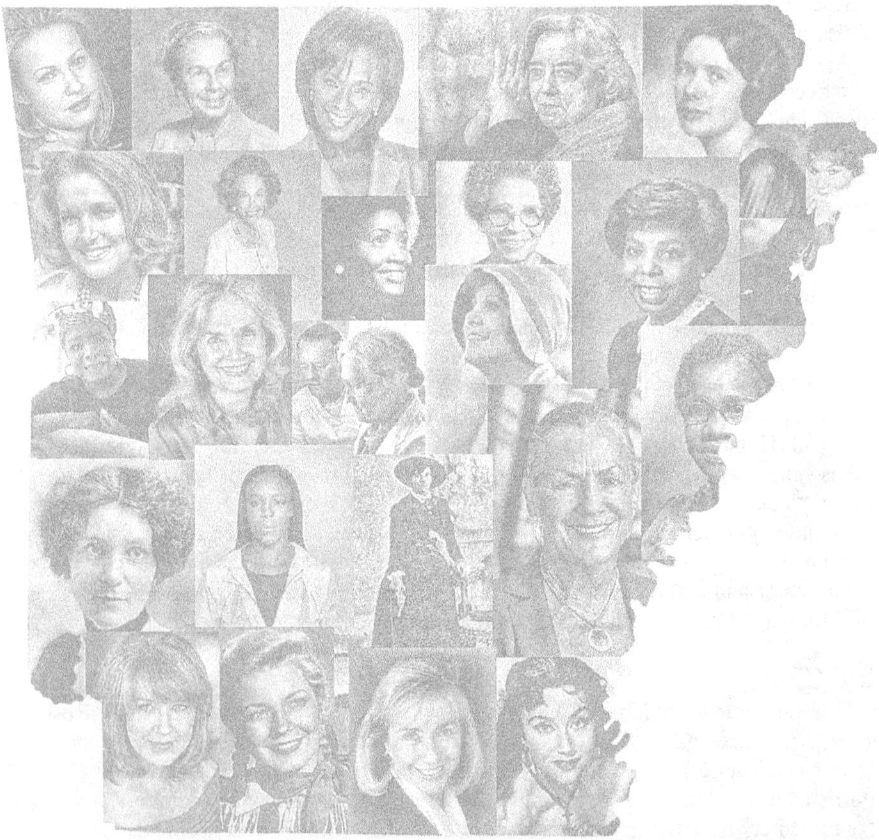

Annie Abrams (1931–)

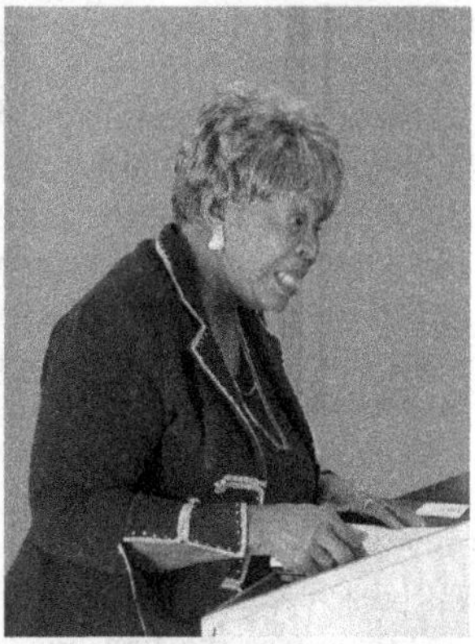

ANNIE ABRAMS IS A NATIONALLY recognized leader in the fields of education, politics, women's issues, senior citizens' concerns, and civil rights. She has been photographed whispering advice to U.S. presidents and other prominent figures on the world stage.

Annie Mable McDaniel was born in Arkadelphia, Arkansas, on September 25, 1931, the eldest of four children born to Queen Victoria Annie Katherine Reed. When she was eighteen months old, McDaniel's father died in a truck crash on the way to his job with the Civilian Conservation Corps (CCC).

After the death of her father, McDaniel's grandfather James Arnold helped to raise her amidst the poverty of the Great Depression. Arnold was a farmer, sawmill worker, and domestic helper. Though he was not literate, he was a strong advocate for education, persuading the local school board to build a schoolhouse nearby and lending his mule to teachers who needed a way to get there. Later in life, his granddaughter would teach him to spell his name.

Until she was thirteen, McDaniel attended the segregated Peake School in Arkadelphia. During her middle-school years, she was sometimes called out of class to serve as a substitute in the elementary school if a teacher was out sick. Her mother was not pleased at that arrangement, as McDaniel was missing her own lessons, and was determined that she would attain a better education.

In 1944, her mother sent her to live in Little Rock with Herbert Denton, the principal of Stephens Elementary, and his wife, Louise Denton, who was McDaniel's cousin. At the Denton home, McDaniel helped take care of their son, Herbert Denton Jr., who later attended Harvard, worked as a foreign correspondent, and became the first black city editor of the *Washington Post.*

McDaniel graduated from Little Rock's all-black Dunbar High School in 1950 and enrolled in Dunbar Junior College, which was located in a wing of the high school. She majored in teacher education, graduating in 1952 with a license in education. McDaniel was offered a scholarship to the prestigious Brandeis University in Massachusetts, but she was unable to attend due to financial circumstances and lost the scholarship. She would later graduate from Little Rock's Philander Smith College.

With her teaching license, McDaniel moved to the small eastern Arkansas town of Marianna. With an agricultural economy based on cotton, Marianna was home to a large African American population, numbering about 4,500. McDaniel taught at the town's three-room segregated elementary school.

She remained in Marianna until 1956. That year, she took a position in Little Rock with the Arkansas Teachers Association (ATA), which supported equality in education for African Americans, school integration, and salary equity for the state's black teachers, who were traditionally paid less than their white counterparts.

Also at about this time, she married Orville Abrams, who worked as a bartender at Little Rock's Riverdale Country Club; the couple had four children.

Working with the ATA in Little Rock during this period led to her involvement with the 1957 desegregation crisis at Little Rock Central High School. Abrams became a close friend of civil rights leader Daisy Bates [SEE ENTRY]. When Bates died in 1999 and her body lay in state in the rotunda of the Arkansas State Capitol, Abrams says she leaned over the coffin and said, "Remember when you couldn't even come in here? Now you are the first black to lie in state here."

Abrams took courses at Philander Smith College, earning a degree in special education in 1962. After her husband suffered a massive stroke in 1970, when their oldest of their children was thirteen, Abrams cared for him until his death in 2000.

In the 1970s, Abrams actively participated in the leadership of the Young Women's Christian Association (YWCA). She was selected to travel to Geneva, Switzerland, in 1978, to represent North America as a YWCA delegate at a United Nations conference addressing institutional racism and discrimination.

In Arkansas, Abrams became involved in many of the state's organizations, including the Arkansas Democratic Black Caucus (though she supported Republican Winthrop Rockefeller for governor), Fair Housing Commission, Little Rock Central High Integration 50th Anniversary Commission, and Martin Luther King Jr. Commission.

Abrams led the drive to establish the annual Martin Luther King Jr. Day parade in Little Rock and the campaign to create Martin Luther King Jr. Drive, which was dedicated in 1992. For her efforts, Abrams received the "Making of the King Holiday Award," which was presented to her by Coretta Scott King in 1993.

Abrams was the first black president of the Little Rock Central High School PTA, became a 2010 inductee into the Arkansas Black Hall of Fame, and received the Brooks Hays Award for Civil Rights Champions. Each year at its King-Kennedy Honors Banquet, the Arkansas Democratic Black Caucus recognizes a civic leader with the Annie Abrams Award for Community Service, named in her honor.

Abrams has been a confidante to U.S. Presidents Bill Clinton and Barack Obama. She has served as a delegate to five national Democratic conventions, ranging from her support of Shirley Chisholm in 1972 to Barack Obama in 2008.

For more information:

Peacock, Leslie Newell. "Living Witness." *Arkansas Times*, February 25, 2010. http://www.arktimes.com/arkansas/living-witness/Content?oid=1013919 (accessed December 8, 2015).

Joey Lauren Adams (1968–)

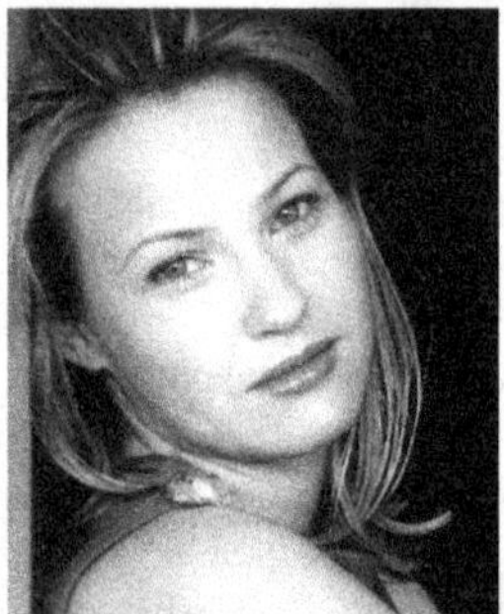

JOEY LAUREN ADAMS IS A POPULAR and critically acclaimed actress, writer, producer, and director. Known especially for her unique voice, Adams has appeared in more than seventy movies and television shows. She won the "Most Promising Actress" award from the Chicago Film Critics in 1997 for her performance in *Chasing Amy*. She starred with Adam Sandler in the hit movie *Big Daddy*, as well as appearing as a regular on TV shows *United States of Tara* and *Switched at Birth*. Adams made her directorial debut in 2006.

The youngest of three children, Joey Lauren Adams was born in North Little Rock, Arkansas, on January 9, 1968. Her father, who was in the lumber business, built the family home in the Overbrook neighborhood of North Little Rock. She graduated from Northeast High School in 1986. It was her high school drama teacher, Carol Ann McAdams, who helped her find a career path in the performing arts after Adams was not chosen to be a cheerleader. In an interview at the Sundance Film Festival in 2013, Adams honored her former teacher by saying, "She was the first person to say I was talented at anything."

At age nineteen, Adams left Arkansas for Hollywood. By the early 1990s, Adams had been cast in several TV shows, including *Top of the Heap*, *Vinnie & Bobby*, and *Married with Children*. She filmed a scene for the movie *Wayne's World 2* in 1993, though her scene was edited out. That same year, she was cast in her first major film role as Simone in Richard Linklater's *Dazed and Confused*. Also in 1993, she appeared in the film *Coneheads* based on a sketch on TV's *Saturday Night Live*. She played Christina, a friend of Connie Conehead.

Adams continued to be cast in a number of small films and TV shows until her 1995 breakthrough role as Gwen in *Mallrats*, which was written and directed by Kevin Smith. The personal relationship between Adams and Smith formed the inspiration for Kevin Smith's next film, *Chasing Amy*, in which Adams played Alyssa Jones. Her performance earned Adams a Golden Globe nomination for Best Actress. In addition to acting, Adams wrote and performed the song "Alive" for the movie soundtrack. Smith later described the critically acclaimed *Chasing Amy* as a "thank-you homage" to Adams, who won the 1997 Chicago Film Critics Award and Las Vegas Film Critics Society Award for Most Promising Actress for her role in the film.

Since that time, Adams has appeared in more than seventy movies and television shows. She is often remembered for playing Layla Maloney, Adam Sandler's love interest in the Hollywood comedy *Big Daddy*. In 2005, she had a guest role in an episode of the popular TV show *Veronica Mars*.

Discussing finding roles, Adams said, "It just gets frustrating playing the girlfriend. It's just this awful feeling, sitting in your house, waiting for a script to come. I like to be more proactive." She said, "For women in their 30s, it's so hard to get good parts." As she herself entered her late thirties, Adams released a film she wrote and directed called *Come Early Morning* in 2006. It starred Ashley Judd, whose performance in Adams's film led film critic Roger Ebert to say, "Ashley Judd gives one of the best performances of her career." The film was shot on location in Arkansas and was selected from almost 2,000 entries for the 2006 Sundance Film Festival, where it was nominated for the Grand Jury prize. Adams was said to have drawn on material from her childhood in North Little Rock for the screenplay.

In 2006, Adams was the recipient of the Women in Film Dorothy Arzner Directors Award.

In 2014, Adams returned to Arkansas for her role as Tonya in the film *All the Birds Have Flown South*, written and directed by brothers Miles and Josh Miller of Little Rock. A fundraiser for the independent film's production was held in Little Rock to seek support for Arkansas movie-making.

Although she has a home in Oxford, Mississippi, Adams has said of her home state of Arkansas: "I love it there. I go home all the time."

For more information:

"Joey Lauren Adams." Internet Movie Database. http://www.imdb.com/name/nm0000725/ (accessed December 8, 2015).

Julie Adams (1926–)

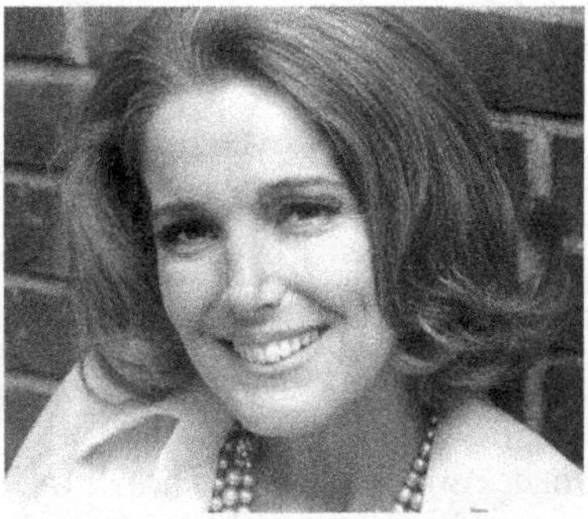

JULIE ADAMS HAS MADE MORE than 150 films and television shows in wide variety of roles spanning an unusually lengthy career as an actress. She may be best remembered for her role in the cult classic *Creature from the Black Lagoon*, although she appeared in significant roles in many other movies. She co-starred with some of Hollywood's top leading men in a remarkable career that spanned six decades. Some of her notable movies from each decade include *Tickle Me* (1965) with Elvis Presley; *McQ* (1974) with John Wayne; *Champions* (1984); *Catchfire* (1990), and *World Trade Center* (2006), directed by Oliver Stone.

She was born Betty May Adams on October 17, 1926, in Waterloo, Iowa, where her mother was visiting. As a child, Adams lived in Blytheville and Malvern, Arkansas. The family moved frequently due to her father's job as a cotton buyer. They later moved to Little Rock, where Adams attended Little Rock High School (now Little Rock Central

High School) and Little Rock Junior College, now the University of Arkansas at Little Rock (UALR). She has said that an elementary school production of *Hansel and Gretel* led to her interest in acting as a career. Her father's first wife, who lived near Los Angeles, offered to help her get started in Hollywood.

In 1946, at age nineteen, Adams left Arkansas for Hollywood, where she studied acting and worked part time as a secretary. Her first movie role was an uncredited appearance as a starlet in Paramount's 1949 movie *Red, Hot and Blue*. Next came a series of low-budget westerns for Lippert Studios in which she was billed as Betty Adams. In 1951, she assisted with a screen test opposite a football player who was under consideration by Universal Studios. He was not offered a job, but Adams was signed to a contract with Universal, where her first name was changed to Julia. In 1955, it would legally be changed to Julie.

Adams's dark eyes were found to photograph especially well. Universal made a publicity splash by insuring her legs with Lloyd's of London. In 1954, still billed as Julia, she was cast in the role for which she is often remembered, as Kay Lawrence in the 3-D thriller *Creature from the Black Lagoon*. Her role was described as "not only lovely, but an intelligent researcher who is both feminine and strong-willed."

Her first film as "Julie" Adams was *Six Bridges to Cross* with Tony Curtis in 1955. In a film called *The Looters*, released that same year, she co-starred with actor Ray Danton. They were married in 1954, and had sons Steven and Mitchell Danton before divorcing in 1981.

Throughout the 1950s, she had a busy film career including 1952's *Bend of the River* with James Stewart; *The Private War of Major Benson* with Charlton Heston in 1955; and *Slaughter on Tenth Avenue* with a young Walter Matthau in 1957.

In 1955, Adams began mixing television roles with her film work. Her TV appearances are remarkable not only for representing a virtual history of popular television from the 1950s to the present, but also in the fact that she was so often asked back to play different roles. Her TV appearances in the 1950s include roles in *Playhouse 90*, *Yancy Derringer*, and *Zane Grey Theater*. In the 1960s, there were roles in *Maverick*, *Bonanza*, *Alfred Hitchcock Presents*, and *77 Sunset Strip*. On *The Andy Griffith Show* in 1962, she played Sheriff Andy's love interest, and on *Perry Mason* in 1963, she played the only one of Perry's clients ever to be convicted. Her 1968 performance on *The Big Valley*, in which Adams terrorizes the formidable Barbara Stanwyck, remains a cult favorite.

The 1970s saw Adams appearing in *Night Gallery*, *Mod Squad*, *Kolchak the Night Stalker*, *Marcus Welby M.D.*, *Streets of San Francisco*, and *Police Woman*. Adams was cast in a co-starring role as James Stewart's wife on *The Jimmy Stewart Show*, a 1971 family situation comedy television series. She was in *Too Close for Comfort* and *Quincy M.E.* in the 1980s as well as having a recurring guest role on *Murder, She Wrote*. Adams appeared on *Melrose Place* and *Beverly Hills 90210* in the 1990s, followed by *Cold Case* (2006), *CSI: NY* (2007), and *Lost* (2008).

In 2011, Adams published her autobiography and Hollywood memoir, *The Lucky Southern Star: Reflections from the Black Lagoon*. Upon its release, she embarked on a national book tour.

In 1999, Adams received a Golden Boot Award for her work in westerns. Among her other honors are the Cinecon Film Career Achievement Award in 2011, and the Rondo Award for the Monster Kid Hall of Fame in 2012. In 2013, she received UALR's Distinguished Alumni Award, being honored at the Clinton Presidential Library in Little Rock. In 2015, she received the prestigious Arkansas Traveler Award while visiting her former hometown of Malvern.

The Academy of Motion Picture Arts and Sciences selected *Creature from the Black Lagoon* as one of thirteen classic horror films to screen during 2012 to celebrate the 100th anniversary of Universal Pictures. After the screening, Adams appeared on stage to answer questions and share reminiscences.

In 2015, Adams and *Creature from the Black Lagoon* were chosen for induction into the Classic Film Hall of Fame in Moraga, California.

Adams resides in Los Angeles. The still photogenic Adams appeared for interviews in 2013 on a Little Rock television station, saying, "I am a very lucky girl from Arkansas."

For more information:

Adams, Julie, with Mitchell Danton. *The Lucky Southern Star: Reflections from the Black Lagoon*. Los Angeles: Hollywood Adventures Publishing, 2011.

Julie Adams. http://www.julieadams.biz (accessed December 8, 2015).

Maya Angelou (1928–2014)

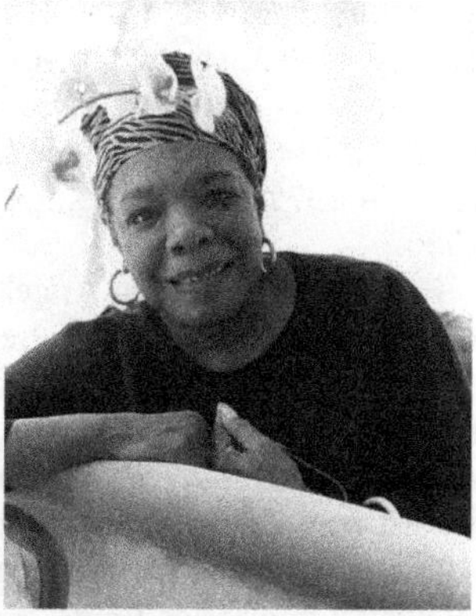

MAYA ANGELOU WAS AN INTERNATIONALLY known author, poet, and performer as well as an activist for women and African Americans. She held dozens of honorary university degrees, along with scores of awards. Her first published book was the autobiographical *I Know Why the Caged Bird Sings*, which focused on her childhood in Arkansas. She was the poet for Bill Clinton's 1993 presidential inauguration and won the Presidential Medal of Freedom, America's highest civilian honor. Angelou has been called "America's Renaissance Woman."

She was born Marguerite Annie Johnson on April 4, 1928, in St. Louis, Missouri, to Vivian Baxter Johnson and Bailey Johnson. Marguerite's brother, one year older than Marguerite, had trouble pronouncing her name. He affectionately called her "Maya," short for "my sister."

Three-year-old Marguerite and her four-year-old brother were sent alone by train to Arkansas in 1931 after the divorce of their parents. In Stamps, Arkansas—a small, mixed-race rural town in the southwestern part of the state—the children lived with their grandparents, Willie and Annie Henderson. Their grandfather owned the town's only grocery store. In her autobiography, Angelou recalls encountering racial prejudice by white customers in her grandfather's store as well as by the community at large.

In 1935, when Marguerite was seven years old, she and her brother visited her mother in St. Louis but soon went back to Stamps after the discovery that Marguerite had been sexually assaulted by her mother's boyfriend. After she revealed the rape to family members, her mother's boyfriend was found dead. The traumatized child believed that in naming the rapist, she had caused his death. She did not speak for about five years, until she was thirteen.

The children moved with their mother to San Francisco, California, where Marguerite attended high school. At fourteen years old, she became the first African American female streetcar conductor in San Francisco.

She earned a scholarship to study dance and drama at San Francisco's California Labor School. At age sixteen, she gave birth to a son, Claude "Guy" Johnson, three weeks after her graduation. To support herself and her son, she worked at a variety of jobs, including as a cook, dancer, cocktail waitress, and prostitute.

In 1951, Angelou married Anastasios Angelopulos, also called Tosh Angelos, a Greek sailor and aspiring musician. They soon divorced. At this time, when she was singing in nightclubs, she created a professional name by combining a variation of her married name with her brother's childhood nickname for her, becoming "Maya Angelou."

In 1954, she began touring Europe and Africa in a production of *Porgy and Bess* sponsored by the U.S. State Department. She then moved with her son to New York City, where she studied modern dance with Martha Graham and Alvin Ailey. She appeared on television and released an album called *Miss Calypso* in 1957, also appearing in the film

Calypso Heat Wave the same year. At the same time, she was writing poems and song lyrics. Around this same time, she met prominent members of the African American community such as Malcolm X and Martin Luther King Jr. After pursuing journalism in Egypt, she later worked at the University of Ghana.

Returning to the United States, Angelou wrote the famous autobiographical work concerning her childhood years in Arkansas, *I Know Why the Caged Bird Sings* (1970). Her experiences in the civil rights movement were the foundation for 1981's *The Heart of a Woman*. Her other autobiographical books include *Gather Together in My Name*; *Singin' and Swingin' and Gettin' Merry Like Christmas*; *A Song Flung Up to Heaven*; and *Mom & Me & Mom*. Her screenplay for the 1972 movie *Georgia, Georgia* was the first screenplay by a black woman to be filmed. In 1998, Angelou became the first black woman to direct a major motion picture, *Down in the Delta*. Her first collection of poems, *Just Give Me a Cool Drink of Water 'fore I Diiie*, was nominated for a Pulitzer Prize in 1972. In 1973, Angelou married Welsh writer Paul du Feu; they divorced in 1980.

Each decade brought Angelou further accolades in a variety of fields. In the 1970s, she was appointed to the Presidential Commission for International Women's Year; received a Rockefeller Foundation Bellagio Center residency; was awarded a Chubb Fellowship by Yale University; won the Coretta Scott King Award; and was named the *Ladies' Home Journal* "Woman of the Year in Communication." She received a Tony Award nomination for her role in the 1973 Broadway play *Look Away* and an Emmy Award nomination for her portrayal of Kunta Kinte's grandmother in 1977's landmark television miniseries *Roots*.

In the 1980s, she received a lifetime appointment to the Reynolds Chair of American Studies at North Carolina's Wake Forest University and was named one of the *Ladies' Home Journal*'s "Top 100 Most Influential Women." She won the Matrix Award from the New York Association for Women in Communications as well as the Fulbright Program Distinguished Lecturer recognition by the U.S. State Department.

At President Bill Clinton's 1993 inauguration, she read her poem "On the Pulse of Morning." Also in the 1990s, she won the Horatio Alger Award, Langston Hughes Medal, National Association for the Advancement of Colored People (NAACP) Spingarn Medal, Peace Abbey Courage of Conscience Award from Wellesley College, and NAACP Image Award.

In 1998, Angelou was inducted into the National Women's Hall of Fame. She was made an honorary American Ambassador by the United Nations Children's Fund (UNICEF), and she read her poem "A Brave and Startling Truth" at the 50th anniversary of the United Nations in 1995. She won a 1993 Grammy Award for Best Spoken Word Album for *On the Pulse of Morning* and again in 1995 for Best Spoken Word or Non-Musical Album for performing *Phenomenal Woman*.

The 2000s saw her win another Grammy for Best Spoken Word Album for *A Song Flung Up to Heaven*. Also in that decade, she had a movie role in Tyler Perry's *Medea's Family Reunion* and started a line of Hallmark greeting cards called Life Mosaic. She was awarded the National Medal of Arts, Marian Anderson Award, Mother Teresa Award, Lincoln Medal, and Presidential Medal of Freedom.

Throughout later life, Angelou retained her compelling speaking voice and powerful physical presence. After suffering from heart ailments, she died at her home in North Carolina on May 28, 2014, at age eighty-six. The following month, the town of Stamps renamed its only park for her. In 2015, the United States Postal Service released a stamp in honor of Angelou.

For more information:

Angelou, Maya. *I Know Why the Caged Bird Sings*. New York: Random House, 1970.

Maya Angelou. http://mayaangelou.com (accessed December 8, 2015).

Katharine Susan Anthony (1877–1965)

KATHARINE SUSAN ANTHONY WAS A NATIONALLY KNOWN author, feminist, pacifist, and suffragist best known for her biographical works, especially her controversial book, *The Lambs*, a study of authors Charles and Mary Lamb. Most of Anthony's biographical works documented the lives of notable women, and they were often written from a psychological point of view. Anthony was also known for her unconventional lifestyle, which modern observers note was far ahead of her time.

Katharine (sometimes spelled Katherine) Susan Anthony was born in Roseville, Arkansas, a small town in today's Logan County. Located on the south bank of the Arkansas River in the western part of the state, Roseville was a busy river port town. Although some of the oldest settlements in western Arkansas were located in the region, the area was sparsely populated. At the time of Anthony's birth, the town of Booneville was the only trading center between Fort Smith and Dardanelle.

Anthony was born on November 27, 1877, the third of four children of Susan Cathey Anthony and Ernest Augustus Anthony, a grocer who later became a police officer. During her childhood, there was a marked decline in Roseville's economy. The family moved first to Paris, Arkansas, and later to Fort Smith on the state's western border.

Anthony attended public schools in Fort Smith and was hired to teach elementary school in the same school district. She continued to live with her parents to save money. She studied at Peabody College for Teachers in Nashville. With her savings, was then able to finance a year of study in Germany, attending the Universities of Heidelberg and Freiburg.

Upon her return to the United States, she earned a bachelor's degree at age twenty-eight from the University of Chicago in 1905. In 1907, Anthony began teaching at Wellesley College in Boston, Massachusetts. In 1910, she was back in Arkansas, working as a public school teacher in Fort Smith. However, she soon moved to the bohemian enclave of Greenwich Village in New York City.

In Greenwich Village, Anthony lived with the woman who became her life partner, Elisabeth Antoinette Irwin, who was a noted psychologist and progressive educator. Irwin, a native New Yorker, had attended the elite Smith College and Columbia University. As a staff member of the Public Education Association, Irwin was active in the revision of public school curricula. In 1921, Irwin founded the Little Red School House in Lower Manhattan, which was described as a program that was broader and more active than Manhattan's public schools and is regarded as New York City's first progressive school.

Anthony and Irwin lived together on Bank Street in Greenwich Village for nearly thirty years. They were members of the intellectual feminist social club Heterodoxy, a term defined as describing opinions or doctrines that varied from an official or orthodox position. The club met in Greenwich Village from 1912 through 1940. During this time, Anthony and Irwin vacationed in a summer cottage at Gaylordsville, Connecticut. They jokingly referred to themselves as "the gay ladies of Gaylordsville."

Anthony left teaching to become a full-time writer, launching a successful career that would last for almost a half century. Her first book was *Mothers Who Must Earn*. Published in 1914, the nonfiction book attacked the abuse of women workers and decried child labor. It was followed by another nonfiction work in 1915 called *Feminism in Germany and Scandinavia*.

Her biographical works include *Margaret Fuller: A Psychological Biography* (1920), *Catherine the Great* (1925), *Queen Elizabeth* (1929), *Marie Antoinette* (1933), *Louisa May Alcott* (1938), *The Lambs: A Story of Pre-Victorian England* (1945), *Dolly Madison: Her Life and Times* (1949), and *Susan B. Anthony: Her Personal History and Her Era* (1954). *Susan B. Anthony* was a biography of the pioneering women's rights advocate who lived between 1820 and 1906, and who some sources say was a distant relative to Anthony. Her last biographical work, *First Lady of the Revolution*, about Mercy Otis

Warren, was published in 1958. In the *New York Times* and other publications, Anthony's books were positively reviewed, and several, such as those about Catherine the Great and Queen Elizabeth, sold more than 100,000 copies. A review of her book about Susan B. Anthony in *Commentary* magazine said, "Katharine Anthony's thoughtful biography reminds us again that America owes a debt to the rebels who have believed that this nation spells equal rights."

Anthony was interested in the field of psychiatry, and her books often discussed the psychological development and motivation of her subjects. Her book about the brother and sister English writers, Charles Lamb and Mary Lamb, became controversial because of Anthony's theory that their work may have reflected incestuous feelings.

Anthony and Irwin lived quietly in Greenwich Village amid a circle of friends that included progressive political and artistic luminaries such as the first female ambassador of the Soviet Union, psychiatrists, feminists, authors, historians, labor leaders, and social reformers. Elisabeth Irwin died in 1942, survived by Anthony as well as two children whom the couple raised and supported.

At age eighty-eight, Katharine Susan Anthony died at St. Vincent's Hospital in New York City after having a heart attack. Her obituary appeared in the *New York Times* on November 22, 1965. Anthony's funeral was held in New York City, and she is buried at Gaylordsville, Connecticut, next to Elisabeth Irwin.

For more information:

"Katharine Susan Anthony and Elisabeth Irwin." *Greenwich Village History*. http://gvh.aphdigital.org/items/show/1227 (accessed December 8, 2015).

Julia "Bernie" Babcock (1868–1962)

JULIA BURNELLE "BERNIE" SMADE BABCOCK was a nationally known author who was recognized for essays, newspaper articles, and more than forty novels. She was the first Arkansas woman listed in *Who's Who of North American Authors* and served as folklore editor for the Depression-era Federal Writers' Project. She created the *Arkansas Sketch Book*, a fine-arts quarterly which was the state's first such publication, featuring work by Arkansas writers and artists. In addition, she established the Arkansas Museum of Natural History and Antiquities, which formed the basis for today's Museum of Discovery in Little Rock.

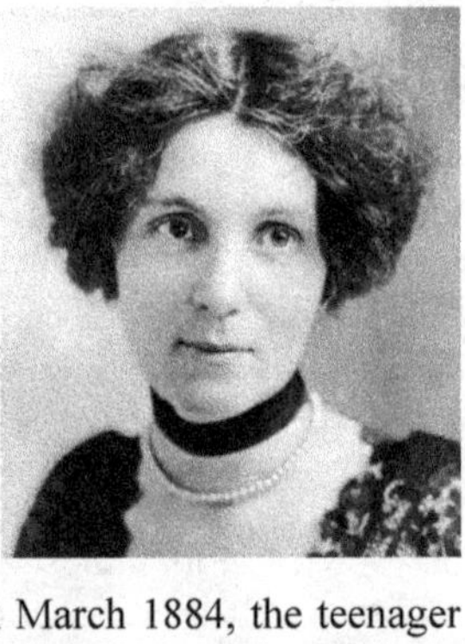

Born on April 28, 1868, in Union, Ohio, Julia Burnelle Smade was the first of six children of Hiram Norton Smade and Charlotte Burnelle Smade. When she was a child, her parents moved the family to Russellville, Arkansas, where her father owned a sawmill. She was raised by her parents to value creativity, education, and independent thinking. Late in life, she said she had been accused of lying in kindergarten, but her mother had said it was a sign the imaginative youngster would grow up to be a writer.

By the time she was fifteen, Julia Smade was a strong supporter of the temperance, or anti-alcohol, movement. In March 1884, the teenager read her powerful essay on the subject at the state convention of the Woman's Christian Temperance Union (WCTU), in which her mother was active.

After high school, she attended the Methodist school Little Rock University where she earned her tuition by serving as housekeeper for the college president. In 1886, she left school to marry William Franklin Babcock. The Bible and Darwin's *Origin of Species* were the first two books she obtained for their home library. The couple had five children in eleven years. Her husband died suddenly in 1897, leaving the twenty-nine-year-old widow to support the family alone.

In an unusual step for a woman of her time, she began working as a writer. Using the name Bernie Babcock, she sent submissions to editors around the nation. Writing at night, she produced a wide variety of books, essays, pamphlets, plays, poems, and stories. In 1900, her first book, *The Daughter of the Republican*, was published; it sold 100,000 copies in six months. Like subsequent works such as *The Martyr*, it focused on the suffering caused by alcohol abuse. Babcock was credited with bringing attention to the Prohibition movement.

Her 1901 novel *Justice to the Woman* concerned female voting rights, rights women in the United States did not gain until 1920.

During her marriage, Babcock and her husband had lived briefly in Vicksburg, Mississippi, where she saw the poor treatment of African Americans. Her play *Mammy*, published in New York, was based on that experience and was the first known drama to have a black woman in the leading role. Later in life, Babcock would supervise the collection of slave narratives for the Federal Writers' Project.

Babcock also took on the controversial topic of evolution in her book *By Way of the Master Passion*. Two biographies, *The Soul of Abraham Lincoln* and *The Soul of Ann Rutledge: Abraham Lincoln's Romance* were especially well received internationally. Babcock's biographical works also include *Light Horse Harry's Boys* about Robert E. Lee and *The Heart of George Washington*.

In addition, she took on difficult contemporary subjects. Based on visits to New York City, she made a study of "submerged poverty people," or what today might be called "the working poor." Her work was presented at a meeting of garment workers who went on strike for higher wages, with 75,000 sympathy strikers ultimately marching down Broadway.

Babcock traveled to Chicago to write for a newspaper but returned to Arkansas. She was a passionate defender of her state, responding to ridicule by world-famous journalist H. L. Mencken (who said the people of Arkansas were "too stupid to see what was the matter with them") by establishing the Arkansas Museum of Natural History and Antiquities in 1927.

With contributions from friends, she opened the museum in a Little Rock storefront. It quickly gained popularity, especially for its display of "King Crowley," a sculpted stone head later discovered to be a fake. In 1929, Babcock donated the museum and its varied collections to the City of Little Rock. It went through several name changes, finally becoming the Museum of Discovery. As the museum changed venues, she was known to live in the basement as the displays were being mounted. Even when she was in her seventies, she climbed ladders to paint murals on the walls.

She corresponded with General of the Army Douglas MacArthur, who had been born in Little Rock. Babcock was instrumental in naming a city park for MacArthur and obtained memorabilia to display in a room of the museum in his honor. However, after a public dispute with Little Rock's Aesthetic Club over a meeting room at the museum (which was then in the Arsenal Building), Babcock retired in 1953 at age eighty-five.

In her new home atop Petit Jean Mountain, Babcock continued to write. In 1959, she published a volume of poetry, *The Marble Woman*. She also took up painting.

She died at home on June 14, 1962, soon after her ninety-fourth birthday. The neighbor who found her reported that Babcock was sitting with a manuscript in her hand. Babcock was buried beside her husband at Little Rock's Oakland Cemetery.

Although Babcock is little remembered today, on the exterior of the Central Arkansas Library System's Main Library in Little Rock, Bernie Babcock's name is carved in stone alongside those of William Shakespeare and Mark Twain.

For more information:

Bernie Babcock Collection. Center for Arkansas History and Culture. University of Arkansas at Little Rock, Little Rock, Arkansas.

Teske, Steven. *Unvarnished Arkansas: The Naked Truth about Nine Famous Arkansans*. Little Rock: Butler Center Books, 2012.

Lucille Babcock (1921–1993)

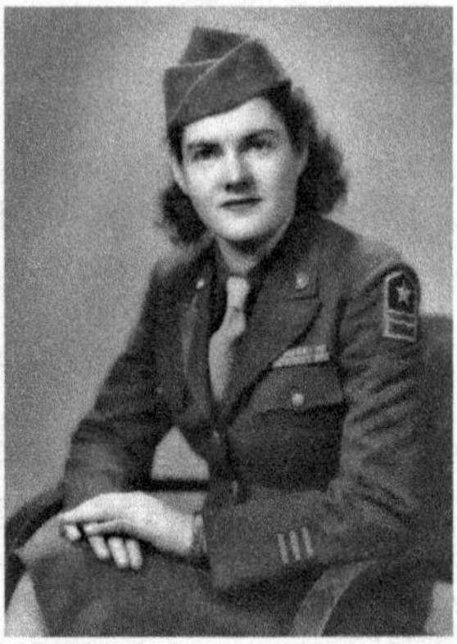

LUCILLE THORNBURG BABCOCK was a noted actress on television and the Broadway stage. She served as president of the Arkansas Poets' Roundtable, founded Little Rock's first community theater group, and was editor of the poetry column in the *Arkansas Gazette*. When she was sixty-five years old and disabled, she achieved national recognition for her heroism.

Lucille Thornburg, often called Lucy, was born on September 30, 1921, one of two children of John Thornburg and Frances Babcock Thornburg, who was daughter of nationally renowned author Julia "Bernie" Babcock [SEE ENTRY]. When Lucy was an infant, her father deserted the family. The family moved into Broadview, a converted barn that Lucy's grandmother Bernie Babcock had purchased.

Thornburg would eventually drop the last name of the father who abandoned the family, preferring "Babcock." As a child, she ran afoul of school officials for fighting, usually while defending someone who was vulnerable, often African Americans. She went to Forest Park Elementary and Pulaski Heights Junior High in Little Rock, although she stopped attending by the tenth grade.

Shortly before her twentieth birthday, with World War II on the horizon, Babcock began driving buses between Little Rock and the Maumelle Ordnance Works, which produced munitions for the army. A "manpower" shortage allowed women like Babcock to work as drivers, shuttling employees to their jobs.

After America entered the war in December 1941, Bernie Babcock appealed to Eleanor Roosevelt to help granddaughter Lucy obtain war work in Washington. At first, Lucy worked as a filing clerk at the Pentagon. Subsequently, Mrs. Roosevelt suggested that Lucy join the Women's Army Corps (WAC).

Lucy married policeman Don Junkins in 1942; their marriage lasted six months. Lucy went through basic training with other WACs and was assigned the job of classification specialist. In that position, she assigned herself to overseas duty.

The ship on which she was traveling was attacked by a suicide bomber at the harbor of Naples, Italy, killing more than 300 Americans. Since Babcock had experience driving buses, she went to work as an ambulance driver. German rocket artillery hit the ambulance she was driving, overturning the vehicle and afflicting Babcock with a back injury that affected her for the rest of her life.

After being transferred to the Middle East Service Command in Egypt, Babcock drove a supply truck between Cairo and Alexandria on supply runs until the end of the war in 1945. A Jeep accident led to her having to wear a brace on her right leg later in life.

With the GI Bill providing educational benefits for veterans, Babcock enrolled at Arkansas State Teachers College in Conway (today's University of Central Arkansas) in 1946. After two years, she left to attend the prestigious school of theater arts at California's Pasadena Playhouse.

Babcock then traveled to New York City, where she performed in radio serials as well as early television soap operas and TV dramas such as *The Hallmark Hour*. The *New York Times* reported on her appearance in the Broadway play *Look Homeward, Angel* as a madam, quoting her comment about her theatrical career: "I was always a madam."

Between New York engagements, she returned to Little Rock. In 1954, she worked as a humane officer for the sheriff's department, and she was hired by Little Rock's KARK-TV to host *Aunt Lucy's Animal Fair*, a Saturday morning television show.

The Little Rock Chamber of Commerce asked her to organize the city's first community theater. Ultimately, the theater's productions were reviewed by New York drama critics.

When Babcock cast African American students from Philander Smith College, there was opposition from the Ku Klux Klan, the segregationist White Citizens' Council, and Governor Orval Faubus. Marcia Camp said in the *Encyclopedia of Arkansas*, "While Babcock was in Oklahoma accepting an award for her contribution to integration, the Community Theater board voted to close the theater. After a cross was burned in her mother's yard, she returned to Broadway."

In 1962, Lucille Babcock returned to Little Rock after the death of her grandmother. Though her health was deteriorating, she became active in small theaters across the state and enrolled at Little Rock University (today's University of Arkansas at Little Rock). She served as president of the Arkansas Poets' Roundtable, where she worked to racially integrate the organization. In 1981, she began serving as editor of a weekly poetry column in the *Arkansas Gazette* after convincing the newspaper's management that the paper needed a poetry column.

In 1987, the sixty-five-year-old Babcock was working on her column in her second-floor garage apartment one morning when she saw a man outside dragging a screaming young woman by the hair. Though Babcock was wearing a back brace and using a cane, she limped down the stairs to beat the attacker with her cane. Yelling to get attention, she slammed the man's leg in his car door until neighbors arrived to hold him for the police.

The *Arkansas Gazette* printed the item on the front page, and the story was carried nationwide, including a lengthy item in the *New York Times*. She was featured in such publications as *Guideposts*, *Newsweek*, and *Reader's Digest*. Babcock received honors from Arkansas governor Bill Clinton and received the Carnegie Hero Award with a prize of $2,500.

At age seventy-two, Babcock succumbed to cancer, dying in her sleep on April 4, 1993. She is buried in Little Rock's National Cemetery.

For more information:

Dean, Jerry. "Lucy Babcock, Hero." *Arkansas Gazette*, March 3, 1990, pp. 1E, 5E.

Reed, Roy. "A Leg in a Brace and White Hair, but Still a Tiger." *New York Times*, September 21, 1987, p. 10.

Daisy Bates (1914–1999)

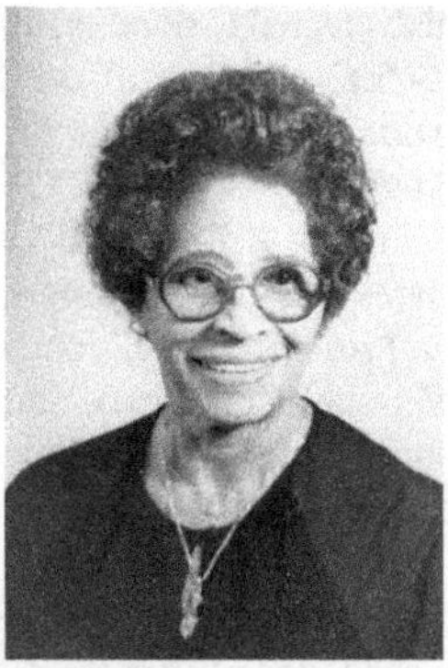

DAISY GATSON BATES was an internationally known civil rights leader, journalist, and author who was a central figure in the 1957 Little Rock desegregation crisis. With her husband, she published the *Arkansas State Press* newspaper, covering issues significant to African Americans. As one of the few female civil rights leaders of her time, she has been called the "Rosa Parks of Arkansas."

Daisy Lee Gatson was born on or around November 11, 1914, and grew up in the southern Arkansas town of Huttig. The identity of her birth parents is unknown. In an article titled "The Death of My Mother," which she wrote later in life, Daisy Bates recalled that when she was seven years old, she was told that her mother had been raped and murdered by three local white men who were known to the community but never arrested. Her father left her with foster parents Susie and Orlee Smith, whom the child grew up thinking of as her biological parents. She has written that her foster father encouraged her to re-channel the hatred she felt after learning of her mother's murder, saying, "Try to do something about it, or your hate won't spell a thing." She said that her strength and desire for change came from this advice.

Gatson attended all-black schools in Huttig, with her formal education apparently ending by the ninth grade. She met Lucious Christopher "L. C." Bates at age fifteen.

Bates was an insurance salesman from Memphis, Tennessee. She moved with him to Little Rock, where they were married in 1942. Beginning in 1941, they published the *Arkansas State Press*, a statewide weekly newspaper aimed at African Americans. The *Arkansas State Press* spotlighted civil rights issues and also covered social news and achievements by black city residents, which mainstream white newspapers generally did not cover. In 1945, Daisy Bates was named city editor and recognized as co-publisher.

Daisy Bates was an active supporter of the National Association for the Advancement of Colored People (NAACP). In 1952, she was elected president of the NAACP's Arkansas coordinating body. In response to her advocacy of school desegregation, she regularly received death threats, crosses were burned at her home, and financial pressure was put on the *Arkansas State Press* until it was forced to close in 1959.

With her involvement with the newspaper and the NAACP, Daisy Bates assumed a leadership role in the court-ordered integration of Little Rock's schools in 1957. Nine black students were selected to attend the all-white Little Rock Central High School. Along with serving as NAACP's public spokesperson, Daisy Bates became the students' advisor as they attempted to enroll. Arkansas governor Orval Faubus called out the state's National Guard to prevent the Little Rock Nine from attending. News stories were carried around the world about the angry mobs in Little Rock. President Dwight Eisenhower federalized the Arkansas National Guard and dispatched the U.S. Army's 101st Airborne Division to maintain order.

Bates and other NAACP figures were arrested and fined, though they eventually won a reversal in the U.S. Supreme Court. The Little Rock Nine were allowed to attend school at Central in 1957, but for the 1958–59 school year, Little Rock high schools were closed in an attempt to thwart desegregation.

The Bates house served as the site of planning sessions, and it continued to be attacked by segregationists. In 2002, the home was named a National Historic Landmark as a pivotal site in civil rights movement.

During the Little Rock crisis, Bates was contacted by Martin Luther King Jr., who offered words of support. King was her guest in 1958 when he spoke at Agricultural, Mechanical, and Normal College (today's University of Arkansas at Pine Bluff), and he invited her to speak at Alabama's Dexter Avenue Baptist Church later that year. She was also elected to the executive committee of the Southern Christian Leadership Conference (SCLC). As one of the few female civil rights leaders of the time, she was the only woman who spoke at the Lincoln Memorial for the landmark March on Washington in August 1963.

From 1957 through 1970, she served on the national board of the NAACP. In 1960, Bates wrote a memoir with an introduction by Eleanor Roosevelt, *The Long Shadow of Little Rock*, which won a National Book Award. Bates joined the Democratic National Committee and worked in Washington DC on anti-poverty programs for the administration of President Lyndon Johnson. In 1965, she suffered a stroke and returned to Little Rock.

In 1968, she moved to the rural black community of Mitchellville in eastern Arkansas to serve as executive director of the Economic Opportunity Agency. She commuted on weekends to Little Rock to be with her husband, who was in declining health.

Among her many honors, she was named one of the top ten newsmakers in the world by the Associated Press and Woman of the Year in 1957 by the National Council of Negro Women. Along with the Little Rock Nine, she received the NAACP's Spingarn Medal.

In 2001, the Arkansas Legislature designated the third Monday in February as Daisy Gatson Bates Day in conjunction with Presidents' Day as an official state holiday. The street running north of Central High School was renamed Daisy L. Gatson Bates Drive. In 1987, Little Rock's Daisy Bates Elementary School was named in her honor, with its first principal being an African American woman.

In later life, Bates resided in a nursing home. She died of a heart attack on November 4, 1999, at age eighty-five. She was the first (and to date, only) African American to lie in state in the Arkansas State Capitol. In 2012, a documentary film called *Daisy Bates: First Lady of Little Rock* premiered on PBS.

For more information:

Bates, Daisy. *The Long Shadow of Little Rock*. Fayetteville: University of Arkansas Press, 2000.

Kearney, Janis E. *Daisy: Between a Rock and a Hard Place*. Little Rock: Writing Our World Press, 2013.

Stockley, Grif. *Daisy Bates: Civil Rights Crusader from Arkansas*. Jackson: University of Mississippi Press, 2005.

Melba Pattillo Beals (1941–)

JOURNALIST MELBA PATTILLO BEALS was a member of the Little Rock Nine, a group of African American students who were the first to integrate Little Rock Central High School in 1957. There, they faced daily threats, intimidation, and violence. Beals wrote about the ordeal in *Warriors Don't Cry: A Searing Memoir of the Battle to Desegregate Little Rock's Central High School*. She also vividly described returning to Little Rock later in life for events commemorating the 1957 crisis.

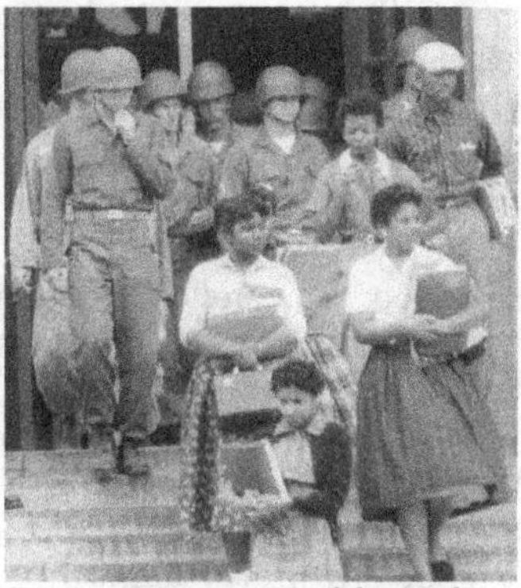

Four young women of the Little Rock Nine exit Central High School. They are (clockwise from top): Elizabeth Eckford, Minnijean Brown, Gloria Ray, and Melba Pattillo. The other young women of the Little Rock Nine were Thelma Mothershed and Carlotta Walls.

Melba Pattillo was born in Little Rock on December 7, 1941, the day that Japan bombed Pearl Harbor, spurring the United States' entry into World War II. She was the first child born to Howell "Will" Pattillo, who worked for the Missouri Pacific Railroad, and secondary school English teacher Lois Peyton Pattillo. Lois Pattillo would become one of the first African American students to graduate from the University of Arkansas (UA) in Fayetteville when she received a master's degree in education in 1954.

As a newborn, Melba Pattillo suffered a serious scalp infection that left her near death. White doctors and nurses did little to help the newborn. Lois Pattillo spoke to a janitor, who told her that he had overheard a doctor mentioning that Epsom salts would help. When the salts were obtained, the baby recovered.

Melba's younger brother, Conrad Pattillo, grew up to have a distinguished career as one of the first African Americans in Arkansas law enforcement. The family lived with Melba's grandmother, India Annette Peyton, without whom Beals says she would not have survived her year at Central.

Melba Pattillo attended Little Rock's all-black Horace Mann High School. When integration was ordered by the courts, she volunteered to transfer to the all-white Central High School. She later said, "I wanted to go because they had more privileges. They had more equipment, they had five floors of opportunities. For me, I understood education before I understood anything else." Pattillo became one of nine black students—dubbed the Little Rock Nine—to enroll at Central, saying that she saw it as a chance to meet new people and do new things.

In August 1957, just before the start of school, she visited relatives in Cincinnati, Ohio. She found it to be welcoming to blacks, "a place where I could be free and I could breathe." Returning to Little Rock in September 1957, however, Pattillo faced angry mobs who yelled, cursed, and spat when she and the other black students tried to register at Central. Arkansas governor Orval Faubus used the state's National Guard to block them from attending. President Dwight Eisenhower federalized the National Guard and ordered in the U.S. Army's 101st Airborne Division to protect the black students.

Melba Pattillo recounted those events in her book *Warriors Don't Cry*, as well as during interviews. She said, "When you're fifteen, you want to be loved and accepted." Instead, the young people faced daily harassment, threats, and violence, including an incident in which a student sprayed acid into Pattillo's eyes. The quick action of the soldier who accompanied Pattillo saved her eyesight. Pattillo also recalled being told by her military escort, "In order to get through this year, you will have to become a soldier. Never let your enemy know what you are feeling."

She also recalled that any white students who smiled at her, were helpful, or were even minimally kind to her were themselves subjected to threats and harassment. Yet she made it through her junior year. However, she was not able to graduate from Central because the governor closed Little Rock high schools for the 1958–59 school year to block integration.

With help from the National Association for the Advancement of Colored People (NAACP), Melba Pattillo moved to Santa Rosa, California, to finish high school there. She recalled being surprised to find that there were white members of the NAACP and that she was sent to live with a white family. Pattillo said that the family treated her as an equal and showed her unconditional love. In 1959, Pattillo finished her senior year at Santa Rosa's Montgomery High School. The school was named for William Montgomery, who was killed at Pearl Harbor on the day of Melba Pattillo's birth—December 7, 1941.

In 1960, she enrolled at San Francisco State University to study journalism. While there, she met fellow student John Beals, whom she married in 1961. The couple had a daughter, but after ten years, they divorced. Melba Beals later adopted two boys.

Melba Beals earned a bachelor's degree at San Francisco State and a master's degree from New York's Columbia University, both in journalism. She wrote for major newspapers and magazines, and worked on the book that would become *Warriors Don't Cry*. She later wrote *White Is a State of Mind*, which begins where the earlier book ended.

Warriors Don't Cry was named the American Library Association's Notable Book for 1995 and won the Robert F. Kennedy Book Award that same year.

Beals earned a doctorate in education from the University of San Francisco, and she taught journalism at Dominican University of California, where she became chair emeritus of the communications department. Beals has worked as a communications consultant, motivational speaker, and television reporter in San Francisco.

Among Beals's many honors are the 1959 Spingarn Medal from the NAACP, which she received with the other members of the Little Rock Nine. In 1999, she and her eight fellow history-makers received the Congressional Gold Medal.

For more information:

Beals, Melba Pattillo. *Warriors Don't Cry: A Searing Memoir of the Battle to Desegregate Little Rock's Central High School*. New York: Washington Square Books, 1994.

———. *White Is a State of Mind*. New York: Putnam Publishing Group, 1999.

Debbye Turner Bell (1965–)

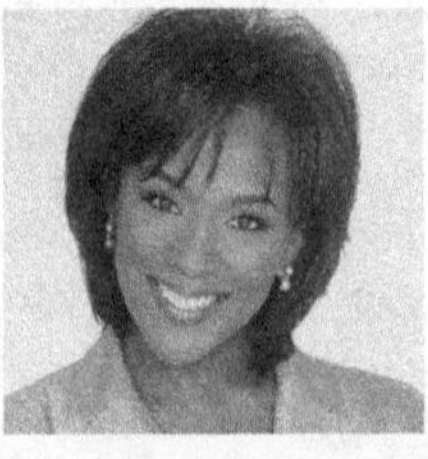

DR. DEBBYE TURNER BELL won the title of Miss America in 1990, becoming the first African American to hold the Miss America crown for an entire year. She went on to a career as a popular national television anchor, talk show host, and motivational speaker in addition to her vocation as a veterinarian. She is a singer and pianist, as well as a talented percussionist, as was seen in her marimba rendition of "Flight of the Bumblebee" for the talent portion of the Miss America pageant.

Debrah Lynn "Debbye" Turner was born on September 19, 1965, in Honolulu, Hawaii, to Gussie Lee Jones Turner and Frederick C. Turner Jr., who was stationed there in the military. Her mother later became an academic counselor. Her father had been one of the first two African American graduates of Arkansas State University (ASU) in Jonesboro, receiving a commission in the infantry along with his bachelor's degree in education. After three combat tours in Vietnam, he returned to ASU in 1969 as an assistant professor of military science, becoming the university's first black faculty member.

Debbye Turner was raised in Jonesboro, setting her goal as a child to become a veterinarian. However, she recognized that there were financial challenges, especially after her parents divorced. When she was thirteen years old, she found information through her local library about the costs of veterinary school. She later said, "Veterinary school is four years, just like medical school. In fact, we learn everything a human physician learns, except they learn about one mammal, the human. Veterinarians must learn about *six* mammals—cats, dogs, horses, cows, pigs, and chickens."

Living with her mother and sister, Suzette, she became focused on a veterinary career. She took advanced science courses, joined leadership clubs, and worked toward attaining top grades in order to be accepted into veterinary school. She became an observer at a local veterinary clinic, and as soon as she turned sixteen, she got a job serving hamburgers at a fast-food restaurant. She also held jobs as a department store clerk and grocery store cashier. She graduated from Jonesboro High School in 1983. In 1986, after majoring in animal science, she graduated cum laude from ASU with a bachelor's degree. In 1991, she received her Doctor of Veterinary Medicine degree from the University of Missouri in Columbia.

In order to obtain money to attend college and graduate school, Turner entered scholarship-related pageants. While in Jonesboro, she was first-runner-up in her initial pageant, Miss Black Teenage World, in 1981. That same year, she won the title of Northeast Arkansas Junior Miss and was a semi-finalist in the 1982 Arkansas Junior Miss pageant. After winning the Jonesboro High School Valentines Sweetheart pageant in 1983, Turner was encouraged to enter the Miss Jonesboro competition. It was her first pageant in the Miss America system, the largest source of scholarships for women in the world.

In the Miss Jonesboro pageants of 1983 and 1984, Turner placed second- and first-runner-up, respectively. In 1985, 1986, and 1987, Turner won three local pageants: Miss Arkansas State University, Miss White River, and Miss Northeast Arkansas. Through these pageants, she went to the Miss Arkansas pageant three times, finishing twice as first runner-up.

When she entered graduate school in 1988 at the University of Missouri, she became eligible for the Miss Missouri system of pageants. Turner won the Miss Columbia pageant and the Miss Missouri pageant. As Missouri's delegate to the Miss America pageant, she was crowned Miss America 1990, becoming the first delegate from Missouri to win the title. She was also the first African American to hold the Miss America title for an entire year, following the 1984 title year split between Vanessa Williams and Suzette Charles after Williams relinquished the crown. With the resultant scholarship, Debbye Turner completed her education to become a veterinarian.

In 1995, she was sought as a television host for KSDK in St. Louis on a program called *Show Me St. Louis*; she received an Emmy nomination for this program. She went on to host a PBS series, *The Gentle Doctor*, and joined CBS News as a feature correspondent. She became the regular correspondent discussing animal issues on CBS's *Early Show* as well as a fill-in anchor. She has also appeared on the *Cats 101* and *Dogs 101* series on the Animal Planet TV channel. Turner has appeared as a guest on such top-rated TV programs as *The Late Show with David Letterman, The Oprah Winfrey Show*, and the *Today* show.

In 2013, she became the host of *Arise America*, on the Arise News network, an internationally broadcast twenty-four-hour news and entertainment channel. In addition, she is a motivational speaker who has appeared before millions of students at schools, colleges, and youth organizations.

In 2008, she married Gerald Bell; they have a daughter. The family resides in New York City.

In addition to hosting the Miss Florida, Miss Georgia, and Miss Missouri pageants, Debbye Turner Bell has also served organizations including the Children's Miracle Network, National Council on Youth Leadership, and National Advisory on Child Health & Human Development Council, an advisory council to the National Institutes of Health.

For more information:

Debbye Turner Bell. http://www.debbyeturner.com (accessed December 8, 2015).

"Miss America and the American Dream." *St. Louis Magazine* (May 1998). http://www.debbyeturner.com/news_stlouismag.html (accessed December 8, 2015).

Diane Blair (1938–2000)

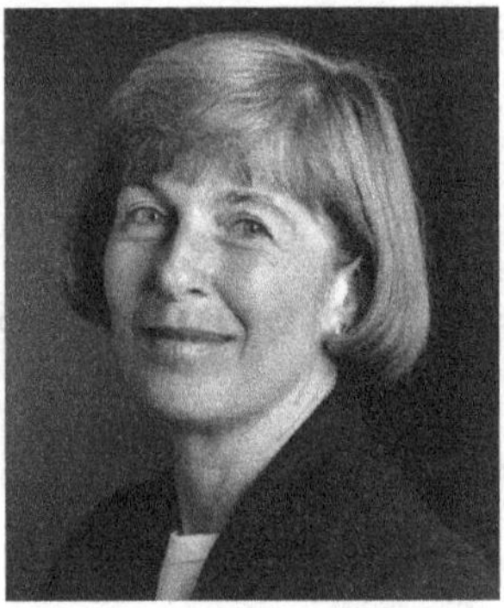

DIANE BLAIR was an educator, political scientist, speaker, and writer. She was a member of the U.S. Electoral College, served as chair of the Corporation for Public Broadcasting, and authored two influential books. She also served as senior advisor and chronicler of the Clinton-Gore presidential campaigns.

After her sudden death, she was eulogized in newspapers across the country. In 2014, more than a decade after her death, she made headlines with the release of her "treasure trove" of notes about the campaign of Bill Clinton and Al Gore.

Diane Frances Divers was born on October 25, 1938, in Washington DC. She had one older sister. Her parents, William Keeveny Divers and Minna Rosenbaum Divers, were both attorneys. Divers grew up in Washington before going to Cornell University in New York to study political science. There, she was a member of Phi Beta Kappa, graduating cum laude from Cornell's Department of Government in 1959.

She returned to Washington after graduation, working as a legislative secretary and speechwriter for Missouri senator Stuart Symington, a two-time presidential hopeful. In addition, she served as analyst for the President's Committee on Government Contracts and research assistant with the Senate Special Committee on Unemployment.

While in Washington, she married Arkansan Hugh Kincaid, an attorney with the U.S. Army Judge Advocate General (JAG) Corps. Moving to Fayetteville in 1963, she earned a master's degree in political science from the University of Arkansas (UA) in Fayetteville in 1967.

In a memoir written by Hillary Clinton [SEE ENTRY], she described Blair as her closest friend during her early years in Arkansas, saying that they played tennis, traded favorite books, and regularly met for lunch. Both women loved politics, and both had traded big-city life for an Arkansas college town because of the men they married.

In 1968, Diane Kincaid began teaching political science at UA. Governor Dale Bumpers appointed her to chair the Governor's Commission on the Status of Women in 1971. On February 14, 1975, the famed "Valentine's Day Debate" took place in the Arkansas General Assembly, during which Kincaid took the "pro" position on passage of the Equal Rights Amendment (ERA) against her opponent, the nationally known conservative activist Phyllis Schlafly. Though the ERA was not successful in Arkansas, the consensus was that Kincaid had easily won the debate.

In 1979, Kincaid published *Silent Hattie Speaks: The Personal Journal of Senator Hattie Caraway*, providing commentary about the first woman elected to the U.S. Senate, Hattie Wyatt Caraway [SEE ENTRY]. Also in 1979, after her marriage to Hugh Kincaid had ended, she married prominent northwestern Arkansas attorney James Burton Blair. The Clintons and Blairs shared many of their most important moments together, including then-governor Bill Clinton performing the Blairs' marriage ceremony, with Hillary Clinton as "best person."

In 1980, Governor Clinton appointed Diane Blair to the Arkansas Educational Television Network Commission. She was on the commission until 1993, serving as chairperson in 1986–87. Blair's second book, *Arkansas Politics and Government: Do the People Rule?* was published in 1988. At the time of her death, she was working on a second edition. Though not specifically written as a textbook, it is still widely used in many Arkansas colleges and universities.

During Bill Clinton's presidential bid of 1992, Blair took a year's leave from UA to serve as a senior advisor, researcher, and chronicler of the cross-country campaign. That year, she was selected to be a member of the U.S. Electoral College. After Bill Clinton won the presidential election, Blair and her husband stayed at the White House on the Clintons' first night there in 1993.

Clinton appointed Blair in 1993 to the Corporation for Public Broadcasting's board of directors, which she later chaired. She was reappointed in 1997 and served so admirably that the organization named its boardroom in her honor. In 1993, Blair was awarded guest scholar status at Washington's famed Brookings Institution.

When Bill Clinton was re-nominated for the presidency in 1996, Blair again took leave from UA to join the 1996 Clinton-Gore re-election campaign. Throughout the campaigns and with full approval from the principals, Blair kept extensive journals and interviewed members of the Clinton-Gore team.

In May 2000, Blair spoke at UA's commencement. A month later, on June 26, 2000, Blair—a non-smoker—died of lung cancer at age sixty-one, several weeks after learning of her illness. She left behind her husband and two children: William and Kathryn. The Clintons were at her bedside in Fayetteville shortly before she died, and both eulogized their friend at her memorial service.

In her honor, the Diane D. Blair Center of Southern Politics and Society at UA was established in late 2000.

After Blair's death, her papers were archived at UA. When the archives were opened to the public in 2010, Hillary Clinton recorded a video honoring Blair's life and work.

In 2014, Blair's name made national headlines with the release of her notes on the Clinton presidential campaigns. Most news reports focused on their "unguarded" look at Hillary Clinton, the former first lady, senator, and secretary of state who then became a presidential candidate. Blair's notes, almost two million documents in all, have been lauded for their scholarly and meticulous quality.

For more information:

Blair, Diane D., and Jay Barth. *Arkansas Politics and Government*. 2nd ed. Lincoln: University of Nebraska Press, 2005.

Diane D. Blair Center of Southern Politics and Society. http://blaircenter.uark.edu/ (accessed December 8, 2015).

Lisa Blount (1957–2010)

LISA BLOUNT was a nationally known actress in film and television who also became an Oscar-winning producer. She was especially acclaimed for her role in 1982's hit movie *An Officer and a Gentleman*, for which she garnered a Golden Globe nomination. She died suddenly in Little Rock at age fifty-three while she was still active in show business, preparing a television pilot.

Lisa Suzanne Blount was born in Fayetteville, Arkansas, on July 1, 1957, to Margaret Louise Martin Blount and homebuilder Glen Roscoe Blount. With her brother Greg, Lisa Blount was raised in Jacksonville, Arkansas, and attended Jacksonville High School.

Although some sources say she graduated from high school in 1975, she instead skipped her senior year to enroll at the University of Arkansas at Little Rock (UALR), where she studied music and theater. In a 2009 interview, Blount said she left school at age sixteen and "acted" her way into college, claiming her diploma must have gotten lost in the mail. "I didn't wait to graduate from high school to get the education I wanted," she said. "I was in Hollywood, set up with my own apartment when I was still a teenager."

In 1977, at age nineteen, she was cast in the movie *September 30, 1955*, which was filmed in Conway, Arkansas. She worked steadily in both movies and television, including TV appearances on *Murder, She Wrote*; *Picket Fences*; and the drama *Profit*, in which she was a regular. Her film work includes *Cut and Run*, *Cease Fire*, *South of Reno*, *Great Balls of Fire!*, *What Waits Below*, *Femme Fatale*, *Prince of Darkness*, *Needful Things*, *Box of Moonlight*, *Chrystal*, and *Randy & the Mob*.

Blount's breakthrough role was playing Debra Winger's character's best friend, Lynette Pomeroy, in *An Officer and a Gentleman*. For her work in that movie, she earned a Golden Globe nomination as the female New Star of the Year in a Motion Picture, and she was voted Favorite Female Newcomer in a 1983 *US* magazine readers' poll.

While filming the movie *Needful Things* in 1992, she met fellow actor Ray McKinnon from Georgia. McKinnon has also worked steadily, with TV appearances on such programs as *Sons of Anarchy*, *Justified*, *Deadwood*, and *The X-Files*, along with movie roles in *The Blind Side*; *O Brother, Where Art Thou?*; *The Net*; and *Apollo 13*.

The couple wed in 1998. With their friend Walton Goggin, Blount and her husband formed Ginny Mule Pictures in 1999. In a 2002 interview, Blount said their goal was to make authentic Southern movies, adding, "We got sick and tired of seeing Northerners make movies about the South."

In 2001, they released *The Accountant*, a film set on a financially troubled Southern farm. Blount produced the film, which was written and directed by her husband. It went on to earn awards such as the 2002 Academy Award for "Best Live Action Short Film."

Blount and her husband moved to Little Rock in 2005. She said the move was partially due to their love of the South as well as because of her health problems. She filmed the series pilot *Outlaw Country* for the FX cable channel, pursued a music project, and performed onstage with actor Johnny Depp and Pearl Jam rocker Eddie Vedder at a rally in Little Rock for the "West Memphis Three." On September 9, 2010, Blount was inducted into the Arkansas Entertainers Hall of Fame.

The following month, on October 27, 2010, Lisa Blount was found dead at home in the Hillcrest neighborhood of Little Rock while her husband was in Atlanta. Blount's mother found her in bed holding a cellphone, which she had last used when she told a friend she was not feeling well. Her mother told authorities that Blount had been suffering for seventeen years with a rare blood disorder that created a painful condition similar to multiple sclerosis. Just prior to her death, Blount had complained of back and neck pain. There was no sign of foul play.

For more information:

"Lisa Blount." Internet Movie Database. http://www.imdb.com/name/nm0089408 (accessed December 8, 2015).

Wilke, Lorraine. "Oscar-Winner Lisa Blount Is Remembered...'As Is and Still Loved.'" http://www.huffingtonpost.com/lorraine-devon-wilke/lisa-blount-memoriam_b_828967.html (accessed December 8, 2015).

Gretha Boston (1959–)

THE NATIONALLY RENOWNED MEZZO-SOPRANO and award-winning actress Gretha Boston was the first person from Arkansas to win Broadway's prestigious Tony Award. In her Tony acceptance speech she thanked her family and friends in Crossett, Arkansas.

Gretha Denise Boston was born in Crossett on April 18, 1959. She was the eldest of seven children born to Delores Tucker Boston and Curtis Boston Sr. Her path to the world of music began at age two with training as a member of the "Kiddie Choir" at the Gates Chapel African Methodist Episcopal (AME) Church. As a fifteen-year-old student attending Crossett High School, she saw her first opera, *Carmen*, at Northeast Louisiana University and was inspired to make a career in opera. She sang in her high school choir and took voice lessons with music department teachers, who encouraged her singing career. Boston graduated from Crossett High School in 1977.

She attended North Texas State University (NTSU, now the University of North Texas) in Denton, Texas, studying music and performance. During her tenure at NTSU, she was invited to sing "God Bless America" before a Dallas Mavericks basketball game. As a member of the college's a capella choir, she recorded Mendelssohn's *Walpurgisnacht* with the Royal Philharmonic Orchestra in London, England.

After graduation from NTSU in 1981 with a bachelor's degree in music and performance, Boston attended the University of Illinois at Urbana-Champaign. There, she was twice recognized by the D'Angelo International Young Artists Competition. She went on to study in New York City with Margaret Hoswell and Maestro Franco Iglesias in addition to working locally in real estate.

In 1991, Boston made her Carnegie Hall debut in Mozart's *Coronation Mass*. She again took the Carnegie Hall stage to perform in Beethoven's Ninth Symphony.

Her work as a choral performer includes Verdi's *Requiem* with the New York Grand Opera. She has played operatic roles such as Amneris in *Aida*, Maddelena in *Rigoletto*, and Maria in *Porgy and Bess*. Boston reached a national audience when she appeared on *An Enchanted Evening: A Salute to Oscar Hammerstein*, which was broadcast on PBS. She has also been seen on television on the *Today* show and *The Late Show with David Letterman* as well as guest starring on *Hope and Faith*, *Law and Order*, and *Law and Order: Criminal Intent*.

Boston portrayed the character of Bloody Mary in the national touring company of the iconic musical *South Pacific*, which starred Robert Goulet. She has also performed in musicals in such roles as Ethel (said to symbolize the legendary Ethel Waters) in *Let Me Sing* and Velma Crowns in *Portraits of Black Women in Church Hats*. She also appeared as Lola in *Jar the Floor*.

While Boston was touring with the opera *Porgy and Bess*, she impressed the producers of *Show Boat*, who invited her to audition for the 1994 revival of the American classic. In that production of *Show Boat*, reimagined by legendary showman Hal Prince, the role of Queenie was built around Boston. The song "Mis'ry's Comin' Aroun'," which had been cut from productions after the show's 1927 premiere, was added to showcase Boston's talent. She was acclaimed by critics for her interpretation of Queenie, reminiscent of the dignity and reserve as personified by African American opera singers such as Leontyne Price. Boston was quoted as saying, "I used to see women going in the morning to clean white folks' houses. They left in the morning with dignity and returned home with dignity. That was all I needed."

For that portrayal, Boston won the American Theatre Wing's 1995 Antoinette Perry

Award for Excellence in Theatre, more commonly known as the Tony Award, for Best Featured Actress in a Musical, despite heavy competition. She was the first Arkansan to be honored with a Tony. Also in 1995, Boston received a Theatre World Award for Outstanding Broadway Debut Artist.

In 1999, Boston was again a Tony Award nominee as Featured Actress in a Musical for her performance in *It Ain't Nothin' But the Blues.* For that role, she was also nominated for the Helen Hayes Award for Outstanding Lead Actress at the Kennedy Center in Washington DC.

Currently residing in New York City, Gretha Boston often acknowledges her home state. When she took the stage to receive her Tony Award, she said, "At this very moment in a little town called Crossett, Arkansas, a ballroom is filled with my parents, my sister, all five of my brothers, along with a host of other family members and friends—thank you for always being my safe haven."

For more information:

Decker, Todd. *Show Boat: Performing Race in an American Musical.* New York: Oxford University Press, 2013.

"Gretha Boston." Internet Movie Database. http://www.imdb.com/name/nm0098253 (accessed December 8, 2015).

Beth Brickell

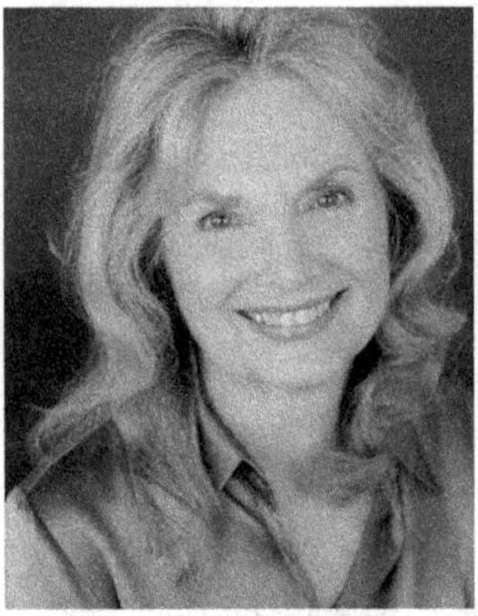

BETH BRICKELL is an actress, producer, and writer with many stage and screen credits, including a leading role on the television series *Gentle Ben.* In recent years, she has concentrated on film production and on her book, *The Disappearance of Maud Crawford*, based on the mystery surrounding the fate of Arkansas attorney Maud Crawford.

Beth Brickell was born on November 13. Some sources, such as the *New York Times*, give her year of birth as 1936, while others say 1937 or 1941. She was born in Brinkley, Arkansas, and raised in Pine Bluff and Camden.

She graduated from Camden High School in 1954 and then attended Arkansas State Teachers College (today's University of Central Arkansas—UCA). Brickell transferred to the University of Arkansas (UA) in Fayetteville, earning a bachelor's degree in political science. She went on to study at the American Film Institute Conservatory in Los Angeles, California, from which she received a master of fine arts degree in 1978.

She worked as a secretary after moving to New York City, where she was cast in television commercials and off-Broadway shows while studying at the famed Actors Studio. She appeared in more than twenty stage productions.

In 1966, she was cast on television's *The Girl from U.N.C.L.E.*, a spin-off of the hit series *The Man from U.N.C.L.E.*, on which Brickell appeared in 1967. During this period, she appeared on TV shows such as *Captain Nice*, *The Green Hornet*, and *The Hero*.

From 1967 to 1969, she starred for two seasons on the popular television series *Gentle Ben* as the wife of Dennis Weaver. The show highlighted the adventures of a Florida Everglades game warden, his family, and a tame bear named Ben.

Through the 1970s, Brickell appeared on such popular TV shows as *Marcus Welby M.D.*, *The Virginian*, *Bonanza*, *Hawaii Five-O*, *Gunsmoke*, *Love American Style*, *Emergency!*, *Adam-12*, and *Fantasy Island.* In 1972, she appeared in the feature film *The Only Way Home*, followed by the 1975 movie *The Posse* (with Kirk Douglas) and 1977's *Death Game*.

In the 1980s, she transitioned to directing after teaching for three years at the Lee

Strasberg Institute in both New York and Los Angeles. She worked on projects such as directing two episodes of the TV drama *Knots Landing*, and she was writer and producer for films including *Little Boy Blue*, *A Rainy Day* (which won several awards, including First Place at the USA Film Festival in Dallas and was broadcast on PBS), and *Summer's End*, which won seventeen film industry awards.

Brickell wrote, directed, and produced 2005's holiday movie *Mr. Christmas*, which won Best Family Film at Hollywood's Moondance Film Festival and an Award of Excellence from the Film Advisory Board in Los Angeles.

In addition to her acting career, she utilized her early interest in politics when she worked for the 1988 Michael Dukakis presidential campaign. In 1992, she organized a fundraiser for Bill Clinton's presidential campaign. She also promoted the campaign of Senator Blanche Lincoln [SEE ENTRY] of Arkansas.

Brickell has served as chair of the Director's Guild of American Women's Steering Committee, an Emmy Awards panelist for the Academy of Television Arts and Sciences, and on the grants committee for the Corporation for Public Broadcasting. She has served on the screening committee for the Hot Springs Documentary Film Festival and has taught screenwriting and cinema at the University of Arkansas at Little Rock.

Brickell is president of her own independent film company, Luminous Films Inc., with the stated mission of making "uplifting character-driven movies that speak to the lives of viewers." Projects in development include an adaptation of the bestselling novel by Mary Medearis [SEE ENTRY], *Big Doc's Girl*. Another, *Disappearance*, is an original screenplay based on an investigative series that Brickell wrote for the *Arkansas Gazette* in 1986.

Brickell's newspaper articles and subsequent book tell the story of Maud Crawford, a prominent woman from Camden who disappeared in 1957. It has been called the most widely publicized mystery in Arkansas history. Crawford, an attorney and civic leader in Camden, vanished from her home, with no body, clue, trace, or motive found during the original police investigation.

Almost thirty years after Crawford's disappearance, Brickell returned to Camden, the town where she grew up. Feeling that the case had not been properly investigated, she suspected a cover-up of Crawford's disappearance and found that even three decades later, townspeople were afraid to talk about it. Brickell, whose life was threatened, remained in Camden for more than a year attempting to unravel the mystery of Crawford's disappearance. Her nineteen newspaper articles ran on the front page of the *Gazette* over a period of five months. The newspaper was threatened with a lawsuit in an effort to stop the articles, but it went on to publish the complete series. The articles were then compiled into a book.

Today, Beth Brickell makes occasional book-signing appearances as she develops the Maud Crawford project. She divides her time between a home in Los Angeles and an Arkansas rural retreat.

For more information:

Brickell, Beth. *The Disappearance of Maud Crawford*. Luminous Films, Inc., 2013.

Luminous Films Inc. www.luminousfilms.net (accessed December 8, 2015).

Helen Gurley Brown (1922–2012)

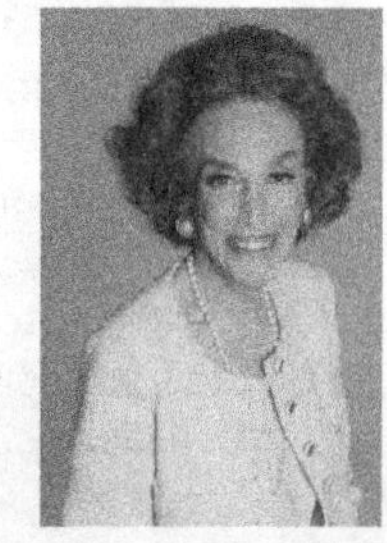

HELEN GURLEY BROWN was a pioneer in advertising, business, and publishing, as well as being an internationally known voice for women's liberation and the sexual revolution of the twentieth century. She attained worldwide fame as author of the bestselling book *Sex and the Single Girl* and as editor-in-chief of *Cosmopolitan* magazine, whose "Cosmo Girl" was said to influence a generation of women.

Helen Marie Gurley was born on February 18, 1922, in Green Forest, Arkansas, to schoolteachers Cleo Sisco Gurley and Ira Marvin Gurley. Helen had an older sister, Mary. When Helen was a child, her father was elected to the Arkansas state legislature and the family moved to Little Rock.

In 1932, Ira Gurley died in an elevator accident at the Arkansas State Capitol as he was preparing to run for Arkansas secretary of state. Helen's mother attended typing school and took in sewing to provide for the family while Helen attended Pulaski Heights Junior High.

In 1937, when Helen Gurley was fourteen, the family moved to Los Angeles, California. A few months later, her sister Mary was stricken with polio. Helen attended John H. Francis Polytechnic High School, where she was in the top ten percent of her class, graduating in 1939. After her graduation, the family moved to Warm Springs, Georgia, where the waters were considered beneficial to polio patients.

Helen Gurley attended Texas State College for Women (now Texas Woman's University) in Denton but was forced to withdraw after one semester for financial reasons. She returned to Los Angeles, where she enrolled at Woodbury Business College, graduating in 1941. In 1947, when Helen Gurley was twenty-four, her mother and sister returned to Arkansas to live with her mother's family in the small town of Osage. Helen remained in Los Angeles.

After working at the William Morris Agency, Music Corporation of America, and Jaffe Talent Agency, she took a secretarial job with the Los Angeles advertising firm of Foote, Cone and Belding in 1948. There, she advanced to writing copy when her employer recognized her writing skills. She would become one of the nation's highest-paid ad copywriters in the early 1960s, which was highly unusual for a woman.

Gurley rose rapidly in advertising, winning three Frances Holmes Advertising Copywriters awards. In 1958, she joined the Los Angeles advertising firm of Kenyon & Eckhardt as copywriter and account executive.

In 1959, at age thirty-seven, she married movie producer David Brown, who went on to produce such films as *The Sting*, *Jaws*, and *Driving Miss Daisy*. With her husband's encouragement, she documented her memories of being an unmarried woman, publishing the book *Sex and the Single Girl* in 1962.

The book became an immediate bestseller. It was published in two dozen countries, stayed on bestseller lists for over a year, was turned into a movie starring Natalie Wood, and revolutionized the perception of a single woman from a sad spinster to the "glamour girl of our times." It covered beauty, dating, finance, and work, as well as sex—a subject previously off limits to "proper" unmarried women.

The book stressed the importance of what came to be known as "self-esteem." According to Brown, a full, rich life was not determined by great beauty, brains, or money, but rather by a woman's belief in herself, her willingness to develop her own potential, and her refusal to remain what Brown called a "mouseburger." In a time when women were expected to remain in the home, Brown emphasized the importance of paid, meaningful, continuing outside employment for women even after marriage.

Based on the book's success, Brown and her husband drafted plans for a magazine aimed at eighteen- to thirty-four-year-old single women. In 1965, she was named editor-in-chief of an existing literary magazine, *Cosmopolitan*, and implemented the plan. *Cosmopolitan*, or simply *Cosmo*, moved away from its staid image and became an upbeat, glitzy, high-profile magazine glorifying the "Cosmo Girl," who epitomized the modern, career-minded woman. Brown's advocacy of the liberated woman and the concept of "having it all" played a significant part in what was termed the sexual revolution.

Helen Gurley Brown remained as *Cosmo*'s editor-in-chief until 1997, defying the existing practice of men editing women's magazines. *Cosmopolitan* became a bestselling women's magazine, sold in more than 100 countries. In 1997, Brown moved from her role as *Cosmopolitan*'s U.S. editor to become international editor for all fifty-nine international editions of *Cosmo*, a position she held until her death.

In 1985, she established the Helen Gurley Brown Research Professorship in magazine publishing at Northwestern University in Chicago. Among her recognitions was induction into the Publishers' Hall of Fame and the American Society of Magazine Editors' Hall of Fame. After her husband died in 2010, Brown gave $30 million to the Columbia University Graduate School of Journalism and the Stanford University School of Engineering to establish the David and Helen Gurley Brown Institute for Media Innovation to develop journalism in the realm of new technologies.

Among her honors are the Matrix Award, Henry Johnson Fisher Award from the Magazine Publishers of America, Editor of the Year by *Advertising Age* magazine, and the Woman of Achievement Award from the Women's Project Theater (posthumously). Brown's published books include *Sex and the Office*, *Helen Gurley Brown's Outrageous Opinions*, *Sex and the New Single Girl* (an updated version of her first book), *Having It All*, *The Late Show*, *The Writer's Rules*, *I'm Wild Again*, and *Dear Pussycat*.

Helen Gurley Brown died at age ninety on August 13, 2012, in New York City following a brief hospitalization. She was eulogized around the world, especially noted for her quips like, "Good girls go to Heaven. Bad girls go everywhere."

For more information:

Falkof, Lucile. *Helen Gurley Brown: The Queen of Cosmopolitan*. Ada, OK: Garrett Educational Books, 1991.

Scanlon, Jennifer. *Bad Girls Go Everywhere: The Life of Helen Gurley Brown*. New York: Oxford University Press, 2009.

Betty Bumpers (1925–)

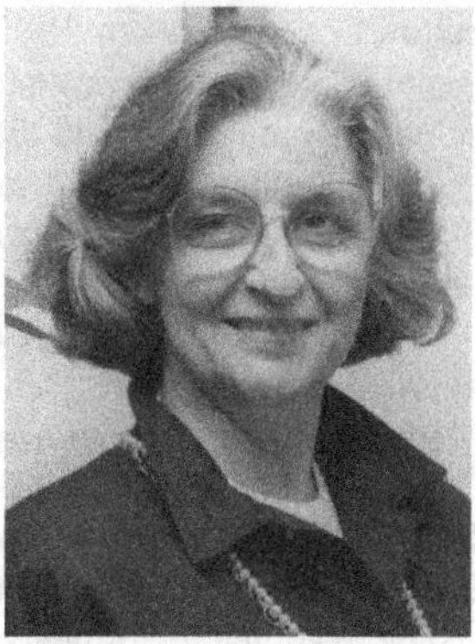

ELIZABETH "BETTY" BUMPERS is known for Peace Links, the international organization she helped create, as well working with First Lady Rosalynn Carter to promote childhood immunization.

Elizabeth Callan Flanagan was born in Grand Prairie, Arkansas, on January 11, 1925. She was the third child of homemaker Ola Callan Flanagan and Herman Flanagan, a farmer, salesman, and auctioneer. Betty grew up in Grand Prairie and in Charleston, both in the western part of the state. She attended high school in Charleston, where one of her classmates was Dale Leon Bumpers, who graduated from Charleston High School in 1943. Although the two dated, they were separated when they attended different colleges and while Dale served in the U.S. Marine Corps.

After America's entry into World War II in 1941, the Flanagan family moved to Fort Smith and later to Iowa before returning to Arkansas. Betty attended the Chicago Academy of Fine Art and the University of Iowa, becoming an elementary school teacher.

She married Dale Bumpers in 1949 while he was in law school at Chicago's Northwestern University. The couple returned to Charleston, where Dale Bumpers established a private law practice and Betty Bumpers taught school. The couple had two sons, Brent and Bill, and a daughter, Brooke. Betty Bumpers was later quoted as saying she "volunteered for everything."

Dale Bumpers lost a 1962 campaign for the Arkansas General Assembly, but he was elected governor in 1970. He was re-elected and served through 1975, when he became a U.S. senator.

As Arkansas's popular first lady and later as a Senate wife, Betty Bumpers focused her energies on children and families. Under her stewardship, Arkansas went from having one of the nation's lowest rates of childhood immunization to one of the highest. Her program in Arkansas was adopted by the U.S. Centers for Disease Control and Prevention

(CDC) as a model for use across the country.

In 1974, Dale Bumpers was elected U.S. senator from Arkansas, and the couple moved to Washington DC. In 1976, First Lady Rosalynn Carter joined with Betty Bumpers to encourage individual states to require that children be immunized before entering school, a goal that was accomplished within two years. After a measles epidemic in 1989–1991 killed more than 200 children in the United States, the women collaborated on the "Every Child By Two" program to ensure immunization for all American children by the age of two. That program was also a success.

Under the Ronald Reagan presidential administration, which began in 1981, Betty Bumpers became concerned about the expansion of nuclear arms by both the United States and the USSR. A conversation with her college-age daughter about her daughter's concerns about the significant threat of nuclear war motivated Bumpers to start a campaign for peace. She felt that the best way to overcome the threat of war and fear of the perceived enemy was through conversations with individual Soviet citizens. Betty Bumpers said, regarding her children's concerns, "I couldn't just sit back and wring my hands."

Bumpers met with congressional wives as well as other women to create Peace Links in Little Rock in 1982. The organization was founded on the belief that average American women could develop positive connections with women in the Soviet Union through a mutual concern about their children and families. Peace Links worked with women's groups to make women aware of the nuclear arms race and the consequences of war.

Peace Links became a national organization with headquarters in Washington, reaching about 30,000 members in forty states as well as Europe and the USSR and sponsoring cultural exchanges. In 1982, Betty Bumpers was attacked in a lengthy speech by a Republican senator who stated that, through her efforts for peace, she was a Communist subversive in league with the Russian KGB.

Peace Links disbanded in 2001 after it was felt that the Cold War had ended with the dissolution of the former USSR, though some chapters continued to work for international peace.

After Dale Bumpers left the Senate in 1999, the couple remained for several years in Washington, where Betty Bumpers continued working with Rosalynn Carter to promote childhood immunization. In 2001, Bumpers testified before the Senate's Health, Labor and Pensions Committee on the need for a national immunization program and for childhood immunizations to be covered by health plans. In 2010, Betty and Dale Bumpers returned to Arkansas, residing in Little Rock. Dale Bumpers died in 2016.

The National Institutes of Health Vaccine Research Center was named for Dale and Betty Bumpers in recognition of their efforts to promote research, childhood immunization, and a wide-ranging national healthcare program. Betty Bumpers received the Woman of Conscience Award from the National Council of Women of the United States, the first Wilton Peace Prize from the Unitarian Universalist Church, the Pediatric Nursing Humanitarian Award, the Surgeon General's Medallion, the Rotary International Polio Eradication Champion Award, and the Centers for Disease Control and Prevention's Champion of Prevention Award. In 2005, Betty Bumpers was inducted into the National Women's Hall of Fame.

For more information:

"Betty Bumpers' Life Story." https://www.youtube.com/watch?v=Sla5_mNPyF4 (accessed December 8, 2015).

Bumpers, Dale. *The Best Lawyer in a One-Lawyer Town: A Memoir*. New York: Random House, 2003.

Elben, Anna L., and Martha Jane Elben. *Betty Bumpers: Champion of Childhood Immunization and Peace*. Lanham, MD: Rowman & Littlefield, 2013.

Sarah Caldwell (1924–2006)

KNOWN FOR PRESENTING OPERAS that were rarely performed because of their difficulty, Sarah Caldwell was an operatic director and orchestra conductor who founded her own opera company, staged more than seventy-five operas, and became the first female conductor of New York's Metropolitan Opera. In later life, Caldwell made her home in Boston, Massachusetts, where, according to the *Boston Globe*, she "made Boston an international operatic capital for three decades."

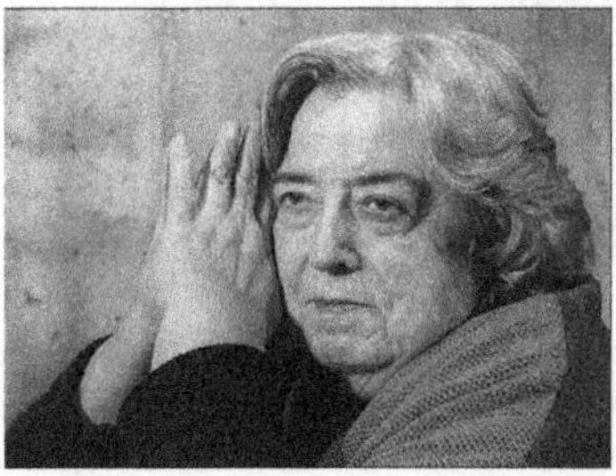

Sarah Caldwell was born on March 6, 1924, in Maryville, Missouri, but grew up in Fayetteville, Arkansas. Her parents divorced when she was an infant. As a child, she often lived with relatives while her mother, Margaret Carrie Caldwell Baker, pursued graduate studies in music. Sarah Caldwell began taking violin lessons as a young child and was recognized as a musical prodigy. By age six, she was giving public concerts. When her mother married Henry McMillan Alexander, a professor of government at the University of Arkansas (UA), the family moved to Fayetteville.

Sarah Caldwell attended Fayetteville High School, graduating at age fourteen. She enrolled at UA to study psychology, having been discouraged by her stepfather from pursuing a career in music. She left after a year and a half. She then became a violin major at Hendrix College in Conway, graduating in 1944.

She won a scholarship to the New England Conservatory of Music to study violin and viola, and received a viola scholarship from the Berkshire Music Center (now the Tanglewood Music Center) in Massachusetts in 1946. In 1947, at age twenty-three, Caldwell staged the opera *Riders to the Sea*.

She served for more than a decade as the chief assistant to mentor Boris Goldovsky, a renowned conductor, lecturer, pianist, and opera impresario. Goldovsky was known to millions for the intermission commentaries that he provided for almost fifty years during radio broadcasts of New York's Metropolitan Opera.

In 1952, Caldwell moved to Boston to lead the Boston University opera workshop. In 1957, with $5,000, she founded the Boston Opera Group, which became the Opera Company of Boston. There, she established a reputation for producing difficult works as well as creative variations on standard operas. She was both stage director and orchestra conductor for most of her productions, attracting top-tier opera stars such as Marilyn Horne, Beverly Sills, and Joan Sutherland.

Sarah Caldwell became one of the few women to conduct the New York Philharmonic and the Boston Symphony. A 1975 cover story in *TIME* magazine called her "Music's Wonder Woman." In 1976, Caldwell became the first female conductor at the world-renowned Metropolitan Opera. There, she directed such opera superstars as José Carreras and Placido Domingo, who later joined with Luciano Pavarotti to become the famed "Three Tenors."

Known for conducting the orchestra while sitting in a director's chair, Caldwell also tried her hand at a non-musical production when she staged the televised 1981 Lincoln Center production of Shakespeare's *Macbeth*.

She served as guest conductor for prestigious orchestras around the world as well as staging operas in such exotic locales as the Forbidden City in Beijing. In 1983, she became artistic director for the New Opera Company of Israel. World-renowned conductor/composer Leonard Bernstein said that he felt her staging of his composition *Mass* was the finest the piece had received.

In 1978, Caldwell was the first recipient of the Kennedy Center Award for Excellence.

In 1996, President Bill Clinton and First Lady Hillary Clinton presented her with the National Medal of Arts. President Bill Clinton said, "She's come a long way from Arkansas, and I'm very proud of her."

Caldwell's Boston opera company was unable to survive financial difficulties, suspending operations in 1991 even after Caldwell expended her personal assets to try to save it. She accepted guest-conducting spots around the world, as well as the post of distinguished professor of music at the University of Arkansas in 1999. There, she directed innovative productions of *La Bohème* and *The Turn of the Screw*.

However, her health was declining, and, in 2003, she moved to Freeport, Maine, where she bought a home. Caldwell died on March 23, 2006, at age eighty-two in Portland, Maine, from heart failure compounded by respiratory problems. She left no immediate survivors. Caldwell was cremated after a private ceremony in Maine. Later, there was a public memorial service in Boston.

Eulogizing Caldwell, the *Boston Globe* stated that she opened the door for subsequent generations of important female operatic directors. In her obituary, the *New York Times* quoted critic Andrew Porter, who wrote in *The New Yorker* that, in her prime, Caldwell had been "the single best thing about opera in America." Beverly Sills, opera star and former chair of the Metropolitan Opera, said, "Some of the most creative work that many of us artists have done has been with Sarah."

For more information:

Caldwell, Sarah, with Rebecca Matlock. *Challenges: A Memoir of My Life in Opera.* Middletown, CT: Wesleyan University Press, 2008.

Kessler, Daniel. *Sarah Caldwell: The First Woman of Opera.* Lanham, MD: Scarecrow Press, 2008.

Veronica Campbell-Brown (1982–)

WORLD-CLASS TRACK AND FIELD STAR VERONICA CAMPBELL-BROWN is a seven-time Olympic medalist. She is only the second woman in history to win two consecutive Olympic 200-meter events, and one of only nine athletes to win world championships at the youth, junior, and senior level of a sport. She was a track star at the University of Arkansas, where she was named an All-American four times, and she became the most decorated Olympic athlete connected with Arkansas.

Veronica Campbell was born on May 15, 1982, to Cecil Campbell and Pamella Bailey Campbell in Clarks Town, Trelawny, Jamaica. She has nine brothers and sisters. Veronica attended Troy Primary and discovered a talent for running when she won foot races at elementary school sports days. She was also strong academically, earning a scholarship to attend Vere Technical High School in Clarendon, Jamaica. With a strong track and field program at Vere Tech, she developed into a formidable sprinter. Her international debut took place at the 1996 Central American and Caribbean Junior Championships (CACJC), at which the fourteen-year-old Campbell won a gold medal in the 4x100-meter relay.

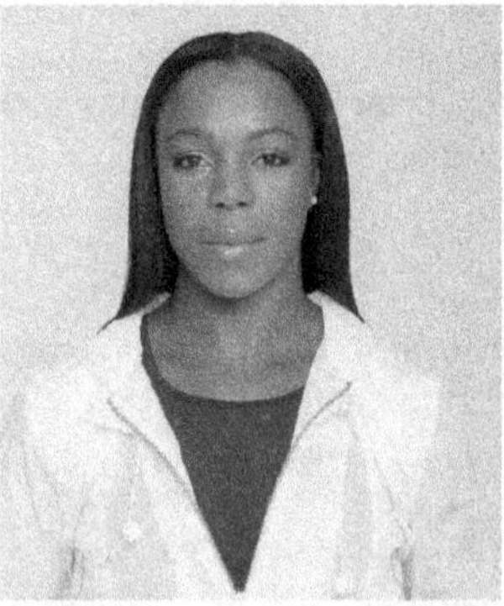

She then began accruing a host of gold medals, including at the 1997 Caribbean Free Trade Association (CARIFTA) Games and the 1998 CACJC. In 1999, she won two gold medals at the inaugural World Junior Championships of the International Association of Athletics Federations (IAAF), the world governing body for track and field. The following year, she became the first female runner to win the sprint double at the IAAF.

In 2000, Campbell came to the United States to further her education after earning a track and field scholarship. She enrolled at Barton County Community College in Great Bend, Kansas, which had an outstanding junior college track program, often competing in meets at the University of Arkansas (UA) in Fayetteville. Campbell set numerous records and won four national junior college titles in the 60-, 100-, and 200-meter events, both indoors and outdoors. At age eighteen, she competed in the 2000 Summer Olympics held at Sydney, Australia, and won her first Olympic medal, taking the silver in the 4x100-meter relay.

At Barton County Community College, she also excelled academically, earning an associate's degree in 2002. She then moved to UA, home of the most successful program in NCAA history under legendary track coach John McDonnell, called the "winning-est" coach in any sport in college athletics.

In McDonnell's program at UA, Veronica Campbell flourished, becoming a leading sprinter and Southeast Conference (SEC) star. She returned to the Olympic Games held at Athens, Greece, in 2004. She earned more Olympic medals, including in races in which she outpaced the favorite. In the 200-meter finals, she became the first Jamaican and first Caribbean woman in the history of the Olympics to win the sprint title. With Campbell anchoring her relay team, Jamaica won the 4×100-meter relay at the Olympics for the first time.

For her achievements at the 2004 Athens Olympics, UA cited her as "the first Razorback women's Olympic gold medalist in school history," adding that she was the "only Razorback woman to ever win multiple gold medals."

In 2006, Campbell graduated from UA with a bachelor's degree in marketing. Between Olympiads, she continued gathering medals, including at the 2007 World Championships, where Campbell won a gold and two silver medals.

Also in 2007, Campbell married fellow Jamaican sprinter and UA alumnus Omar Brown, changing her name to Veronica Campbell-Brown.

At the opening ceremony for the 2008 Olympics in Beijing, China, Campbell-Brown carried the Jamaican flag during the Parade of Athletes, the first female athlete associated with Arkansas to receive the honor of carrying her nation's flag in the opening ceremony. Closing out the 2008 season, Campbell-Brown was selected as the top 200-meter runner in the world by *Track and Field News*, also making the top ten in the magazine's "Woman of the Year" ranking.

At the 2012 Olympic Games in London, she qualified in both the 100- and 200-meter events, winning a bronze medal in the 100 meters. In the 200-meter race, she was less than a quarter of a second from taking another bronze. Running in the 4×100-meter relay, she and her Jamaican team took home a silver medal, just slightly behind the U.S. team, which won the event with a new world's record.

So far in her career, she has earned nearly fifty medals, including twenty-seven gold, sixteen silver, and three bronze. Aside from Olympic competition, Campbell-Brown has been a five-time world champion. According to the *Encyclopedia of Arkansas*, thirty Arkansas Olympians—male and female—have won Olympic medals, and "Veronica Campbell-Brown leads this group, with seven medals."

In 2009, Campbell-Brown was inducted into University of Arkansas Sports Hall of Honor. That same year, she was appointed a United Nations UNESCO Goodwill Ambassador. She stated that she would use that role to promote gender equity in sports. Currently living and training in Florida with her husband, she is the founder of the Veronica Campbell-Brown Foundation, which provides support to schoolchildren in Jamaica.

For more information:

Stanbrough, Mark. *Motivational Moments in Women's Track and Field.* Emporia, KS: Roho Publishing, 2013.

Veronica Campbell-Brown. http://www.veronicacampbellbrown.com (accessed December 8, 2015).

Hattie Caraway (1878–1950)

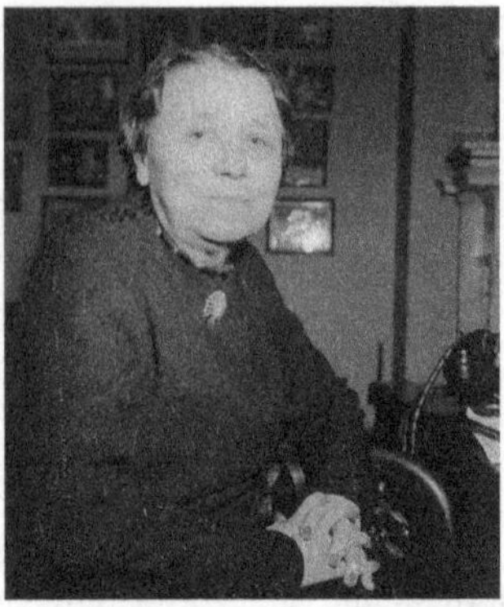

SERVING FROM 1931 TO 1945, HATTIE WYATT CARAWAY of Arkansas was the first woman elected to the U.S. Senate, the first woman re-elected to the Senate, the first woman to preside over the Senate, and the first woman to chair a Senate committee. She was a strong supporter of America's veterans, and she was instrumental in the first federal funding for construction on Arkansas college campuses. Many of the buildings she arranged funding for are still standing.

Hattie Wyatt was born to William Carroll Wyatt and Lucy Burch Wyatt on February 1, 1878, near Bakersville, Tennessee. Theirs was a large farm family, with a number of step-brothers and step-sisters from her father's first wife, along with Hattie's siblings George, Dick, and Mosie.

At age four, she moved with her family to Hustburg, Tennessee, where she helped on the family farm and in her father's general store. With a goal of becoming a schoolteacher, she sought an education beyond the county's one-room schoolhouse. With financial help from an aunt, Hattie enrolled at Dickson Normal College in Dickson, Tennessee, where she earned a bachelor's degree in 1896.

After teaching school, she married fellow Dickson student Thaddeus Horatius Caraway in 1902. They moved to Jonesboro, Arkansas, where Hattie Caraway was a homemaker and raised three sons—Forrest, Paul, and Bobby—while her husband climbed the political ladder. The family moved to Maryland when Thad Caraway was elected to the U.S. House of Representatives in 1912.

In 1920, the first year American women were allowed to vote, Thad Caraway was elected to the U.S. Senate. He served until his sudden death on November 6, 1931. Under Arkansas law, there had to be a special election to fill the vacant Senate seat. The state's leadership designated Hattie Caraway to run, and she won the special election on January 12, 1932, thus becoming the first woman elected to the U.S. Senate.

On May 9, 1932, she became the first woman to preside over the Senate. To the surprise of many, she announced her intention to run for a full term in her Senate seat.

Senator Huey P. Long of Louisiana campaigned for Caraway in Arkansas in 1932, attracting national media attention. Caraway won the election with more votes than all the six men who ran against her put together, also winning in counties where she and Long had not campaigned.

After Long's death, Caraway ran for re-election in 1938. Her opponent was Congressman John McClellan, whose campaign slogan was "Arkansas needs another man in the Senate." Caraway won, becoming the first woman re-elected to the Senate. In 1944, she ran again but was defeated by William Fulbright. When her term ended, Caraway was given a rare standing ovation in the Senate by her male colleagues. With no predecessors or mentors, it was a sign she had had held her own admirably.

As the lone woman in the Senate, Caraway was covered extensively by the press. However, without a microphone in the Senate chamber, she did not make the lengthy speeches her male colleagues were known for, becoming known derisively after her death as "Silent Hattie." She spoke well, however, in committee meetings, where she could converse in normal tones.

From 1933 to 1944, Caraway served as chair of the Committee on Enrolled Bills, becoming the first woman to chair a Senate committee. She served on the Senate Agriculture Committee, also overseeing flood control, which was an important issue for predominantly rural Arkansas. She was especially known for responding to the hundreds of letters that poured into her office and for her efforts to help her constituents.

Caraway was a strong supporter of Franklin D. Roosevelt's New Deal as a means to combat the effects of the Great Depression. She seconded FDR's nomination for re-election at the 1936 Democratic National Convention in Philadelphia. She did not always support either Roosevelt or Long, however, as she was very much a traditional Southerner of her era. She joined other senators from the "Solid South" in voting against anti-lynching and anti-poll-tax legislation, viewing them as unconstitutional. She was also anti-alcohol, opposing the repeal of Prohibition.

She never lost her belief in the power of education. At a time when the state legislature did not appropriate money for construction on Arkansas college campuses, she arranged federal funding from New Deal agencies. Her efforts brought a great number of buildings to colleges, including today's Arkansas State University, Arkansas Tech University, the University of Central Arkansas, and the University of Arkansas. With the onset of World War II, she sought to keep Arkansas colleges open when students, staff, and faculty left to join the armed services. Caraway worked with the Department of War to bring Army College Training Detachments to Arkansas campuses. She was also a Senate sponsor of the legislation known as the GI Bill, guaranteeing educational benefits to veterans.

Caraway was the first woman in the Senate to co-sponsor the proposed Equal Rights Amendment in 1943, strongly supporting equal pay for equal work. She also worked for the Equal Nationality Treaty of 1934, which extended numerous nationality rights to women. When she left the Senate, President Roosevelt appointed Caraway to the U.S. Employees' Compensation Commission and the Employees' Compensation Appeals Board.

After suffering a stroke, seventy-two-year-old Caraway died in Falls Church, Virginia, on December 21, 1950. Her body was brought back to Arkansas, where she was buried next to her husband at Oaklawn Cemetery in Jonesboro.

For more information:

Hendricks, Nancy. *Senator Hattie Caraway: An Arkansas Legacy*. Charleston, SC: History Press, 2013.

Kincaid, Diane, ed. *Silent Hattie Speaks: The Personal Journal of Senator Hattie Caraway*. Westport, CT: Greenwood Press, 1979.

Malone, David. *Hattie and Huey: An Arkansas Tour.* Fayetteville: University of Arkansas Press, 1989.

Irene Castle (1893–1969)

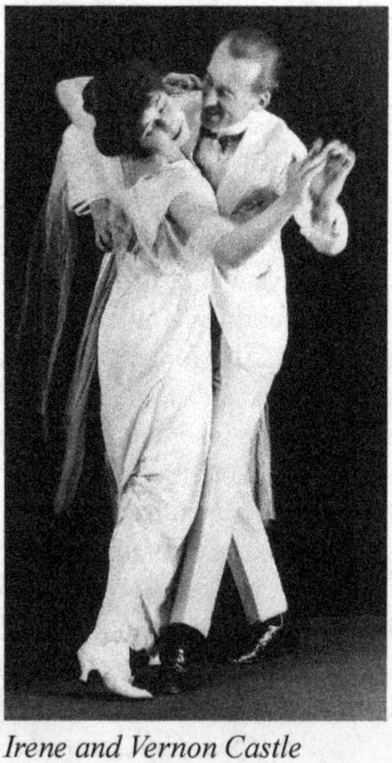

Irene and Vernon Castle

IRENE CASTLE was an internationally known show business star and fashion trendsetter from the World War I era through the 1930s. Along with her husband and dance partner, Vernon Castle, she is credited with popularizing ragtime and modern ballroom dance. Later in life, she lived in Eureka Springs, Arkansas, where she worked for animal rights, saying she would rather be remembered for that effort than for her show business career. In 1939, her life was made into a hit Hollywood movie, *The Story of Vernon and Irene Castle*, in which she was portrayed by Ginger Rogers.

She was born Irene Foote in New Rochelle, New York, on April 17, 1893. Irene was the second daughter of homemaker Annie Thomas Foote and Dr. Hubert Townsend Foote, a prominent physician. Irene attended boarding school and studied dance with famed instructor Rosetta O'Neill, but she did not graduate from high school. As a teenager, she loved to swim and also appeared in amateur theatricals, often singing a popular number of the day, "The Yama-Yama Man."

At the New Rochelle Rowing Club in 1910, she met British citizen Vernon Castle, who was part of a comedy show. He had moved to New York in 1906, finding work as a comic actor, dancer, and singer through noted impresario Lew Fields. In his comedic routine, Vernon Castle often played the part of a drunk man who tried to dance elegantly but kept falling down. At Castle's request, Irene Foote auditioned for Lew Fields, who hired her for a small dancing part, her first professional job.

Over her father's objections, Irene Foote married Vernon Castle in 1911. The couple found work as a dance act in Paris, France. They became the rage of Parisian society by performing the latest American ragtime dances such as the turkey trot. After their success was widely reported in America, they triumphantly returned to New York in 1912. In 1914, they became a tremendous hit in Irving Berlin's first Broadway show, *Watch Your Step*. They popularized music for dancing such as ragtime, jazz, and African rhythms. In New York, they opened a dancing school, a nightclub, and a restaurant. Dance lessons could cost up to a thousand dollars an hour. They wrote a bestselling book on dance, appeared in a newsreel about social dancing, and starred in a number of silent films of the era.

Vernon and Irene Castle were international stars, even introducing their own dance sensation, the Castle Walk. Irene Castle was a fashion trendsetter, popularizing flowing gowns, short full skirts, and loose waistlines. She is also credited with introducing a short hairstyle called the "bob," which was worn by "flappers" in the 1920s, as well as wearing a necklace across the forehead called a "Castle Band," which was later seen on Diana, Princess of Wales, in 1985. In a pioneering move, the Castles traveled with an African American orchestra. When their life story was filmed, Irene Castle protested when their black manservant was portrayed by a white actor.

When World War I erupted in Europe in 1914, Vernon Castle left for England to volunteer. He survived flying 300 combat missions for Britain's Royal Flying Corps, but after being assigned to train new pilots, he was killed in an airplane crash in 1918.

After his death, Irene Castle appeared in shows, but she was unhappy performing solo. In 1919, she married the socially prominent Robert Treman, who was reported to have then lost her money in the stock market. They divorced in 1923. That same year, she married Chicago Blackhawks owner Frederic McLaughlin, with whom she went on to have two children: daughter Barbara and son William. McLaughlin died in 1944. In 1946, she married Chicago advertising executive George Enzinger.

In 1939, the Castles were dramatized in a hit Hollywood movie starring Fred Astaire and Ginger Rogers called *The Story of Vernon and Irene Castle*. Castle served as a technical advisor, but she objected to the film as over-fictionalized.

When she was living near Chicago, she became a staunch defender of animal rights and campaigned against cruelty to animals, ultimately founding an Illinois animal shelter called Orphans of the Storm. The shelter is still active in helping stray dogs.

To celebrate Mother's Day 1954 with her son, she visited him in Eureka Springs, Arkansas. She found that the climate was better for her health than that of her home in Lake Forest, Illinois. She and her husband bought a farm near Eureka Springs, which also became a sanctuary for stray dogs. She sold some of her jewelry collection, saying she would use the proceeds for things that were now more important to her, such as rose bushes and peach trees.

In 1958, she published a memoir, *Castles in the Air*. She continued working for animal rights throughout the remainder of her life. Seventy-five-year-old Irene Castle died of heart failure on January 25, 1969, at the Eureka Springs Municipal Hospital. She is buried next to Vernon Castle at New York's Woodlawn Cemetery.

For more information:

Castle, Irene. *Castles in the Air*. Garden City, NY: Doubleday, 1958.

Golden, Eve. *Vernon and Irene Castle's Ragtime Revolution*. Lexington: University Press of Kentucky, 2007.

"Irene Castle." Internet Movie Database. http://www.imdb.com/name/nm0145274 (accessed December 8, 2015).

Mamie Clark (1917–1983)

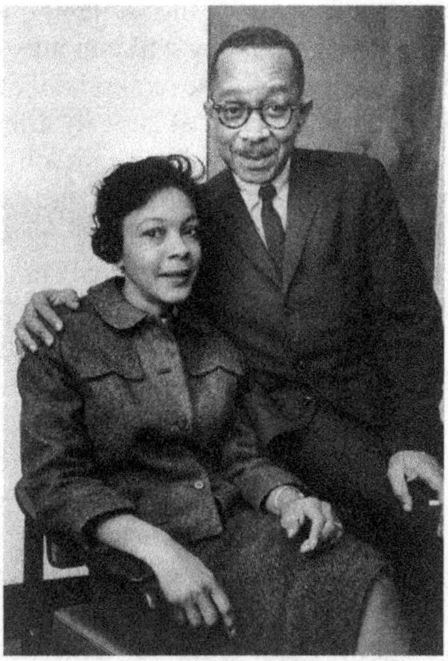

Scholars and civil rights activists Mamie and Kenneth Clark.

DR. MAMIE PHIPPS CLARK conducted landmark research that played a central role in the civil rights movement, influencing the 1954 *Brown v. Board of Education* decision, which determined that racial segregation in public schools was unconstitutional. The research experiments, which had their roots in Clark's Arkansas childhood, are still referenced in discussions about racial equality today.

Mamie Katherine Phipps was born in Hot Springs, Arkansas, on April 18, 1917. She was the elder of two children born to Dr. Harold Phipps, who was a physician, and Kate Florence Phipps, who assisted in his medical practice. The Phippses also managed a small hotel for African American patrons who came to "take the waters" in Hot Springs but were not permitted to stay at hotels with white people.

Although her family was prominent in Hot Springs, Mamie Phipps was still forced to attend segregated public schools, graduating from Pine Bluff's Langston High School in 1934 at age sixteen. At an early age, she was aware of the differing societal norms for white and black people, contributing to her future research in racial identity among black children.

She won a scholarship to historically black Howard University in Washington DC, where she studied math and physics. In her sophomore year, she found that the social sciences were more appealing than what she called the "detached and impersonal approach of the mathematics teachers (and, I believe, particularly towards female students)."

At Howard, Phipps met Kenneth Clark, a graduate student in psychology. Clark and the head of Howard's psychology department influenced her decision to transfer to that field of study. In 1937, Phipps and Clark eloped during her senior year. The couple would later have two children, Kate and Hilton.

In 1938, Mamie Clark graduated with high honors and received a fellowship to enter the master's degree program in psychology at Howard. During the summer, she worked as a secretary for civil rights attorney William Houston. Her master's thesis was based on research into self-identification among black nursery school children. In her research, she used tests that involved different-colored dolls. Mamie Clark then entered the doctoral program at New York's Columbia University as the only female black student pursuing a doctoral degree in psychology. In 1943, she became the second black person to receive a doctorate in psychology from Columbia, with the first being her husband.

Even with her doctorate, she found it difficult to find a job as a psychologist in New York, repeatedly being passed over for whites. She worked at a variety of clerical jobs until joining the Riverdale Home for Children in 1946, where she conducted psychological tests and counseled homeless young black people. As there were virtually no mental health services for African Americans in Harlem, coupled with the fact that many black youths were misdiagnosed by social agencies as retarded, the Clarks created the Northside Center for Child Development in 1946. From 1946 to 1979, Mamie Clark served as executive director of the center, which still serves the Harlem community.

Mamie Clark is known for the research that grew out of her master's thesis. The "Doll Experiment" involved a child being given two dolls, one white with yellow hair and the other brown with black hair. Even among African American children, there was a clear preference for the white doll among all children in the study. The preference was even stronger among children attending segregated schools. The Clarks were called as expert witnesses in several school desegregation cases, testifying that segregation harms children and society at large by affecting self-image.

Along with shedding light on internalized racism, the Clark studies were also precursors to psychological research into concepts of self-esteem. Ultimately, in the landmark *Brown v. Board of Education* case, the U.S. Supreme Court declared that the concept of "separate but equal" in education was unconstitutional because it resulted in African American children feeling inferior in the community.

Along with serving on advisory groups for nonprofit agencies, Clark served on boards for Mount Sinai Medical Center, the New York Mission Society, the New York Public Library, the Metropolitan Museum of Modern Art, and the Teachers' College at Columbia University. In 1973, Clark was elected a director of the American Broadcasting Company (ABC), becoming the first woman and the first African American to sit on the board of the communications conglomerate. The thirteen-member board met monthly to plan all major policy and programming decisions for ABC's television network, radio stations, and associated companies.

Mamie Clark received numerous awards, both with her husband and individually, including the Nicholas Murray Butler Silver Medal from Columbia University and the Four Freedoms Award in the category of Freedom of Speech. Her books include *Prejudice and Your Child*, *Dark Ghetto*, *A Relevant War Against Poverty*, *A Possible Reality*, and *Pathos of Power*.

At age sixty-six, Dr. Mamie Phipps Clark died on August 11, 1983, at her home in New York City.

For more information:

Abbott, Shirley. "Mamie Phipps Clark, a Hot Springs Woman Who 'Overcame the Odds.'" *The Record* 47 (2006): 15–22.

Markowitz, Gerald, and David Rosner. *Children, Race, and Power: Kenneth and Mamie Clark's Northside Center*. Charlottesville: University Press of Virginia, 1996.

Chelsea Clinton (1980–)

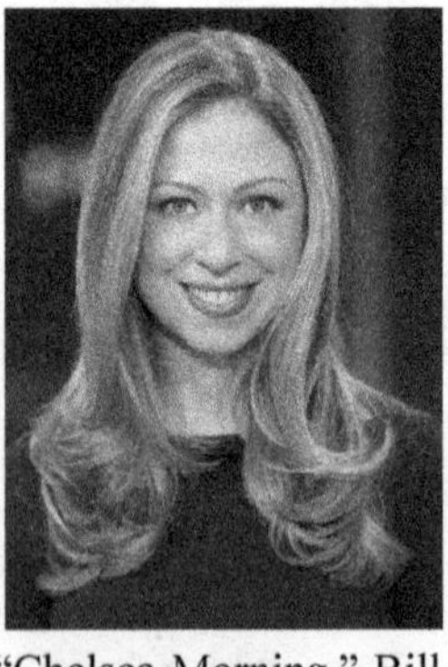

CHELSEA CLINTON is the only child of former U.S. president Bill Clinton and former U.S. secretary of state and senator Hillary Rodham Clinton [SEE ENTRY]. She has served as a special correspondent for NBC News, a public speaker, and an active participant in interfaith organizations. She also works with the Clinton Foundation and Clinton Global Initiative.

Chelsea Victoria Clinton was born in Little Rock on February 27, 1980. In Hillary Clinton's memoir, she stated that the name was inspired by a walk through the Chelsea district in London, England. Hearing the Joni Mitchell song "Chelsea Morning," Bill Clinton said, "If we ever have a daughter, we should name her Chelsea."

When their daughter was born, Bill Clinton was serving his first term as Arkansas's governor and attorney Hillary Rodham Clinton was a partner at Little Rock's Rose Law Firm. Despite busy schedules, the Clintons made Chelsea the center of their lives. As a two-year-old, she accompanied her parents on Bill Clinton's gubernatorial campaign.

Chelsea Clinton attended Forest Park Elementary, Booker Arts and Science Magnet Elementary School, and Horace Mann Junior High—all public schools in Little Rock.

On January 20, 1993, Bill Clinton was inaugurated as U.S. president, and the family moved to the White House in Washington DC. For reasons of security and privacy, Chelsea was enrolled in the private Sidwell Friends School. She had begun taking dance classes in Arkansas at age four, and she continued her dance training at the Washington School of Ballet for several years.

While at Sidwell, Chelsea Clinton was the center of intense media debate regarding whether she should be able to retain her privacy. Most journalists felt that she should be left alone due to her age. When she turned thirteen, Chelsea Clinton's physical appearance became the target of ridicule by commentators such as Rush Limbaugh and on TV programs such as *Saturday Night Live*.

After graduation from Sidwell in 1997, Chelsea Clinton went on to earn her undergraduate degree in history at California's Stanford University, master's degrees from Oxford University in England and Columbia University in New York, and a doctoral degree from Oxford in 2014.

Bill Clinton served as U.S. president from 1993 to 2001. During his turbulent presidency, Chelsea Clinton was often considered a valid journalistic subject as an eyewitness to family drama and historical events. Despite family objections, a cover story titled "Grace Under Fire" was published in *People* magazine in 1999 with a cover photo of Chelsea and Hillary Clinton. During the last year of Bill Clinton's presidency, Chelsea Clinton assumed White House hostess responsibilities when her mother was campaigning for the U.S. Senate. She also attended state dinners with her father and traveled with him on several overseas trips.

During 2007 and 2008, Chelsea Clinton campaigned extensively on American college campuses in support of her mother's bid for the Democratic presidential nomination. At the 2008 Democratic National Convention in Denver, Colorado, Chelsea introduced Hillary Clinton with a video tribute, calling Clinton "my hero and my mother."

Chelsea Clinton has worked in New York City for the consulting firm McKinsey & Company and the Avenue Capital Group as well as teaching graduate classes at Columbia University's Mailman School of Public Health. In 2010, Clinton accepted a position at New York University (NYU) as assistant vice-provost for the global network with a focus on international recruitment strategies. At NYU, she was co-founder and co-chair of the Institute for Multifaith Leadership. For her work in advancing interfaith issues, she received an award, along with Imam Khalid Latif and Rabbi Yehuda Sarna, from the Temple of Understanding for her contributions to cross-cultural education in campus life.

In 2011, Clinton began work as a special correspondent for *NBC Nightly News*, with a contract allowing her to continue her education and work with her family's Clinton Foundation. The focus of her assignment was reporting feature stories about "Making a Difference." She left the network in 2014 to become more involved with the Clinton Foundation and Clinton Global Initiative.

The Bill, Hillary & Chelsea Clinton Foundation describes its mission as convening businesses, governments, nonprofits and other non-governmental organizations (NGOs), and individuals to improve global health and wellness, increase opportunity for women and girls, create economic opportunity and growth, and help communities address the effects of climate change. After co-chairing a fundraising project, Chelsea Clinton became the foundation's vice chairwoman. She has also served on boards including the School of American Ballet, Common Sense Media, and Weill Cornell Medical College.

In 2010, Clinton married investment banker Marc Mezvinsky. They reside in New York City, and their daughter, Charlotte Clinton Mezvinsky, was born in 2014.

Clinton's book for young people, *It's Your World: Get Informed, Get Inspired & Get Going!*, was published in 2015 to inspire young people to help make a difference in the world. Chelsea Clinton has been quoted as recalling her grandmother's adage: "Life is not about what happens to you, but what you do with what happens to you."

For more information:

Clinton, Chelsea. *It's Your World: Get Informed, Get Inspired & Get Going!* New York: Philomel Books, 2015.

Clinton, Hillary Rodham. *Living History*. New York: Simon and Schuster, 2003.

Hillary Rodham Clinton (1947–)

HILLARY RODHAM CLINTON was the first lady of Arkansas, first lady of the United States, U.S. senator from New York, and U.S. secretary of state. She is the only former first lady to have run for U.S. president.

Hillary Diane Rodham was born in Chicago, Illinois, on October 26, 1947, the oldest of three children. Her father, Hugh Ellsworth Rodham, had a textile business, and her mother, Dorothy Howell Rodham, was a homemaker.

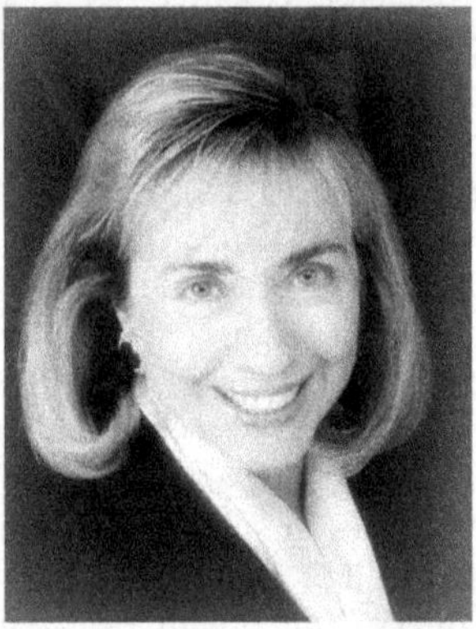

When Hillary Rodham was four, the family moved to suburban Park Ridge, Illinois, where she became an excellent student and a class leader. She was a member of the National Honor Society and was interested in politics from a young age. She was active in her Methodist youth group, organizing a babysitting service for immigrants. She earned numerous Girl Scout merit badges and won community service awards from the Daughters of the American Revolution (DAR).

In 1965, she was voted Most Likely to Succeed upon graduation from Maine Township High School South, where she was in the top five percent of her class. That year, she left for Wellesley College in Massachusetts, graduating in 1969 with high honors. As Wellesley College Government Association president, she was the first student to give the commencement address, which was featured in *Life* magazine.

After a summer working for what became the Children's Defense Fund, she entered Yale Law School in New Haven, Connecticut, in the fall of 1969, where she was one of twenty-seven women in a class of 235. She served on the editorial board of the *Yale Review of Law and Social Action*. During her second year of law school, Rodham met fellow student Bill Clinton of Arkansas.

In 1972, Rodham and Clinton worked on George McGovern's presidential campaign. After law school graduation in 1973, Bill Clinton returned to Arkansas to teach law while Rodham moved to Washington DC, working for the Children's Defense Fund and later for the House Judiciary Committee.

Rodham was offered many lucrative jobs on the East Coast, but she later said that she "followed her heart" to Arkansas, where she joined Clinton in Fayetteville and joined the faculty at the University of Arkansas (UA) School of Law. There, Rodham taught criminal and constitutional law and ran a legal services clinic while Bill Clinton embarked on a career in politics.

Bill Clinton first ran for political office in 1974 in a race for the U.S. House of Representatives. He lost to an extremely popular incumbent, though by only four percentage points; the strength of his campaign was credited to Hillary Rodham's organizational skills.

In 1975, the couple wed in a small ceremony in Fayetteville. The bride said she would keep the name Hillary Rodham to separate her professional life from her husband's, to avoid apparent conflicts of interest, and because "it showed that I was still me."

In 1976, Bill Clinton was elected Arkansas's attorney general. Hillary Rodham taught law in Little Rock and directed the school's legal aid clinic. She was hired by Little Rock's prestigious Rose Law Firm and became the first woman named full partner there. In 1978, she worked on Bill Clinton's successful gubernatorial campaign and continued to work as an attorney at the Rose Law Firm, twice being named to the list of "The 100 Most Influential Lawyers in America" by the *National Law Journal*.

Their daughter Chelsea Clinton [SEE ENTRY] was born in 1980, the same year that Bill Clinton lost the governor's race, though he regained the governorship in 1982. That same year, Hillary took the Clinton name, which some said was for political reasons and others said was out of consideration for their child. From 1982 to 1992, she continued working as a lawyer and helped Bill Clinton to win four re-election campaigns for governor.

When Bill Clinton ran for U.S. president in 1992, women came forward with stories of their romantic affairs with the candidate. The publicity multiplied when Bill and Hillary Clinton went on television's *60 Minutes* in an interview airing immediately after the 1992 Super Bowl. Addressing the subject of the allegations, Hillary Clinton said, "You know, I'm not sitting here—some little woman standin' by my man like Tammy Wynette. I'm sitting here because I love him, and I respect him, and I honor what he's been through and what we've been through together. And you know, if that's not enough for people, then heck, don't vote for him." The backlash was severe, including from Wynette herself. Hillary Rodham Clinton became a household name. Two months later, she again caused a stir when she appeared on TV's *Nightline*, saying, "I suppose I could have stayed home and baked cookies and had teas, but what I decided to do was to fulfill my profession which I entered before my husband was in public life."

In 1992, Bill Clinton became president, with Hillary Rodham Clinton as first lady. Early in his presidency, he named her to lead the President's Task Force on Health Care Reform, the first U.S. first lady to direct such a project. Opponents said they disapproved of an unelected person doing that job, and the effort failed. Hillary Clinton testified before a federal grand jury in 1996 regarding the Whitewater land development deal, becoming the only first lady ever to be subpoenaed. No wrongdoing was found.

In 1998, what Hillary Clinton called "the most devastating, shocking and hurtful experience of my life" took place when her husband revealed his improper relationship with a White House intern. After Hillary Clinton's decision to stand by him, even during his impeachment hearings, her national approval ratings increased to about seventy percent, the highest they had ever been.

Hillary Clinton also served as White House hostess and steward of its historical legacy. She chaired the Save America's Treasures program to match federal funds with private donations to preserve historic items and sites, and she expedited the creation of the First Ladies Historic Site in Canton, Ohio.

Hillary Clinton hosted state dinners, a gala honoring the White House bicentennial, and a New Year's celebration at the turn of the twenty-first century. She headed the White House Millennium Council and hosted Millennium Evenings, a lecture series focusing on the future. She also created the White House Sculpture Garden.

In 1996, her book *It Takes a Village—And Other Lessons Children Teach Us* was a bestseller. Also while she was first lady, Hillary Clinton wrote *Dear Socks, Dear Buddy: Kids' Letters to the First Pets* and *An Invitation to the White House: At Home with History*.

During her time in the White House, Hillary Clinton traveled to seventy-nine countries, becoming America's most-traveled first lady. In 1995, she made a speech in Beijing, China, at the Fourth World Conference on Women, citing abuses to women around the world, including in China itself. In doing so, she was said to resist pressure from both the Chinese government and her husband's administration.

Leaving the White House following Bill Clinton's second term, the couple moved to the Manhattan suburb of Chappaqua, New York. In 2000, Hillary Clinton was elected U.S. senator from New York, the first woman to become senator from that state. In the Senate, Clinton kept a low profile, became known for her hard work, and built bipartisan relationships.

In 2003, Clinton's memoir *Living History* was published and became one of the top five bestselling nonfiction books of the year.

In 2007, Clinton announced her candidacy as Democratic nominee for president of the United States. She won several primaries during the lead-up to the 2008 election, but she ultimately lost the nomination to Barack Obama. After his election, President Obama appointed Hillary Clinton as secretary of state. In her four years in that position, Clinton visited over 100 countries and traveled almost a million air miles. She stepped down as secretary of state in early 2013. The following year, she published her memoir of heading the State Department in the book *Hard Choices*, which also sold well. On April 12, 2015, Clinton announced that she would again be a candidate for the presidency of the United States in a bid to be the 2016 Democratic nominee.

Her independence and public involvement have often made her a subject of controversy, but her support of women's and children's issues has won her many admirers. Summing up her career to date, Hillary Clinton said, "I have never been as good or as bad as my most fervid supporters and opponents claimed."

For more information:

Clinton, Hillary Rodham. *Hard Choices*. New York: Simon & Schuster, 2014.

———. *Living History*. New York: Simon & Schuster, 2003.

Rhonda Coullet (1945–)

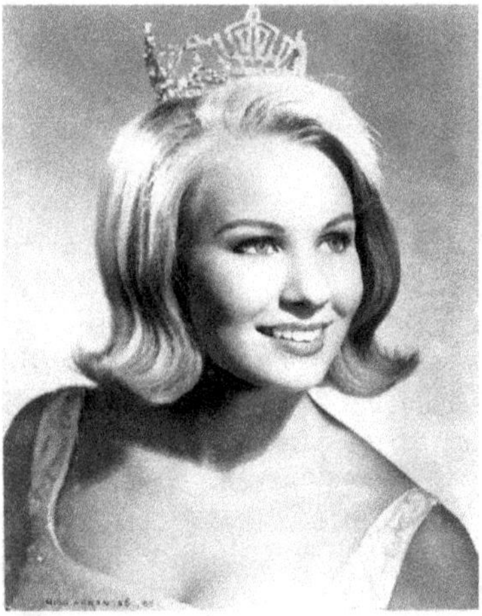

RHONDA OGLESBY COULLET is an actress, playwright, singer, and songwriter. She appeared in leading roles on Broadway, restaged the musical *Hair* for a European tour, wrote a critically acclaimed musical, and performed on *Saturday Night Live*. She may be best known in her home state for being the only Miss Arkansas ever to relinquish the crown.

Rhonda Lee Oglesby was born on September 23, 1945, in Magnolia, Arkansas, and was raised in Stamps, Arkansas. She and her brother, Scott, were born to Horace Oglesby and Cecil Hudson Oglesby, both employees of International Paper Company.

When Rhonda Oglesby was ten years old, the family moved to Pine Bluff, Arkansas. There, she attended Sam Taylor Elementary School and Pine Bluff High School, where she was a cheerleader. She graduated in the class of 1963.

Her talent as a singer led to a music scholarship from the University of Arkansas (UA) in Fayetteville. As a freshman, she toured Europe with UA's Schola Cantorum choir, and she sang with the UARKettes. She represented UA in the 1965 Miss Arkansas Pageant, a preliminary competition for the Miss America Pageant. Performing as a vocalist, Oglesby was crowned Miss Arkansas 1965. Oglesby then represented Arkansas in the Miss America Pageant at Atlantic City, New Jersey, that September, though she was not a finalist.

In her autobiographical work, *Runaway Beauty Queen*, she observed that instead of having opportunities to showcase her talents by performing as a singer, she faced "endless appearances at one-car parades and ribbon-cutting ceremonies wearing a bright smile, high heels, and a tight girdle." After three months as Miss Arkansas, she was nowhere to be found. In November 1965, newspaper reports stated, "Miss Arkansas has abdicated her throne amid an air of mystery." Just prior to her disappearance, she had been scheduled to appear in Little Rock for the Arkansas Livestock Exposition. Miss Arkansas Pageant officials reported receiving a telegram from Oglesby stating, "Will not be living in Arkansas. Please consider this my resignation as Miss Arkansas. Signed Rhonda."

Oglesby moved to Los Angeles, California, where she pursued a career in show business. There, she joined a production of *Hair* in 1968, six months after its Broadway debut. She was soon elevated to a lead female role as Jeanie, and she went on to restage the musical for touring productions in Europe, where she remained for three years.

In 1970, she married musician and sound designer Armand Coullet; they divorced in 1980.

After moving to New York City, Rhonda Coullet worked steadily in such shows as *National Lampoon's Lemmings* and *The National Lampoon Radio Hour*, appearing with and befriending actors including John Belushi, Chevy Chase, Bill Murray, and Gilda Radner. After Belushi's 1982 death, Rhonda Coullet wrote and sang a tribute song called "West Heaven" for a segment on TV's *Saturday Night Live* produced by Belushi's widow. She also appeared in the all-star cast of the cult movie *Mr. Mike's Mondo Video*.

On Broadway, Coullet played leads in such shows as *The Robber Bridegroom* and *Pump Boys and Dinettes*, also appearing in lead roles in off-Broadway productions as well as regional pre-Broadway productions.

Coullet recorded songs for television programs such as *Captain Kangaroo* and *Sesame Street*. In 1988, she narrated "Indians, Outlaws, and Angie Debo," which was shown on the first season of *The American Experience* on PBS.

She wrote the song "Bigger Than the Both of Us" for Jimmy Buffett's 1984 *Riddles in the Sand* album. In late 1984, Buffett released the song as a single, making the Top 100 Country chart. She was a back-up singer for Buffett, Cher, and Spinal Tap. In 1992, she recorded *The American Secret*, an album of her own songs. Several were later included in her theatrical production, 2005's *Runaway Beauty Queen*.

Runaway Beauty Queen or The Lost Pleiad, with book, music, and lyrics by Rhonda Coullet, has received strong reviews around the country. It originally starred Coullet as "Sis," the character based on herself, but Coullet has since taken on the role of the grandmother, "Mamaw." At its 2010 Martha's Vineyard production, co-produced by Judith Belushi, the *Martha's Vineyard Times* called it smart and affecting, adding, "It is the music of a gritty, unconventional, poignant, funny, and successful life story sung with a foot-stomping Arkansas twang."

For more information:

"Pine Bluff Beauty Says She Is Quitting Miss Arkansas Title." *El Dorado Times*, November 18, 1965, p. 29.

"Rhonda Coullet." Internet Movie Database. http://www.imdb.com/name/nm0183429 (accessed December 8, 2015).

Runaway Beauty Queen. http://www.runawaybeautyqueen.com (accessed December 8, 2015).

Gail Davis (1925–1997)

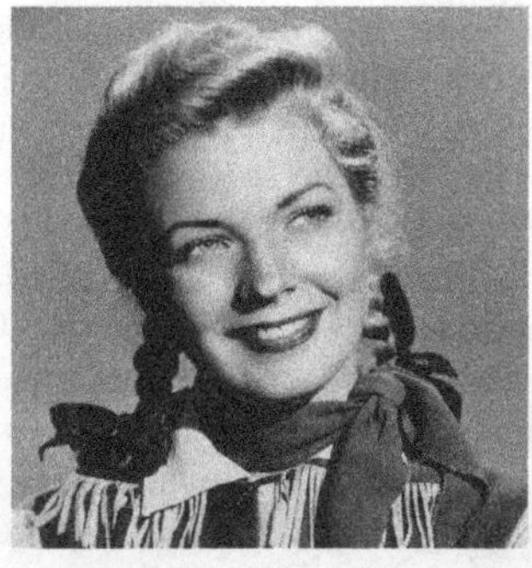

GAIL DAVIS became the first woman to star in a television western when she portrayed a legendary sharpshooter in a groundbreaking series. She appeared in numerous films and TV shows, received a star on the Hollywood Walk of Fame, and was inducted into the National Cowgirl Hall of Fame. Gene Autry called her "the perfect Western actress," and many women later said they were influenced by watching Davis as Annie Oakley, a female character in a traditionally male role.

Gail Davis was born Betty Jeanne Grayson on October 5, 1925. Her mother was a homemaker, and her father, William Grayson, was a physician in McGehee, Arkansas. The small town of McGehee did not have a hospital, so she was born at a hospital in Little Rock.

Dr. Grayson became state health officer for the Arkansas State Board of Health in 1933. When Betty Jeanne was eight years old, the family moved from McGehee to Little Rock. Though she rode horses and was a tomboy, she enjoyed singing and dancing throughout her childhood. She appeared in local talent shows and won beauty contests, including one in which she was named "Most Beautiful Baby in Arkansas."

After graduation from Little Rock Senior High School (now Central High School), she studied at Harcum Junior College for Girls in Bryn Mawr, Pennsylvania. There, she studied at Harcum's Experimental Theatre with Richard Nash, the playwright and screenwriter for *The Rainmaker*.

Betty Jeanne Grayson completed her college education at the University of Texas in Austin, taking drama and dance. While at the university, she met and married her first husband, Robert Davis, in 1945.

The couple moved to Hollywood to pursue film work. She worked as a hatcheck girl until a talent agent arranged a screen test for her. She was signed to an MGM contract in 1946. She later told an interviewer that she could not use her married name "Betty Davis" since it would be confused with Bette Davis, and her maiden name conflicted with Kathryn Grayson. She said the name Gail Davis was suggested by the casting department.

After appearing in several minor roles, she made her major motion picture debut in 1947's *Romance of Rosy Ridge*, starring Van Johnson. In 1948, she was cast in a supporting role with star Roy Rogers in a western, *The Far Frontier*.

Davis worked steadily in movies from 1948 to 1953, appearing in more than thirty feature films. Most were westerns, but she also appeared in others, such as *Flying Leathernecks* with John Wayne. Her work included about twenty films for the production company of Gene Autry, who really discovered her potential.

Beginning in 1950, she guest-starred on the new medium of television, notably on westerns. She made multiple appearances on *The Adventures of Kit Carson*, *The Cisco Kid*, *The Lone Ranger*, *Range Rider*, and *The Gene Autry Show*. Autry had been hoping to find a western star to whom girls could relate, saying, "Boys have had their idols.... Why not give the girls a Western star of their own?"

Gail Davis would become that star. At just over five feet tall and weighing less than 100 pounds, Davis was a charming heroine on *Annie Oakley*, which ran from 1954 through 1956, and was re-run in the 1960s. She starred as a rancher who wore pigtails and stopped criminals by outsmarting them or shooting the guns out of their hands. She rode horses and did many of her own stunts. In the show, Davis solved crimes with handsome deputy sheriff Lofty Craig. As Davis was the first woman to star in a TV western, many young women later said they were influenced by her performance in a traditionally male role.

When the TV series ended, she appeared as Annie Oakley in the 1959 film *Alias Jesse James*, which starred Bob Hope and featured appearances by Roy Rogers, Fess Parker as Davy Crockett, and James Garner as Bret Maverick.

In 1960, Davis was awarded a star on the Hollywood Walk of Fame on Hollywood Boulevard. She toured North America with Gene Autry's traveling Wild West rodeo show as an expert horseback rider. Many people especially remember her on a 1961 episode of *The Andy Griffith Show* called "The Perfect Female" in which she played Sheriff Andy's love interest and demonstrated her trademark sharpshooting. It would be her final appearance as a performer. Davis discovered she was typecast as Annie Oakley. In an interview, she later said, "Directors just couldn't envision me in a sexy part or playing a heavy. I was always going to be Annie Oakley."

With Robert Davis, she had one child, Terrie, but the marriage ended in divorce in 1952, soon after her daughter's birth. She later married recording executive Richard Pierce and then businessman Carl Guerriero.

With Guerriero, she moved to the San Fernando Valley in California and worked as a talent agent. She made numerous guest appearances at western shows and film festivals. In 1994, she received the Golden Boot Award from the Motion Picture and Television Fund for positive portrayals in the western tradition.

On March 15, 1997, Gail Davis died of cancer in Los Angeles at age seventy-two. She is buried in Hollywood's Forest Lawn Cemetery. In 2004, she was inducted posthumously into the National Cowgirl Hall of Fame.

For more information:

"Gail Davis." Internet Movie Database. http://www.imdb.com/name/nm0204625 (accessed December 8, 2015).

Magers, Boyd. "Do You Remember…'Annie Oakley'?" Western Clippings. http://www.westernclippings.com/remember/annieoakley_doyouremember.shtml (accessed December 8, 2015).

Iris DeMent (1961–)

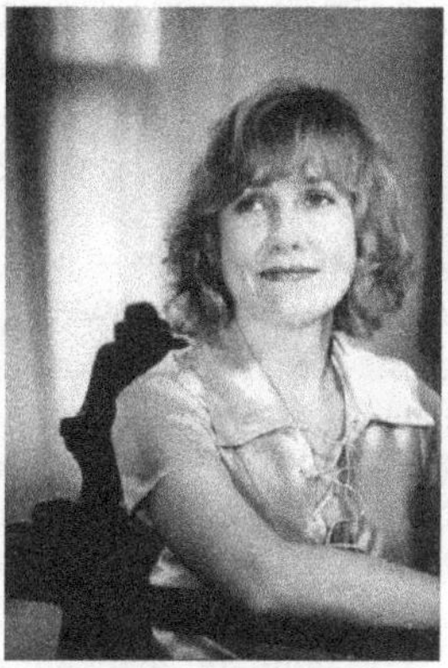

IRIS DEMENT is a Grammy Award–nominated singer and songwriter whose distinctive voice has led to praise from critics and fans. The socio-political topics of her bluegrass, country, folk, and gospel songs have led to comparisons with Bruce Springsteen. Her debut recording was called an essential album of the 1990s by *Rolling Stone* magazine. She has been featured on Garrison Keillor's popular radio show *A Prairie Home Companion* and in the movie *Songcatcher*. Her music has been used in films including the 2010 version of *True Grit*.

Iris Luella DeMent was born on January 5, 1961, near Paragould, Arkansas. She was one of a total of fourteen children whose father was Patric Shaw DeMent. His second wife, Flora Mae DeMent, gave birth to eight of the children, of whom Iris was the youngest.

The family farmed on an island called Indian Hill in the St. Francis River of northeast Arkansas, with her father also working in a factory.

When Iris was three, her father lost his factory job after an attempt to unionize. The family was forced to sell the farm, moving to California, where they lived until Iris was seventeen. In time, her parents and some of her brothers and sisters moved back to Arkansas.

The family followed the Pentecostal tradition. On her website, Iris DeMent wrote, "Growing up, a lot of what I understood about my parents—and many of the adults in my life that were nurturing me—I understood through music. I remember noticing that people seem to be most their real selves when they were in the music. My dad would cry, my mom would wave her arms around when they sang church music." Along with gospel, Iris was also influenced by country music. Her father had once played fiddle, while her mother played piano and sang along with the children. Iris's older sisters Zelda, Reba, Regina, and Faye had a gospel group, the DeMent Sisters, that recorded an album.

Iris DeMent left high school in California and supported herself by cleaning houses and working as a waitress. In her late twenties, living in Kansas and then in Nashville, Tennessee, DeMent considered a career as a singer-songwriter. She performed at open-mic nights in clubs and coffeehouses in the evenings while keeping her jobs during the day. DeMent married Elmer McCall in 1991, but the marriage ended in divorce.

Her first album, *Infamous Angel*, was released in 1992 by Rounder/Philo Records, which specialized in folk music. With liner notes by singer-songwriter John Prine, it had such strong sales that it was re-released the following year by Warner Bros.

From this album, the song "Our Town" was used in the final episode of the TV series *Northern Exposure*. Her rendition of "Whispering Pines" was used in Robert Redford's movie *The Horse Whisperer.* Another song, "Let the Mystery Be," was used in the movie *Little Buddha* starring Keanu Reeves and has been covered by other musicians, including 10,000 Maniacs.

DeMent's subsequent albums expanded on the themes of families, religion, and small-town life. *Infamous Angel* was followed by 1993's *My Life*, which was nominated for a Grammy Award as Best Contemporary Folk Album. Her third album, *The Way I Should* in 1996, featured DeMent's most politically themed work, which garnered comparisons with Bruce Springsteen and other songwriters known for socially conscious work. For *The Way I Should*, DeMent again earned a Grammy nomination for Best Contemporary Folk Album. It touches on topics including government policy, religion, sexual abuse, and the Vietnam War with such songs as "Quality Time," "There's a Wall in Washington," and "Wasteland of the Free."

Iris DeMent appeared in the 2000 movie *Songcatcher* with Janet McTeer and Aidan Quinn, in which she played the character Rose Gentry and sang on the soundtrack.

In 2002, DeMent married musician Greg Brown. In 2004, she recorded *Lifeline*, an album of gospel music. Her rendition of a song on this album, "Leaning on the Everlasting Arms," was used in the closing credits of the 2010 film *True Grit*.

Sing the Delta, released in 2012, contained more of DeMent's original songs, and 2015's *The Trackless Woods* featured songs based on the work of Russian poet Anna Akhmatova (1889–1966). DeMent said she was inspired to read Akhmatova as a way to connect with her Russian daughter, whom DeMent and her husband adopted. The family lives in rural Iowa and also has a home in Kansas City, Missouri.

The *Oxford American* magazine included DeMent's work on its Southern music compilation and said that her voice "is capable of carrying so much exultation on the one hand and so much sorrow on the other, with so little costumery or ornamentation, that it can seem as if she has lived an entire life inside every note she delivers."

For more information:

Brockmeier, Kevin. "Iris DeMent." *Oxford American* 58 (2007): 129–134. Online at http://www.oxfordamerican.org/magazine/item/612-tangled-in-wishes (accessed December 8, 2015).

Iris DeMent. http://irisdement.com (accessed December 8, 2015).

Melinda Dillon (1939–)

THE AWARD-WINNING MELINDA DILLON is an actress who has appeared in numerous movies, plays, and television shows. She has been nominated for two Academy Awards, and she earned a Tony Award nomination for her first Broadway play. She is especially known for her memorable roles in the films *Absence of Malice*, *Close Encounters of the Third Kind*, and *A Christmas Story*, as well as the television adaptation of John Grisham's *A Painted House*, which was set in Arkansas.

Melinda Rose Dillon was born in Hope, Arkansas, on October 13, 1939. She is the daughter of Norine Barnett Dillon and stepfather W. S. Dillon, a U.S. Army colonel.

Melinda Dillon attended Hyde Park High School in Chicago, Illinois. She studied acting at Chicago's Goodman School of Drama from 1958 to 1961 as well as at Lee Strasberg's Actors Studio in New York City. Dillon was invited to join Chicago's famed improvisational troupe Second City in 1961, the same year Joan Rivers joined. Character actor Richard Libertini would soon also join Second City. In 1963, he and Melinda Dillon were wed. They were married until 1978 and are the parents of one child, Richard Libertini Jr.

In 1962, playwright Edward Albee was readying his play *Who's Afraid of Virginia Woolf?* for its Broadway premiere, first offering it to Lee Strasberg's Actors Studio. Strasberg proposed several cast members for the play and for the director, Alan Schneider, all of whom were associated with the Actors Studio. Melinda Dillon was a protégée to Schneider, who proposed her for the role of Honey. Although she was a Broadway newcomer, she was hired for the role even though a fellow cast member objected because she was taller than him. Dillon went on to play the role, receiving a Tony Award nomination for Best Performance by a Featured Actress and winning a New York Drama Critics Award.

Her other stage work includes *You Know I Can't Hear You When the Water's Running* and Paul Sills's *Story Theatre*. She also had guest-starring roles on television shows such as *Bonanza*, *The Jeffersons*, *CHiPs*, and *Picket Fences*. However, most of her work has been in motion pictures. Dillon's first movie was 1969's *The April Fools* with Jack Lemmon. In 1976, she co-starred with David Carradine in *Bound for Glory*, the film biography of Woody Guthrie. In it, she played two characters and was nominated for a Golden Globe for Best Female Acting Debut.

The following year, Dillon played a mother whose child is abducted by aliens in Steven Spielberg's *Close Encounters of the Third Kind*. For that role, she was nominated for an Academy Award for Best Supporting Actress and won the Saturn Award from the Academy of Science Fiction, Fantasy & Horror Film. In 1981, she appeared in a pivotal role as Paul Newman's alibi in *Absence of Malice*, bringing her another Academy Award nomination for Best Supporting Actress.

Because of repeated annual showings on television during the holiday season, Melinda Dillon may be best known for her work in the 1983 movie *A Christmas Story*. In that film, she plays the mother of a boy who wants an air rifle for Christmas. In 2012, *A Christmas Story* was chosen for preservation in the National Film Registry by the Library of Congress for being "culturally, historically, or aesthetically significant."

Dillon earned another Saturn Award nomination for her work in *Harry and the Hendersons*. She had a key role in Barbra Streisand's *The Prince of Tides*, and she was nominated for a Screen Actors Guild Award for her work in *Magnolia*.

A sampling of her other film work includes Sylvester Stallone's *F.I.S.T.*; *How to Make an American Quilt*; *Reign Over Me*; *Seeking a Friend for the End of the World*; *Sioux City*; *Slap Shot*, with Paul Newman; and the cult favorite *To Wong Foo, Thanks for Everything, Julie Newmar*.

Her major television work includes the beloved TV adaptation of John Grisham's *A Painted House*, which was both set and filmed in Arkansas; a nuclear war–themed installment of *The Twilight Zone* in 1985; and *Heartland*. She received a Prism Award nomination for her performance on *Law & Order: Special Victims Unit*, and she earned a CableACE award nomination for HBO's *State of Emergency*.

After working with her, iconic filmmaker Steven Spielberg said that Melinda Dillon "gives off a lovely light."

For more information:

Bottoms, Stephen J. *Albee: Who's Afraid of Virginia Woolf?* New York: Cambridge University Press, 2000.

Halliwell, Leslie. *Halliwell's Filmgoer's and Video Viewer's Companion.* 9th ed. New York: Charles Scriber's Sons, 1988.

"Melinda Dillon." Internet Movie Database. http://www.imdb.com/name/nm0227039/?ref_=fn_al_nm_1 (accessed December 8, 2015).

Crescent Dragonwagon (1952–)

CRESCENT DRAGONWAGON is the award-winning author of dozens of books in various genres, including children's books, novels, poetry, and cookbook-memoirs. In the early part of her career, she also wrote many articles for publications ranging from *Cosmopolitan* to *Fine Cooking* to the *New York Times*. Her children's book *Half a Moon and One Whole Star* won the Coretta Scott King Book Award as well as being named a Reading Rainbow Selection. Her novel *The Year It Rained* was a *New York Times* Notable Book, while her *Passionate Vegetarian* won a James Beard Award. In addition, she is the developer and leader of the Fearless Writing workshops. Dragonwagon lived for over three decades in Eureka Springs, Arkansas. There, she and her husband, Ned Shank, co-founded Dairy Hollow House, a country inn and restaurant that they ran for eighteen years. She later helped reinvent it as the nonprofit Writers' Colony at Dairy Hollow.

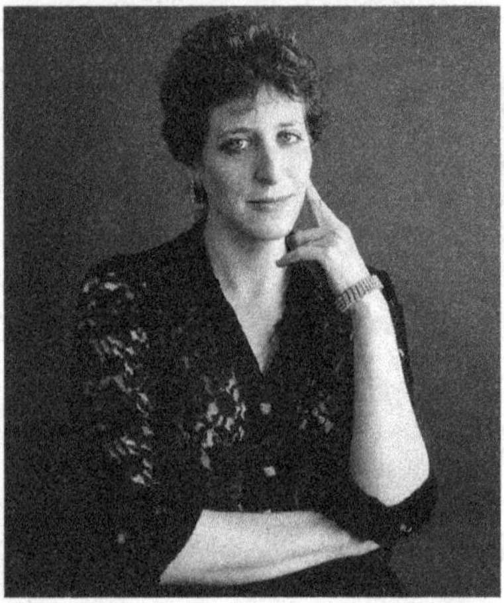

Dragonwagon was born Ellen Zolotow in New York City on November 25, 1952. Her mother, Charlotte Shapiro Zolotow, a vice president at HarperCollins, was a noted writer, editor, and publisher of many children's books. Her father, Maurice Zolotow, was also well known in the publishing world as a biographer of such celebrities as Marilyn Monroe and John Wayne.

She attended school in Hastings-on-Hudson, New York, but did not finish high school. She left home at sixteen, and she married Texas archeologist Mark Parsons in 1970. She then became Crescent Dragonwagon; the full story of her name change can be found on her website (under "Is That Your Real Name?"). The two lived for a year in a commune in Brooklyn, New York, then for a second year in a commune they co-founded in Missouri.

In 1971, her first cookbook, *The Commune Cookbook*, was published by Simon & Schuster, while her first children's book, *Rainy Day Together*, was published by Harper & Row. A year later—eighteen years old and separated from her husband—Dragonwagon moved to Eureka Springs. She continued to write, worked as a cook at the town's Crescent Hotel, and became part of the local community. Her second children's book, *When Light Turns into Night*, was published in 1975, the year her first marriage ended in divorce. In 1977, she published a short biography of Stevie Wonder, about whom she had originally written a magazine story.

In 1978, Dragonwagon married artist/writer/historic preservationist Ned Shank. Along with a friend, musician Bill Haymes, they opened Dairy Hollow House, named for a valley on the outskirts of Eureka Springs where the town's last local dairies had been located. It was the first bed-and-breakfast inn at Eureka Springs, the first in the Ozark Mountains, and one of the first two in the state of Arkansas.

In 1988, they added a restaurant featuring "nouveau'zarks cuisine," built around local, regional and seasonal produce. One reviewer called her "the Alice Waters of the Ozarks," and she is considered one of the pioneers of what is now called the farm-to-table movement. Among the inn's well-known guests were Bill and Hillary Clinton, feminist author Betty Friedan, actress Mercedes McCambridge, and singer Andy Williams.

Two of her cookbooks, *The Dairy Hollow House Cookbook* and *Dairy Hollow House Soup & Bread*, drew from recipes served at the restaurant. They became nationally renowned, drawing praise from *Gourmet*, the *New York Times*, *Southern Living*, and *Travel and Leisure*.

At Decatur House, a historic mansion two blocks from the White House in Washington DC, Dragonwagon and Shank served brunch to more than 1,200 people for Bill Clinton's first presidential inauguration. The event, featuring Arkansas musicians and decorated with quilts borrowed from the Historic Arkansas Museum, drew acclaim for its food and atmosphere from the *New York Times*, the *Washington Post*, and CNN.

The couple closed the inn in 1998 to begin its transition to the nonprofit Writers' Colony at Dairy Hollow (WCDH). Established in 1999, the colony has hosted more than a thousand writers from more than thirty-three countries. It is still in operation, though Dragonwagon's only connection with it is historical.

Ned Shank was killed in 2000 when he was hit by a pickup truck while riding a bicycle. Two years after his death, Dragonwagon left Dairy Hollow for Vermont, where she purchased what had been her family's summer home. In 2002, she was joined there by Academy Award–nominated filmmaker David Koff. After Koff's death in 2014, Dragonwagon continued to write, publishing a popular blog and presenting Fearless Writing workshops. One of her students was famous chef Julia Child, who took the course in 2000, when she was over eighty years old.

Dragonwagon's first novel, *To Take a Dare*, was co-authored with Pulitzer Prize–winning playwright Paul Zindel, and it has recently been reissued. Her more recent cookbooks include *The Cornbread Gospels* and *Bean by Bean*. Her children's books include *Home Place*, *This Is the Bread I Baked for Ned*, *Alligator Arrived with Apples*, *Bat in the Dining Room*, and *All the Awake Animals Are Almost Asleep*. She recently assisted with the publication of *Changes*, the first posthumously published book by her mother, Charlotte Zolotow.

Dragonwagon's work has been recognized by the American Library Association, National Conference of Christians and Jews, and National Council of Teachers of English. She continues to write for print and the Internet, along with teaching workshops and serving as literary executor for her mother. She divides her time between Vermont, Arkansas, and New York.

On her website, she describes what she does as, "Cooking, eating, living, loving, writing, reading, thinking. Listening, tasting, sniffing. Cozying up to mystery at midlife. I think we're all part of the narrative life tells itself about itself."

For more information:

Crescent Dragonwagon. http://dragonwagon.com/ (accessed December 8, 2015).

Elizabeth Eckford (1941–)

ELIZABETH ECKFORD was one of the group of African American students who came to be known as Little Rock Nine. They were the first black students to attend the all-white Little Rock Central High School in 1957. The dignified fifteen-year-old Eckford became the face of the struggle in one of the most famous photographs in history in which she is shown walking alone through a screaming white mob. The iconic picture was published around the world and brought international attention to the Little Rock crisis by humanizing the struggle in the person of Elizabeth Eckford. The *New York Post* called Eckford "probably the most widely known high school student in the whole United States," and she received up to fifty letters a day from around the world.

Elizabeth Ann Eckford was born in Little Rock on October 4, 1941. She was the second to oldest of six children born to Oscar Eckford, who was a dining car maintenance worker for the Missouri Pacific Railroad, and Birdie Eckford, who taught laundering and ironing skills at the Arkansas School for the Blind and Deaf Negro. As a girl, Birdie Eckford had lived in a rural Arkansas community, but she moved to Little Rock for a better education, attending the all-black Dunbar Junior High. Her daughter Elizabeth would later attend the same segregated school. The Eckford family members became known for their intelligence and seriousness, with the children being strictly brought up.

Elizabeth was a studious child who loved to read. It was expected that she would go to college, though no one was sure how it would be funded. The family found that even having a telephone was too expensive. Elizabeth was inspired by attorney Thurgood Marshall, who had argued the *Brown v. Board of Education* U.S. Supreme Court case, the suit that opened the way for integration. Since Little Rock Central offered the best education in the city, she thought that attending the school might help attain her goal of becoming a lawyer.

The story and photos of Elizabeth Eckford's first day at Central on September 4, 1957, have been seen around the world for half a century. The crisp, white cotton skirt she and her sister had made for her first day of school to enter eleventh grade were later consigned to her mother's attic. She had no desire to see it again after that day.

Because she had no telephone and could not be notified of a change in plans the night before, Eckford had arrived at Central on September 4 by herself on a public bus. She was blocked by Arkansas National Guardsmen who had been called in by the state's governor to keep the black students from entering. Turned away at gunpoint, she tried to make her way through the jeering crowd to a bench where she could wait for another bus to take her to her mother's workplace. At one point, Eckford turned to a kindly looking older white woman; the woman spat on her. Some reporters tried to shield Eckford as the crowd closed in, chanting to lynch her. One reporter advised her not to let the mob see her cry. The bus arrived about a half hour later.

Dramatic photos were taken by news photographers. Published on front pages around the world, they showed the fifteen-year-old girl being taunted by an angry white mob about 400 strong. It is said that seeing photos of Eckford led President Dwight Eisenhower to federalize the National Guard and call in the U.S. Army's 101st Airborne Division to protect the black students.

Though the soldiers remained at Central for the remainder of the year, they were unable prevent the constant harassment of the black students, such as when Eckford was thrown down a flight of stairs and had a rock thrown at her in class. It was said that because she was the "face" of Central's desegregation, Eckford was singled out in order to drive her away, with the other Little Rock Nine students presumed to follow.

With the city's high schools closed the following year by Governor Orval Faubus to thwart integration, Eckford did not graduate from Central High School. She took correspondence and night courses to earn enough credits for a high school diploma.

Eckford attended Knox College in Galesburg, Illinois, and Central State University in Wilberforce, Ohio, earning a bachelor's degree in history. She served in the U.S. Army for five years as a pay clerk and information specialist, writing for the newspapers at Fort McClellan and Fort Benjamin Harrison. She also served as a social studies teacher, welfare worker, employment interviewer, and probation officer—the latter in her hometown of Little Rock.

On 1997, on the fortieth anniversary of the Central High crisis, Eckford appeared with Hazel Bryan Massery, a white Central High School student who appeared in several of the 1957 photographs, her face contorted with rage as she screamed at Eckford. The two women made public appearances together promoting positive race relations and reconciliation, but their cordial relationship did not last. A poster titled "Reconciliation" was printed with past and present photos of the two women. For its second printing, Eckford asked that a small sticker be attached that said: "True reconciliation can occur only when we honestly acknowledge our painful, but shared, past—Elizabeth Eckford."

Among her honors are the Spingarn Medal from the National Association for the Advancement of Colored People (NAACP) and the Congressional Gold Medal, the nation's highest civilian award, which was awarded to the members of the Little Rock Nine.

Eckford returned to Little Rock to be closer to her parents, and she ultimately lived in the same home where she had lived in 1957. She is the mother of two sons, one of whom was shot and killed by Little Rock police at age twenty-six after pointing a rifle at officers.

For more information:

Little Rock Central High School National Historic Site Visitor Center. Little Rock, Arkansas. http://www.nps.gov/chsc (accessed December 8, 2015).

Margolick, David. *Elizabeth and Hazel: Two Women of Little Rock*. New Haven: Yale University Press, 2011.

Joycelyn Elders (1933–)

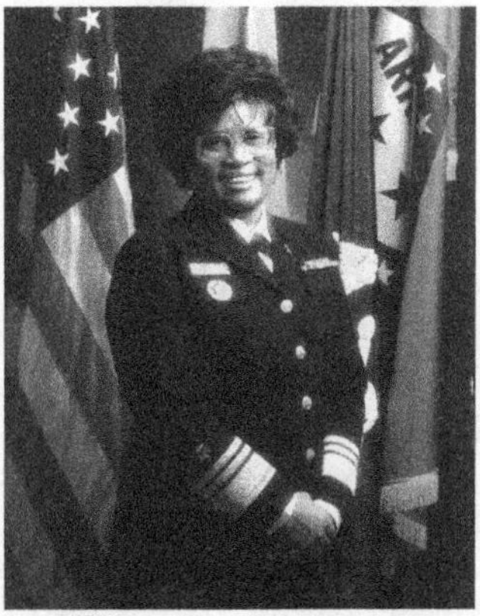

IN 1993, JOYCELYN ELDERS became the first African American surgeon general of the United States. She openly discussed controversial issues such as drug and alcohol abuse, sex education, drug legalization, tobacco usage, and national health care. Critical attacks from opponents led to her resignation as surgeon general.

She was born Minnie Lee Jones on August 13, 1933, in Schaal, Arkansas, an unincorporated rural community in the southwestern part of the state. She was the eldest of eight children born to Curtis and Haller Jones, who were sharecroppers. Their home was a three-room cabin without electricity or an indoor toilet. Like their parents, all of the children worked in the cotton fields.

The community was racially segregated, and she attended an all-black school thirteen miles from home. She valued education, citing a memory of being taught to read by her mother, who had an eighth-grade education (which was considered a good education for an African American woman at that time).

In high school, Jones displayed academic ability, going on to become valedictorian of her class. Upon graduation in 1949, she earned a scholarship to the historically black Philander Smith College in Little Rock. Even with a scholarship, her attendance was in doubt because her father did not want to let her go and paying for it was a problem. Her grandmother persuaded Minnie Lee's father to let her attend, and the entire family picked extra cotton to earn the $3.43 for her bus fare to Little Rock. She not only became the first in her family to attend college, but the college's physical exam marked the first time she had ever seen a doctor. She had an interest in biology and chemistry, with a goal to become a lab technician.

In college, she took the name Minnie Joycelyn Lee, though Joycelyn is sometimes erroneously spelled "Jocelyn." She set a goal of becoming a physician after attending a lecture by Edith Irby Jones, the first African American to graduate from the University of Arkansas Medical School (later the University of Arkansas for Medical Sciences—UAMS).

She graduated from Philander Smith in 1952 with a bachelor's degree in biology. She worked as a nurse's aide at a Veterans Administration hospital in Milwaukee, Wisconsin, before joining the U.S. Army in 1953. While in the army, she trained as a physical therapist. With educational benefits provided to veterans under the GI Bill, in 1956, she entered UAMS in Little Rock, becoming the second African American female student to attend the school.

While performing physical exams for the basketball team at Little Rock's all-black Horace Mann High School, she met the team's coach, Oliver Elders, whom she married in 1960. The couple had two sons.

Joycelyn Elders earned her MD degree from UAMS in 1960. She interned at the University of Minnesota Hospital in Minneapolis and performed her residency in pediatrics at UAMS. In 1967, Elders earned a master's degree in biochemistry. Beginning in 1967, she served as chief pediatric resident and professor of pediatrics at UAMS. She performed research in endocrinology, which pertains to the pineal and pituitary glands, pancreas, ovaries, testes, thyroid, hypothalamus, gastrointestinal tract, and adrenal glands. She published scholarly papers and received board certification as a pediatric endocrinologist in 1978, the first person in Arkansas to do so.

Noting that, in the 1980s, about twenty percent of Arkansas children were born to teenage mothers, Elders spoke publicly regarding adolescent sexuality and contraception, which garnered her acclaim as well as criticism. Bill Clinton, during his time as governor, considered teen pregnancy a social and economic problem for the state. In 1987, he named Elders director of the Arkansas Department of Health. In that role, she advocated for a controversial program to provide contraceptives to public school students, drawing attacks from conservatives. In 1989, with Elders's support, the Arkansas legislature approved a sex education program for public schools that included hygiene, personal responsibility, and substance abuse prevention. During her tenure, early childhood screenings increased tenfold and immunization for the state's two-year-olds almost doubled. In 1992, she was elected president of the Association of State and Territorial Health Officers.

After he took office as president of the United States in 1993, Bill Clinton appointed her as U.S. Surgeon General, making her the first African American to be named to the position. At her confirmation hearings in September 1993, she was supported by former surgeon general C. Everett Koop as well as the American Medical Association.

Like many surgeons general before her, she spoke openly about health-related issues. She suggested exploring drug legalization to reduce crime, promoted sex education, and recommended that contraceptives be provided in schools. She spoke openly about AIDS, tobacco-related disease, and drug and alcohol abuse. Under fire from political opponents, Elders resigned in December 1994.

She returned to UAMS as a researcher and professor of pediatrics, and she was later named professor emerita. She continues to lecture extensively, and she has spoken on television against abstinence-only sex education programs, which she considers ineffective. She has also stated she favors legalizing marijuana, saying, "I think we consume far more dangerous drugs that are legal: cigarette smoking, nicotine and alcohol." She also openly supports public health education, has continued to speak on health issues such as AIDS, and favors national health care. She has said, "The greatest contraception in the world is a good education."

For more information:

Elders, Joycelyn. *Joycelyn Elders, MD: From Sharecropper's Daughter to Surgeon General of the United States*. New York: Morrow, 1996.

Dale Evans (1912–2001)

DALE EVANS was an actress, author, singer, and songwriter who rose to worldwide fame as America's "Queen of the West" alongside her husband, "King of the Cowboys" Roy Rogers. Evans wrote twenty-eight inspirational books and composed about 200 songs, including "The Bible Tells Me So" as well as "Happy Trails."

She was born Frances Octavia Smith on October 31, 1912, at her grandparents' home at Uvalde, Texas, though her family lived in the nearby small town of Italy. Her father, Walter Smith, was a farmer who also owned a hardware store, and her mother, Betty Hillman Smith, was a homemaker.

Some sources claim the child was named Lucille Wood Smith at birth, with the name changed to Frances Octavia while she was an infant. A birth certificate was later issued in the name of Lucille Wood Smith, but her mother insisted that she was born Frances Octavia and that the recordkeepers were wrong.

At the age of three, the child soloed in her gospel singing debut at church. When she was seven, the family moved to Osceola, Arkansas, to grow cotton. She later said that the family's first year in Arkansas was "neither financially rewarding nor joyous."

She entered school in Osceola at age seven. She skipped several grades but then suffered a nervous breakdown and was ordered to spend the summer in bed. Even then, she took piano lessons until her instructor quit in frustration, saying that the child improvised her own songs.

She continued her schooling at age twelve as a high school freshman. At a dance, she met an older boy, Thomas Fox, and she eloped with him at age fourteen. They moved to Memphis, Tennessee, where their son, Thomas Fox Jr., was born when she was fifteen. She was seventeen when they were divorced in 1929.

As a single parent in Memphis, she took business courses and worked as a secretary while aspiring to become a singer. Her boss helped her find singing jobs on radio programs sponsored by his company. She became a local radio show regular under the names Frances Fox and Marian Lee.

Some sources state that she married August Wayne Johns in 1929, divorcing in 1936. In her autobiography, she does not mention this union.

She moved with her son to Chicago, Illinois, in 1930, where she found few job prospects—and she was then diagnosed with malnutrition. She moved from Chicago to Louisville, Kentucky, where she found a job at a radio station. There, the manager renamed her "Dale Evans" because it was easy for radio announcers to pronounce.

Next, she found work as a singer at a Dallas radio station. While in Texas, she married Robert Dale Butts in 1937. They moved to Chicago, where she sang with big bands. One engagement took her to Los Angeles. There were no job offers there, but a Hollywood agent took her as a client. He told her to remove her wedding ring and pretend her son was her younger brother.

By 1942, Evans had found work as a contract player at 20th Century Fox, appearing in the films *Orchestra Wives* and *Girl Trouble*. She became a regular on the Edgar Bergen/Charlie McCarthy radio show broadcast nationally from Hollywood. Moving to Republic Pictures in 1943, she worked in such westerns as *In Old Oklahoma* with John Wayne. In 1944, *The Cowboy and the Senorita* paired her with cowboy star Roy Rogers. They proved enormously popular, co-starring through the 1940s in films such as *Yellow Rose of Texas* and *Lights of Old Santa Fe*.

Dale Evans and her husband divorced in 1945. The next year, Rogers's wife died after giving birth to their son, Roy Rogers Jr. (called Dusty). In 1947, Rogers and Evans were married, and they ended the falsehood about her son being her brother.

In addition to Dale's son and Roy's children (Cheryl, Linda Lou, and Dusty), the couple had a daughter, Robin, in 1950. Robin died two years later of complications from Down's Syndrome, inspiring Dale to write a book in her honor, *Angel Unaware*. The couple became foster and adoptive parents to other special-needs children. Two died early, and to honor their lives, Evans wrote the books *Dearest Debbie* and *Salute to Sandy*.

In 1950, Dale Evans wrote the song "Happy Trails," which Roy Rogers went on to use as his theme song. Writing the lyrics on an envelope, she taught the melody to Rogers only minutes before their radio show.

The couple made thirty-five films together and founded their own company, Roy Rogers Productions. They created *The Roy Rogers Show*, which ran from 1951 to 1957, followed by *The Roy Rogers and Dale Evans Show* and *Happy Trails Theatre*. In these, the couple continued their cowboy/cowgirl roles, with Evans riding her trusty buckskin horse, Buttermilk. In addition to recording several solo albums of religious music, Evans starred in her own weekly Christian TV program, *A Date with Dale*, from 1996 until her death in 2001. The couple owned a ranch in Apple Valley, California, and founded the Roy Rogers–Dale Evans Museum in nearby Victorville, where they often greeted fans.

Roy Rogers died in 1998. At age eighty-nine, Evans died of heart failure on February 7, 2001. She is buried beside Rogers at Sunset Hills Memorial Park in Apple Valley, California.

Evans holds three stars on the Hollywood Walk of Fame, was inducted into the Texas Country Music Hall of Fame and the Cowgirl Hall of Fame, and received the Cardinal Terrence Cook Humanities Award.

For more information:

Rogers, Dale Evans. *Rainbow on a Hard Trail*. Tarrytown, NY: Revell Books, 1999.

Rogers, Dale Evans, and Roy Rogers, with Carlton Stowers. *Happy Trails: The Story of Roy Rogers and Dale Evans*. Waco, TX: Word Books, 1979.

White, Raymond. *King of the Cowboys, Queen of the West: Roy Rogers & Dale Evans*. Madison: University of Wisconsin Press, 2006.

Barbara Fairchild (1950–)

GRAMMY AWARD–NOMINATED BARBARA FAIRCHILD is a singer and songwriter of country and gospel music who is best known for her 1973 hit "The Teddy Bear Song." It reached the top spot on the country charts, was a success on the pop charts, and became her signature song. Fairchild was inducted into the Christian Music Hall of Fame and was nominated for a Visionary Award by the Christian Music Hall of Fame.

Barbara Fairchild was born on November 12, 1950, to farmers Ulys Fairchild and Opal Archer Fairchild. Barbara was born at a hospital in Lafe, Arkansas, and was raised on the family farm in nearby Knobel. At age five, she first performed for an audience at a school talent show. In 1963, when she was thirteen, the family moved to St. Louis, Missouri. Two years later, Fairchild released her first single, a country song called "Brand New Bed of Roses," which became a regional hit. At age fifteen, she was a regular on local television.

Fairchild graduated from St. Louis's Southwest High School in 1968 and moved to Nashville, Tennessee. She signed with several record labels as a singer and songwriter, but she found limited success until she signed with Columbia Records in 1969. Her recording of "Love Is a Gentle Thing" hit the top seventy on country charts. Her next single, "A Woman's Hand," was also a modest success. In 1970, she had her first Top 40 hit with "A Girl Who'll Satisfy Her Man." She continued a string of Top 40 hits between 1970 and 1972, including "Love's Old Song" and "Thanks for the Mem'ries." During this time, she also released the albums *Someone Special*, *Love's Old Song*, and *A Sweeter Love*.

The album *A Sweeter Love* included her biggest hit and the tune that became her trademark, "The Teddy Bear Song." In it, the singer wishes she could go back to the simple innocence of a teddy bear after enduring problems in life and a broken love affair. This 1972 recording became the biggest hit of her career, earning the number-one spot on the country charts for several weeks as well as reaching number thirty-two on pop charts and being nominated for a Grammy Award. She would receive another Grammy nomination in 1988 for "Lullaby for Teddy" in the Music for Children category.

Her follow-up, both as an album and a single, was titled "Kid Stuff." It was released in 1973 and charted as a number-two country hit as well as on the Billboard Hot 100. Again, it involves childhood themes, such as memories of playing house juxtaposed against a current adult relationship. In 1974, she had another hit with "Baby Doll," followed over the next three years with successful albums containing singles such as "Standing in Your Line," "Little Girl Feelin'," "Mississippi," "Cheatin' Is," and "Let Me Love You Once Before You Go."

By 1975, she was touring with a four-piece band that included her then-husband, steel guitarist Randy Reinhard. In the late 1970s and early 1980s, she lived in San Antonio,

Texas, with Reinhard and her three children. Fairchild and Reinhard eventually divorced, and she married evangelical minister and singer Milton Carroll in 1982. They divorced in 2002, and she later married Roy Morris, a gospel singer and songwriter.

Returning to Nashville in 1986, Fairchild concentrated on gospel music. In 1989, she was invited to join the gospel group Heirloom, and she has had a successful career in Christian music, both solo and with others. In 1991, Fairchild released a solo gospel album, *The Light*, and moved to Branson, Missouri, the following year.

In Branson, she performed for two years with the *Mel Tillis Show* and also appeared with the *Jim Stafford Show*. In 1993, she began her own show in Branson as well as a weekly Sunday morning worship service at Branson's Music City Centre with her husband. With Branson as home base, Fairchild and Morris also began touring regularly with a program of country, gospel, and patriotic music. A tour titled "Take America Back" honored U.S. troops and veterans.

Fairchild is spokesperson for Feed the Children, a sponsor for the Foster Grandparents program, and a member of Concerned Women for America, which describes itself as a legislative action committee of conservative women that promotes biblical values and family traditions. Fairchild has appeared on numerous television shows including *Hee Haw*, *A Salute to Country Music*, *The 700 Club*, a three-part special called *A Country Homecoming*, and the documentary *Heaven on Earth*.

In 2009, Fairchild was inducted into the Christian Music Hall of Fame.

For more information:

Barbara Fairchild. http://www.barbarafairchild.com (accessed December 8, 2015).

Roberta Fulbright (1874–1953)

ROBERTA WAUGH FULBRIGHT became a prominent businesswoman after the sudden death of her husband, an event that left the family with financial challenges. She was an influential bank president, business owner, civic activist, and newspaper publisher. Her son, J. William Fulbright, went on to a distinguished career in the U.S. Senate. In 1976, Roberta Fulbright was one of only thirteen women nationwide honored with inclusion in the book *Mothers of Achievement in American History, 1776–1976*.

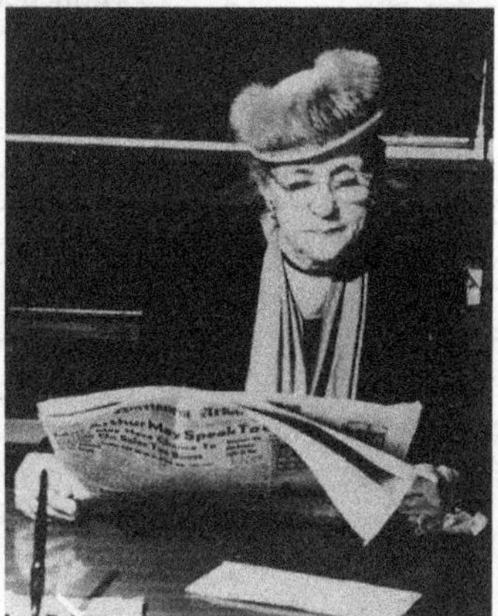

Roberta Waugh was born on February 14, 1874, in Rothville, Missouri. Her parents were homemaker Martha "Pattie" Stratton Waugh and farmer James Waugh. She had three brothers and enjoyed a comfortable childhood. She attended public school in Rothville, graduated from high school in Kansas City, and attended the University of Missouri for two years to attain a teacher's certificate. After doing so, she taught school in Chariton County, Missouri.

In 1894, she married Jay Fulbright, who owned a bank and had other business interests in Sumner, Missouri. The couple would have six children. Of their life, author Randall Woods said, "Jay and Roberta Fulbright epitomized white, middle-class America in the age of Theodore Roosevelt."

In 1906, the family moved to Fayetteville, Arkansas, in the northwest corner of the state. Jay Fulbright had set out to seek business ventures in Memphis, Tennessee, combining business with a family trip by bringing Roberta and their children. They stopped in Fayetteville, where Jay's parents had settled. After visiting Memphis, Jay decided he preferred to try banking in the friendly atmosphere of Fayetteville, much to the delight of his wife.

Roberta Fulbright quickly became involved with local civic, church, and cultural activities. Valuing education, she especially appreciated the town being home to the University of Arkansas (UA), which she hoped her children would attend. Their spacious home became a popular destination for neighbors. Roberta Fulbright had helped her husband at his bank in Sumner, but after becoming pregnant again in 1910 at the age of thirty-six and giving birth to twins, she was occupied with her children.

Jay Fulbright bought and sold a number of Fayetteville businesses. In addition to banking and real estate, these would ultimately include mercantile and grocery businesses, a hotel, a lumber company, a soft-drink franchise, and a newspaper called the *Fayetteville Daily Democrat*, which was of particular importance to Roberta due to her interest in journalism and politics.

The family prospered until 1923 when fifty-six-year-old Jay Fulbright died suddenly. This was followed by legal challenges to the Fulbright businesses, many of which stemmed from the belief that, as a woman, Roberta Fulbright had no place in business. She sold what she needed to, consolidated where she could, and generally turned their precarious financial situation around. What became known as the Fulbright Investment Company had outside managers, but some of their enterprises were run by Roberta. With her management of Citizens Bank and the Bank of Elkins, she was one of only three female bank presidents in Arkansas in 1936.

She was most active as publisher of the *Fayetteville Daily Democrat*, which later became the *Northwest Arkansas Times*. She wrote a column called "As I See It," which described its intent with its title. She was an advocate for various civic projects and commented on state, local, and national government.

She retained a female editor, Lessie Stringfellow Read [See Entry], and became the voice of change in dealing with corrupt local politicians. She was threatened with boycotts, lawsuits, and violence, but she held fast until reform was enacted.

Fulbright became a powerful voice in statewide politics. However, she was ensnared in a political storm between factions that led to the dismissal of her son William as president of UA in 1941. In 1942, with the backing of his mother, he won a seat in the U.S. House of Representatives. In 1944, he was elected to the U.S. Senate, defeating the governor who had ousted him. She convened the first meeting of the Arkansas Newspaper Women in 1949, the same year a volume of her poetry titled *Sea (See) Foam and Dashes of Spray* was published.

At age seventy-nine, Roberta Fulbright died of heart failure at her Fayetteville home on January 11, 1953.

In 1976, to honor the American bicentennial, she was one of only thirteen women nationwide to be profiled in *Mothers of Achievement in American History, 1776–1976*. The book was compiled by the American Mothers Committee (later American Mothers, Inc.), which had been founded by Sara Delano Roosevelt, Mamie Eisenhower, J. C. Penney, and Norman Vincent Peale with a mission of improving the lives of mothers and families in the United States and around the world.

Two buildings on the UA campus had been named for Roberta Fulbright, but they were later demolished. In 2012, the university named the Roberta Fulbright Dining Hall for her, recognizing not only her own achievements but her influence on national and international statesmanship through her son, Senator J. William Fulbright, who served for more than thirty years.

For more information:

American Mothers Committee. *Mothers of Achievement in American History, 1776–1976*. North Clarendon, VT: C. E. Tuttle Co., 1976.

Stuck, Dorothy D., and Nan Snow. *Roberta: A Most Remarkable Fulbright*. Fayetteville: University of Arkansas Press, 1997.

Ellen Gilchrist (1935–)

NOVELIST, POET, AND SHORT-STORY WRITER ELLEN GILCHRIST is a noted author who won a National Book Award for her 1984 collection of short stories *Victory Over Japan*. Along with numerous awards and recognitions such as a National Endowment for the Arts Grant in Fiction, she has been an educator and a commentator on National Public Radio's *Morning Edition.*

Ellen Louise Gilchrist was born on February 20, 1935, near Vicksburg, Mississippi, spending part of her childhood on her grandparents' plantation in Issaquena County, Mississippi. With an older brother, Dooley, she was the second child of Aurora Alford Gilchrist and William Garth Gilchrist. Her father's work as an engineer took the family to a number of locations around the region when he was hired to build airports for the U.S. Army Corps of Engineers. The adventures of Gilchrist's recurring fictional character, Rhoda Manning, and Rhoda's brother, Dudley, are said to be modeled on many of these childhood experiences.

Growing up, she was an imaginative child and a passionate reader. At age fourteen, she wrote a column called "Chit and Chat About This and That" for a local newspaper in Franklin, Kentucky. She attended Vanderbilt University in Nashville, Tennessee, working toward a bachelor's degree in philosophy. At age nineteen, while she was at Vanderbilt, she married engineering student Marshall Walker. They went on to have three children. The couple divorced and later remarried, though they ultimately divorced again. She subsequently married and divorced two other men.

In 1967, Gilchrist received a bachelor's degree in philosophy from Millsaps College, a private liberal arts school in Jackson, Mississippi. There, she studied creative writing under noted Mississippi author Eudora Welty, who went on to win the Pulitzer Prize for fiction. Inspired by Welty, Gilchrist wrote short stories and poetry while working at various jobs in publishing and journalism, such as serving as a contributing editor for New Orleans's *Vieux Carré Courier* from 1976 to 1979. Her first book of poetry, *The Land Surveyor's Daughter*, was published in 1979. This was followed by another poetry collection in 1986: *Riding Out the Tropical Depression: Selected Poems, 1975–1985*.

However, it is in the realm of fiction that she became most recognized, especially her short-story collections, which debuted with 1981's *In the Land of Dreamy Dreams*. It received popular and critical success. In 1984, she published her next short-story collection, *Victory Over Japan*, which won the National Book Award for Fiction in 1984. It was described in *People* magazine as "a collection of pungent and funny short stories. Her heroines are free-spirited Southern belles, the fastest-talking hellions below the Mason-Dixon line."

Her subsequent collections of short stories include *Drunk with Love*; *Light Can Be Both Wave and Particle*; *The Age of Miracles*; *Rhoda: A Life in Stories*; *The Courts of Love*; *Flights of Angels*; *Ellen Gilchrist: Collected Stories*; *I, Rhoda Manning, Go Hunting With My Daddy and Other Stories*; *Nora Jane*; and *Acts of God*.

I Cannot Get You Close Enough: Three Novellas (1990) is sometimes included as both a short-story collection and as part of her body of work as a novelist. The prolific author has published novels including *The Annunciation*, *The Anna Papers*, *Net of Jewels*, *Starcarbon: A Meditation on Love*, *Sarah Conley*, *The Cabal*, and *A Dangerous Age*. Her 1994 historical novel set in ancient Greece, *Anabasis: A Journey to the Interior*, marked something of a departure from her Southern-themed work, though it also centered on a strong female character.

Gilchrist was a regular commentator on National Public Radio's *Morning Edition* in 1984 and 1985, often discussing Southern themes. Those commentaries were published in her 1987 book *Falling through Space: The Journals of Ellen Gilchrist*.

While living in Fayetteville, Arkansas, Gilchrist enrolled in creative-writing courses at the University of Arkansas (UA). In 2000, UA named her a visiting professor, and she joined the faculty in 2001, teaching creative writing. From this experience, she wrote a memoir, *The Writing Life* (2005), discussing issues such as alcoholism, balancing artistic endeavors with family life, and teaching students the art of writing.

She continues to live in Fayetteville while also having a home in Ocean Springs on Mississippi's Gulf Coast. She has won the Mississippi Academy of Arts and Science Award for Fiction, and is a three-time winner of the Mississippi Institute of Arts and Letters Literature Award. In 2015, China Grove Press initiated the first Ellen Gilchrist Prize for Short Fiction to honor the author's legacy as a writer.

Gilchrist's writing was described by a *London Times* reviewer as swinging between "the familiar and the shocking, the everyday and the traumatic....She writes about ordinary happenings in out of the way places, of meetings between recognizable characters from her other fiction and strangers, above all of domestic routine disrupted by violence."

Gilchrist herself once said, "All you have to do to educate a child is leave him alone and teach him to read. The rest is brainwashing."

For more information:

Bauer, Margaret Donovan. *The Fiction of Ellen Gilchrist*. Gainesville: University Press of Florida, 1999.

Gilchrist, Ellen. *The Writing Life*. Jackson: University Press of Mississippi, 2005.

Hooper, Brad. *The Fiction of Ellen Gilchrist: An Appreciation*. Westport, CT: Praeger, 2005.

Mary Lowe Good (1931–)

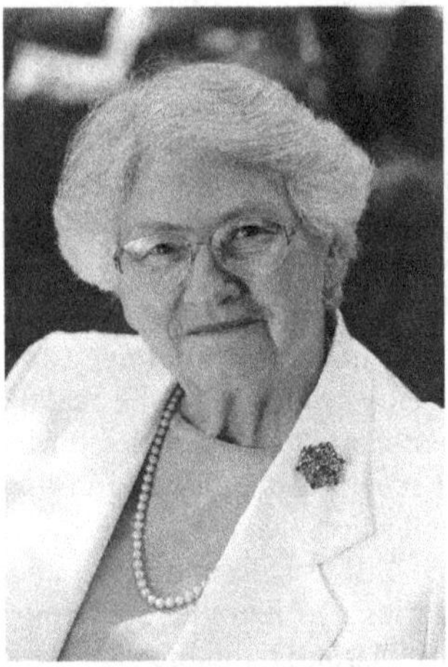

DR. MARY LOWE GOOD went to a high school that did not offer chemistry, yet she went on to become a nationally renowned chemist, industrial innovator, professor, and government leader. Good was the first woman in Arkansas to earn a PhD in the "hard" sciences, and she was the first woman elected to the board of the American Chemical Society. She has held leading government positions under the administrations of four presidents.

One of four children, Mary Lowe was born in Grapevine, Texas, on June 20, 1931. Her parents were teacher and librarian Winnie Mercer Lowe and school principal John Willice Lowe. In 1942, the family moved to Kirby, Arkansas, later moving to Willisville, Arkansas, a small town of fewer than 200 people in the southwestern portion of the state. The rural school she attended offered neither chemistry classes nor a chemistry lab, but Mary read a biography of French scientist Marie Curie, noting later in life, "There weren't very many role models for women in the sciences in the '50s."

Intending to become a home economics teacher, Lowe attended Arkansas State Teachers College in Conway (today's University of Central Arkansas—UCA). She began focusing on chemistry and physics due to an influential professor, graduating from UCA with a bachelor's degree in 1950. Her professors encouraged her to attend graduate school. A fellowship enabled her to study radiochemistry at the University of Arkansas (UA) in Fayetteville. She was not yet eighteen years old when she went to graduate school, and she received her first government clearance as a nineteen-year-old atomic energy research assistant.

In 1952, she married fellow UA graduate student and her lab partner in physical chemistry, William Jewel Good. While she was still in graduate school, the first of her two sons was born. Mary Lowe Good received a master's degree in 1953, followed by a PhD in 1955, both from UA.

From 1954 to 1958, she was director of the radiochemistry laboratory and assistant professor of chemistry at Louisiana State University in Baton Rouge. In 1958, Good and her husband moved to New Orleans when both were offered positions at the newly created Louisiana State University, New Orleans, the first university in the South to open as a fully integrated institution. From 1974 through 1978, she was Boyd Professor of Chemistry, the first woman to achieve the university's most distinguished rank. She then returned to Baton Rouge to develop a new program as the Boyd Professor of Materials Science, Division of Engineering Research.

Along with her academic duties and laboratory work, she published several books and more than 100 articles in refereed journals. In 1972, Good was the first woman elected to the board of the American Chemical Society, becoming board chair in 1978 and serving as the society's president in 1987.

In 1980, she was recruited to serve as vice president and director of research for the Engineered Materials Research division at Signal Research Center (later Allied-Signal). She oversaw a staff of 400 scientists and technicians, with annual sales of approximately $3 billion. Through several mergers, her titles would include president and director of research for Signals Research Center, president of Allied-Signal Engineered Materials Research, and senior vice president of technology, in which she coordinated three research centers. One of the projects she oversaw was to determine if the newly emerging technology of the Global Positioning System (GPS) would have an application for the general public.

In 1980, Good was appointed to the National Science Foundation board by President Jimmy Carter, becoming the first woman to chair that board. She was appointed again by President Ronald Reagan. In 1991, President George H. W. Bush appointed her to the President's Council of Advisors on Science and Technology. During each advisory position, she continued to work at Allied-Signal.

In 1993, Good left Allied-Signal to become U.S. undersecretary for technology in the Department of Commerce under the Bill Clinton administration. In that position, she led the Clean Car Initiative in developing a hybrid gas-electric car and encouraged the government to fund research on emerging technologies.

In 1997, Good became the Donaghey University Professor at the University of Arkansas at Little Rock (UALR), then became the founding dean of the Donaghey College of Engineering and Information Technology. When she retired in 2011, she was named dean emeritus of UALR's College of Engineering and Information Technology and special advisor to the chancellor for economic development.

She has served on numerous boards, including being elected president of the American Association for the Advancement of Science, succeeding world-famous scientist Stephen Jay Gould. Good was the founding chair of the Alliance for Science & Technology Research in America (ASTRA) and is a nationally recognized leader in the support of Science, Technology, Engineering, and Mathematics (STEM) education, especially for women.

A small sampling of her awards includes the Garvan-Olin Medal; *Industrial Research and Development Magazine*'s Scientist of the Year; American Institute of Chemists Gold Medal; Othmer Gold Medal; Heinz Award; and the Vannevar Bush Award, the highest honor from the National Science Foundation. She was also the first woman to receive the Industrial Research Institute Medal, Glenn Seaborg Medal, Priestley Medal, and Philip Hauge Abelson Prize.

She continues advocating women in STEM programs and was one of five national dignitaries honored in 2012 at the inaugural *U.S. News* STEM Leadership Hall of Fame. Dr. Good once said, "You've got to take the opportunities as they appear."

For more information:

"Dr. Mary Good, Founding Dean." http://ualr.edu/eit/mary-good/ (accessed December 8, 2015).

Senate Committee Session on Commerce. *Nomination of Mary Lowe Good to Be Undersecretary of Commerce for Technology: Hearing Before the Committee on Commerce, Science, and Transportation, United States Congress*. Washington DC: July 27, 1993. Reprint edition, London: Forgotten Books, 2012.

Yount, Lisa. *A to Z of Women in Science and Math*. New York: Facts on File, 1999.

Kay Goss (1941–)

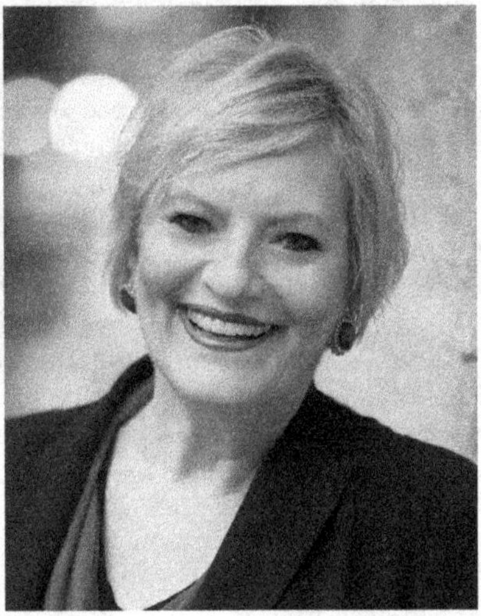

KAY GOSS is an author, educator, historian, lecturer, legislative assistant, and emergency management official. Her friendship with U.S. congressman Wilbur D. Mills led to the first full-scale biography of the powerful Arkansas congressman. She has served as senior assistant for intergovernmental relations for two Arkansas governors and was appointed associate director of the Federal Emergency Management Agency (FEMA), where she served from 1994 to 2001.

Kay Collett Goss is a native of Fayetteville, Arkansas. She is a 1963 graduate of the University of Arkansas (UA), where she majored in political science, public administration, and government, with a minor in history. She earned a master's degree from UA in 1966 before embarking on doctoral studies in public administration at West Virginia University.

In 1971, as assistant professor of political science at UA, she worked to establish congressional internships, coming into contact with Wilbur D. Mills, who served in Congress from 1939 to 1977. When she later worked in Washington DC as legislative assistant to Congressman Ray Thornton, she was able to observe Mills first-hand as the influential chairman of the House Ways and Means Committee.

While in Washington, she met and married Gene Goss, who served as Mills's chief of staff for the final fourteen years of his congressional tenure. They have one daughter.

From 1982 through 1993, Kay Goss served as senior assistant for intergovernmental relations for Arkansas governor Bill Clinton. She coordinated emergency management and emergency medical services and fire service, along with public safety and law enforcement agencies and activities. She continued serving for Clinton's successor as governor, Jim Guy Tucker.

In 1994, she was nominated by U.S. president Bill Clinton to replicate her work on a national scale by serving as associate director of FEMA. She was confirmed unanimously by the U.S. Senate, becoming the first woman to serve in the position. She served through the end of Clinton's presidency in 2001. Her areas of responsibility included overseeing national preparedness and directing training exercises as well as planning for 1999's possible "Y2K" worldwide computer breakdown at the turn of the new millennium, which did not take place.

She worked with fellow Arkansan James Lee Witt of Paris, Arkansas, who Clinton appointed as FEMA director in 1993. In 1996, FEMA was given cabinet rank. During the tenure of Witt and Goss at FEMA, the agency was able to recover from a previously poor reputation. By 1996, an *Atlanta Journal-Constitution* editorial said that FEMA developed "a sterling reputation for delivering disaster-relief services," through preparedness, customer service, and willingness to listen to local and state officials. During Goss's term at FEMA, there were almost 350 disaster areas declared in all fifty states.

While at FEMA, Goss also directed the Emergency Management Institute in

Emmitsburg, Maryland; the Mount Weather Emergency Assistance Center in Berryville, Virginia; and the NATO Civil Emergency Planning Staff in Brussels, Belgium.

After the 1994 Oklahoma City bombing, Goss and her staff launched the FEMA Higher Education Program and later, the National Interagency Task Force on Counterterrorism, which would eventually be housed at the U.S. Department of Justice. In 1996, Goss was appointed to chair the National Emergency Food and Shelter Program. The information base and available funds were broadened to more than 10,000 shelters nationwide with support from President and Mrs. Clinton.

Other successes during her FEMA tenure include the Capability Assessment for Readiness Program, which evolved into the Emergency Management Accreditation Program, and an international effort with Turkey to provide emergency management training to that country, which often faces devastating earthquakes.

After leaving office in 1977, Wilbur Mills sat with Goss for hundreds of hours of interviews. Goss incorporated this material into her book *Mr. Chairman: The Life and Legacy of Wilbur D. Mills*, published in 2012. She has also written four other books: *The City Manager Plan in Arkansas*, *The Politics of Constitutional Revision in Arkansas*, *The Arkansas Constitution: A Reference Guide*, and *The Emergency Management Handbook*, along with hundreds of articles. She has lectured extensively throughout all fifty states and in many foreign countries.

After her work with FEMA in the Clinton administration, Goss worked with a number of public and private entities such as Homeland Security and Electronic Data Systems. In 2011, she formed her own company, World Disaster Management, LLC.

At UA, she served as a visiting professor of political science and interim director for international studies, as well as UA's first executive in residence. In addition, she has served as adjunct faculty at the University of North Carolina, University of Nevada at Las Vegas, and Istanbul Technical University.

Among her honors are the Lifetime Achievement Award from the Wilbur D. Mills Treatment Center for Alcoholism and Drug Abuse; the International Network of Women in Emergency Management Hall of Fame; and election to chair the Training and Education Committee for the International Association of Emergency Managers.

She is president of the Foundation for Higher Education's Accreditation in Emergency Management; first vice president of the International Network of Women in Emergency Management; and vice president of the Every Child Is Ours Foundation, which launched World Disaster Management Community College in Kanana, South Africa, in 2012. She has also served on the advisory board of the Wilbur D. Mills Treatment Center, which includes the Kay Goss Women's Health Center in Searcy, Arkansas.

For more information:

"Barnes and ... A conversation with Kay Collett Goss." http://www.aetn.org/programs/barnesand/goss (accessed December 8, 2015).

"Goss Joins Political Science as Executive in Residence," *University of Arkansas News*, March 10, 2014. http://news.uark.edu/articles/23654/goss-joins-political-science-as-executive-in-residence (accessed December 8, 2015).

Elizabeth Ward Gracen (1961–)

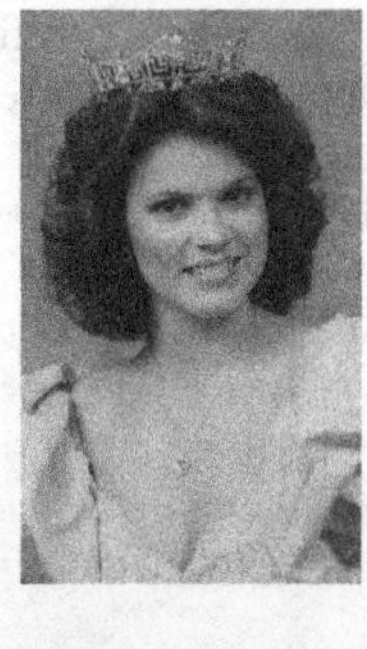

ELIZABETH WARD GRACEN of Arkansas was named Miss America in 1982. She was implicated in rumors surrounding extramarital affairs by then-governor and later U.S. president Bill Clinton, and she became the first former Miss America to pose nude for *Playboy* magazine. After embarking on an acting career, she became known for her role as Amanda in the series *Highlander* and its spin-off, *Highlander: The Raven*.

Grace Elizabeth (some sources list the name as Elizabeth Grace)

Ward was born on April 3, 1961, in Ozark, Arkansas, and raised in nearby Booneville, Arkansas. Her parents were Patricia Hampe Ward, who was a registered nurse, and Jimmy Young Ward, who was a poultry plant supervisor. She was their eldest child, having a younger brother and sister. The family moved to Russellville, Arkansas, where Elizabeth graduated from Russellville High School in 1979. She attended Arkansas Tech University in Russellville as an accounting major.

At this time, Ward became active in beauty competitions. During her senior year in high school, she was 1979's first runner-up in the local Junior Miss Pageant. She entered that year's Miss Lake Dardanelle Pageant, where she also finished as first runner-up. The next year, she won. As Miss Lake Dardanelle 1980, she went on to the Miss Arkansas Pageant, where she finished first runner-up, after winner Lencola Sullivan [SEE ENTRY].

Ward was eligible to compete in the Miss National Sweetheart Pageant in Illinois, which had been created for the runners-up from Miss America–affiliated competitions. The event has no official ties to the Miss America Organization, but, since 1980, five Miss National Sweetheart winners have gone on to win both their state and the Miss America title. Ward was named Miss National Sweetheart of 1980.

After winning the Miss White River pageant, Ward competed again for Miss Arkansas and won the title in 1981. Reprising her rendition of the song "After You've Gone" at the Miss America Pageant in Atlantic City, Ward went on to win the crown as 1982's Miss America. The only other time a Miss Arkansas won the Miss America title was in 1964 when El Dorado's Donna Axum [SEE ENTRY] was crowned. (Future Miss America Debbye Turner [SEE ENTRY], who grew up in Arkansas, competed as Miss Missouri.)

Ironically, several months earlier, Terri Utley of Cabot, Arkansas, was crowned Miss USA, affiliated with the Miss Universe pageant. Utley became the first and only Miss USA titleholder from Arkansas. This made 1982 the only time titleholders for both Miss America and Miss USA were from the same state in the same year.

Ward utilized her Miss America scholarship money to study acting at HB Studios in New York City. She moved to Hollywood in 1987 to pursue a film and television career. At that time, she changed her name to Elizabeth Ward Gracen because there was already an actress named Elizabeth Ward in the Screen Actors Guild.

She began her movie career in 1987 with two movies filmed in Arkansas: *Three for the Road* (still billed as Elizabeth Ward) with Charlie Sheen and 1988's *Pass the Ammo*, which also featured 1983's Miss America, Debra Sue Maffett. Gracen's subsequent film work includes *Sundown: Vampire in Retreat*; *Discretion Assured*; *The Expert*; *Final Mission*; *Kounterfeit*; *Coherence*; and *Marked for Death*, opposite Steven Seagal.

She acted in made-for-TV movies such as *83 Hours Till Dawn*, with Peter Strauss; *Death of the Incredible Hulk*; Shelley Duvall's *Strange Case of Dr. Jekyll and Mr. Hyde*; *Interceptor Force 2*; and Sidney Sheldon's *The Sands of Time*. She also appeared in TV series such as *Charmed*, *Extreme*, *Renegade*, and *Queen of Swords*. Her most well-known role is as Amanda in the popular television series *Highlander* and in *Highlander: The Raven*, centering around her character. She posed nude for the May 1992 issue of *Playboy* magazine, appearing on the cover and in a pictorial, becoming the first former Miss America to do so.

As she continued her acting career, rumors emerged in the 1992 presidential campaign about Gracen's previous involvement with candidate Bill Clinton. She called a press conference to deny the alleged incident, which was said to have taken place in 1983. In 1998, Gracen recanted her previous denial of the Clinton incident amidst an investigation of Clinton by the Office of the Independent Counsel. The most serious charge was that she had been raped by Clinton. A subpoena was issued for her to testify in court, but with her acting work keeping her out of the United States, she did not appear. She issued a statement admitting involvement with Clinton, though maintaining that the one-time encounter in 1983 was consensual.

In 1982, Gracen married her college sweetheart, Jon Birmingham, divorcing two years later. In 1989, she met actor Brendan Hughes, whom she married and later divorced. In 1992, she married Adam Murphy; their daughter, Quinlan Murphy, was born in 2005.

Gracen made her directorial debut in 1998 with a documentary short feature called *The Damn Deal* about female impersonators. She has done voice work for the radio anthology *Suspense*, airing on Sirius XM. According to the Miss America Organization website, she has worked to develop a cooking show and hosts tours to locales such as Tuscany, Venice, and the Napa Valley. She also offers classes in the "Fan Kata" technique featured on *Highlander: The Raven*.

For more information:

"Elizabeth Gracen." Internet Movie Database. http://www.imdb.com/name/nm0001286 (accessed December 8, 2015).

"Elizabeth Ward." Miss America. http://www.missamerica.org/our-miss-americas/1980/1982.aspx (accessed December 8, 2015).

Bette Greene (1934–)

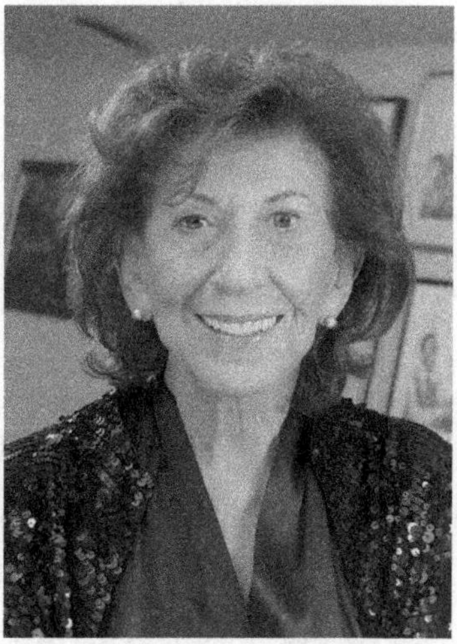

BETTE EVENSKY GREENE is an award-winning author whose Arkansas childhood provides the backdrop for much of her writing. Growing up Jewish in a small Arkansas town during the Great Depression and World War II, she wrote works that often focused on themes of experiencing prejudice and being an "outsider." Her most famous work, *Summer of My German Soldier*, is based on her Arkansas childhood and has become popular in classrooms as well as with general audiences. It was made into an award-winning television movie.

Bette Evensky was born on June 28, 1934, in Memphis, Tennessee, about thirty miles from Parkin, Arkansas, the town in which her family lived. Her parents were Sadie Steinberg Evensky and Arthur Evensky, who owned a general store in Parkin called Evensky's Dry Goods, where young Bette sometimes worked. The Evenskys were frequent visitors to Memphis; as they were the only Jewish family in the small rural town of Parkin, Memphis was where they attended synagogue.

Evensky often felt lonely during her childhood. Her parents were busy with their store, and as a Jewish girl in a fundamentalist Christian town, she experienced isolation from other young people and the community at large. Evensky was raised primarily by her family's African American housekeeper, Ruth, who would become the model for a character of the same name in *Summer of My German Soldier*.

Moving with the family to Memphis when she was thirteen, Evensky graduated from Memphis's Central High School in 1952. She attended the University of Alabama; Memphis State University (now the University of Memphis); Alliance Française in Paris, France (which became the background for her novel *Morning Is a Long Time Coming*); Columbia University in New York; and, in 1972, Harvard University. Much of her coursework was in the area of creative writing, though she holds no known undergraduate degrees.

She always had an interest in writing, later stating that she became a professional writer at age nine when Parkin's McKnight Dairy barn burned to the ground. Evensky wrote the story and sent it to the *Commercial Appeal* in Memphis. The newspaper ran the story with her byline, paying her eighteen cents. She later said that, from that moment, she "was hooked on writing." While attending Memphis State, she worked with the *Commercial Appeal* as a student correspondent, later becoming a full-time reporter. She became a contributor to the weekly *Hebrew Watchman*, and she also worked as a reporter for the Memphis Bureau of United Press International.

After enrolling at New York's Columbia University, Evensky met and married physician Donald Sumner Greene in 1959, moving with him to Brookline, Massachusetts, near Boston. The couple had two children, Carla and Jordan.

After the birth of her daughter Carla, Greene began the five-year process of writing *Summer of My German Soldier*. After almost twenty rejections, the book was published in 1973. It has gone on to become a popular and award-winning young-adult classic that is widely taught in classrooms. The novel is a fictional account by twelve-year-old Jewish girl Patty Bergen. She lives with abusive parents among the self-righteous citizens of the fictitious Arkansas town of Jenkinsville during World War II. The story concerns the friendship between Patty and an escaped German prisoner of war (POW). In addition, the plot focuses on other alienated people in town, including African Americans and a Chinese grocer.

The story is historically accurate. During World War II, a number of POW camps were established in the United States. More than 20,000 German and Italian POWs were held throughout the state of Arkansas. The German POW camps were located in places such as Camp Chaffee (later called Fort Chaffee), Camp Dermott, and Camp Robinson, with smaller camps established at former facilities of the Civilian Conservation Corps (CCC). With many young men leaving the state for the military or war work, there was a labor shortage in farming and lumbering. POWs were trucked into the countryside to cut wood, chop cotton, or do other work in exchange for a small payment they could use for incidentals.

Summer of My German Soldier was a 1973 National Book Award finalist, was listed as an American Library Association Notable Book, won the *New York Times* Outstanding Book Award, and earned the Golden Kite Society children's book writer's award. When it was made into a TV movie, it scored a ratings hit, and it won the Humanitas Prize for promoting human dignity. At the 1979 Emmy Awards, Esther Rolle won an Emmy as Outstanding Supporting Actress for her role as the housekeeper. The film was also nominated for Outstanding Writing and Outstanding Drama.

Greene's subsequent works were also well received. The book *Philip Hall Likes Me. I Reckon Maybe.* was named a Newbery Honor Book in 1975. It won the *New York Times* Outstanding Book Award, *New York Times* Outstanding Title Award, American Library Association Notable Children's Book Award, Child Study Association Children's Book Award, and the Kirkus Choice Award.

Greene's *Them That Glitter and Them That Don't* won the Parents' Choice Award from the Parents' Choice Foundation. Her other books include *Morning Is a Long Time Coming*; *Get On Out of Here, Philip Hall*; *A Writer's Survivor Kit*; *I've Already Forgotten Your Name, Philip Hall!*, and *The Drowning of Stephan Jones*. *Summer of My German Soldier* has been adapted into a musical with Greene's collaboration, and *The Drowning of Stephan Jones* was optioned as a motion picture.

For more information:

"Bette Greene." Internet Movie Database. http://www.imdb.com/name/nm0338677/ (accessed December 8, 2015).

Gallo, Donald, ed. *Speaking for Ourselves: Autobiographical Sketches by Notable Authors of Books for Young Adults*. Urbana, IL: National Council of Teachers of English, 1990.

Greene, Bette. "The Spring of My Harding Lecture." *Arkansas Times*, April 28, 2000, pp. 8–9.

Tess Harper (1950–)

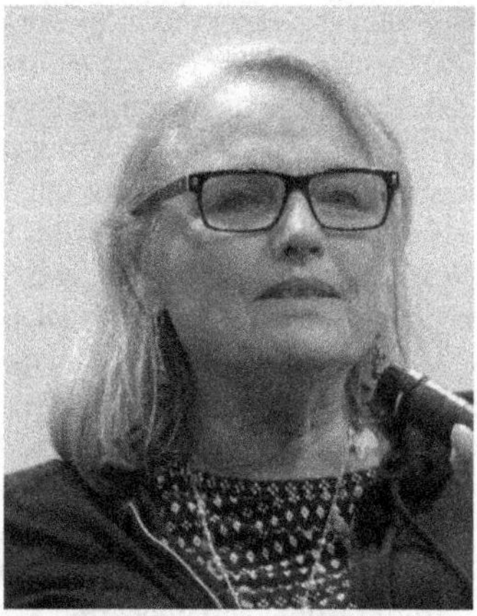

TESS HARPER is a Golden Globe and Academy Award nominee who is known for her extensive television and film work, including a Golden Globe nomination for her first movie role in 1983's *Tender Mercies*. In addition to television work on such shows as *Breaking Bad*, *CSI*, *Grey's Anatomy*, *Law & Order Special Victims Unit*, and *True Detective*, she has appeared in movies including *Crimes of the Heart* and *Far North*, both with Jessica Lange; *Silkwood* with Cher and Meryl Streep; and *No Country for Old Men* with Tommy Lee Jones.

Tessie Jean Washam was born on August 15, 1950, in Mammoth Spring, Arkansas, a town of about a thousand people. She was the eldest of three children born to Rosemary Langston Washam and Ed Washam, who owned Washam's Hardware Store. She has called her childhood "Norman Rockwellish," adding, "The doors weren't locked; everyone knew everyone; everyone was related to everyone. The people in town had families that had been there for four or five generations."

She stated that she had pale, sensitive skin, which often kept her from playing outdoors, so she spent a great deal of time on the front porch with books noted on a reading list provided by her school's English teacher/librarian. "I loved the word," she has said.

Washam graduated from Mammoth Spring High School in 1968, winning the speech award during her senior year. She later told an interviewer, "The night I graduated from high school was one of the saddest nights of my life. I cried. I knew a door was closing and I didn't know what the next one that was opening up would bring."

She enrolled at Arkansas State University–Beebe, a two-year college north of Little Rock. The school had a well-respected music and theater teacher, and it was in the drama department that Washam found a home. There, she performed in such shows as *Little Mary Sunshine* and *Arsenic and Old Lace*.

She went on to Southwest Missouri State University in Springfield, where she would graduate in 1972 with degrees in science, education, and theater. While at Southwest, she met fellow drama student Ken Harper, whom she married in 1971. At this time, she was acting in college theater productions, dinner theater, and children's theater, as well as working as a street performer at theme parks such as Dogpatch USA, in Harrison, Arkansas, and Silver Dollar City in Branson, Missouri.

Ken and Tess Harper moved to Houston, where Tess performed at Houston's Main Street Theatre. In 1976, the couple divorced. Tess Harper moved to Dallas, where she found work in industrial training films and local television commercials.

In 1983, a Hollywood regional casting agent who was in Dallas saw one of Harper's TV commercials and contacted the director of the film *Tender Mercies* to arrange for Harper to audition. The director, Australian Bruce Beresford, later said he did not know he could find actors in Dallas. He added that Harper brought a rural quality to the role without appearing simple or foolish. Harper's first movie role, in the leading part of Rosa Lee, the estranged wife of co-star Robert Duvall's character, brought her a Golden Globe Award nomination. Duvall won the Academy Award for Best Actor for his performance opposite Harper.

Harper has worked steadily after her film debut in *Tender Mercies*, alternating between movies and television. She often plays a strong Southern woman and has said that growing up in Arkansas, specifically the Ozarks, has influenced her work. Harper was nominated for a 1986 Academy Award as Best Supporting Actress for her performance as Chick in the film *Crimes of the Heart* alongside Diane Keaton, Jessica Lange, Sissy Spacek, and

Sam Shepard. Her other film work includes *Silkwood, Far North, The Man in the Moon, The Jackal*, and *Loggerhead.* For her role in the Oscar-winning film *No Country for Old Men*, she shared an award for ensemble acting with her co-stars in recognitions given by the National Board of Review and the Screen Actors Guild. Harper won the Best Actress award from Method Fest for the 2004 short film *Lonely Place*.

Her extensive television work includes mini-series and TV movies such as *Celebrity, Chiefs, Reckless Disregard*, and *Starflight: The Plane That Couldn't Land.* She has had recurring roles on TV series such as *Breaking Bad, Christy, Crash*, and *Early Edition*, and she has appeared in Hallmark Channel holiday movies including *A Christmas Wish* and *The Christmas Heart*. She was nominated for a CableACE Award as Best Actress in a Dramatic Series for 1991's *The Hidden Room*.

Harper has also made guest appearances on TV series such as *Criminal Minds*; *Murder, She Wrote*; *One Tree Hill*; *Touched by an Angel*; and *The Twilight Zone*.

Harper has been a supporter of the Hot Springs International Film Institute, attending the film festival and appearing at the event.

For more information:

Bloodworth, Julie. "An Ozarks Woman in the Movies: An Interview With Tess Harper." *OzarksWatch* 4 (Fall 1990). http://thelibrary.springfield.missouri.org/lochist/periodicals/ozarkswatch/ow402e.htm (accessed December 8, 2015).

"Tess Harper." Internet Movie Database. http://imdb.com/name/nm0002128 (accessed December 8, 2015).

Charlaine Harris (1951–)

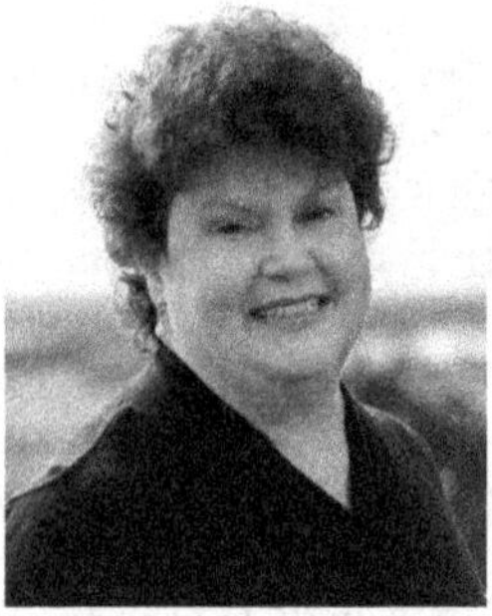

CHARLAINE HARRIS is a bestselling fantasy/mystery writer whose work was the basis for the HBO television series *True Blood*. She is especially known for her dark humor as well as for pioneering Southern vampire mysteries and the urban fantasy genre.

Jean Charlaine Harris was born on November 25, 1951, in Tunica, Mississippi, to Robert Harris, who was a school principal, and Jean Harris, who was a librarian. They also had a son, Ashley. She says that she grew up in a family of readers, which she feels was a great advantage.

Harris knew she wanted to be a writer when she was in the fourth grade. She said: "When I could hold the pencil and form the words, writing was all I ever wanted to do in my life." She says she felt like an outcast in school because there were few people with whom she could share her thoughts. Her parents encouraged her to become a schoolteacher, though she says that through her college years, she did not know what she was going to do.

She attended Southwestern (which later became Rhodes College) in Memphis, where she majored in English and communication arts, receiving a bachelor's degree in English in 1973. At Southwestern, she wrote poems (self-described as concerning "ghosts and teenage angst") and saw her one-act plays produced. Immediately after college, she married; she and her first husband later divorced. During that time, she worked in the darkroom of a newspaper, as a typesetter, and for Federal Express.

In 1978, Harris married chemical engineer Hal Schulz; they had three children. They moved to Arkansas in the 1980s, settling in the town of Magnolia in the southwestern part of the state. She says that her husband gave her an electric typewriter as a wedding present and encouraged her to stay home and write a book.

Harris took a creative-writing class at the University of Missouri–St. Louis, which was taught by Shannon Ravenel, who has been a leading editor for a number of prestigious publishing companies. Ravenel recommended Harris's manuscript to a major publisher, which accepted the book for publication. The subsequent novel, *Sweet and Deadly*, was published in 1981. Set in Mississippi, it has been described as "the story of a murder that embroils a small-town reporter in mystery that hits close to home."

She wrote another stand-alone mystery, *A Secret Rage*, before beginning her Aurora Teagarden series in 1990. This eight-book series features a librarian who continually becomes involved with crimes. It was the basis for several Hallmark Channel TV movies. In 1996, Harris embarked on the five-book Lily Bard series set in the fictional small town of Shakespeare, Arkansas. Bard, portrayed as a well-educated cleaning woman and sometime detective, is described as a darker and more troubled heroine than Teagarden.

Then came the thirteen-book Southern vampire series about a telepathic barmaid named Sookie Stackhouse who has a vampire boyfriend named Bill. *Dead Until Dark*, the first book in this series, won the Anthony Award for Best Paperback Mystery in 2001. Subsequent books in this series follow the heroine as she becomes involved with mysteries involving vampires, werewolves, and other supernatural creatures. This popular series has been published world-wide, and it came to the attention of Alan Ball, creator of the HBO television series *Six Feet Under*. Based on Harris's books, the series *True Blood* premiered on HBO in 2008, running for seven seasons. Though they are based on her work, Harris did not write scripts for the program.

In 2005, the prolific author embarked on a new series of books about a woman named Harper Connelly. Connelly is struck by lightning, becoming able to locate dead bodies and see their last moments through the eyes of the deceased. The first book in the series, *Grave Sight*, is set in the fictional town of Sarne, Arkansas. In 2010, it was announced that this series would be developed for the Syfy television network. Harris's *Cemetery Girl* series of graphic novels appeared in 2014.

After a lengthy residence in Magnolia, Harris and her husband moved to Texas soon after *True Blood*'s debut on HBO in 2008. In 2014, she published *Midnight Crossroad*, the first novel in a new series set in Midnight, Texas.

Harris has served as co-editor for a popular anthology series with Toni L. P. Kelner, also known as Leigh Perry. These feature stories concerning the supernatural, with individual entries coming from writers of mystery and urban fantasy. Harris has been a longtime member of writers' groups including the American Crime Writers League, the International Crime Writers Association, Mystery Writers of America, and Sisters in Crime. She also belongs to the Horror Writers Association, Romance Writers of America, and Science Fiction Writers of America. Among her awards are the Agatha Award for best novel (*Real Murders*); Anthony Award for best paperback original (*Dead Until Dark*); Goodreads Choice Best Fantasy (*Dead and Gone*); and Goodreads Choice Best Paranormal Fantasy (*Dead in the Family*).

Harris has said, "I've always been interested in the paranormal, the horrible, weird and strange."

For more information:

Charlaine Harris. http://www.charlaineharris.com (accessed December 8, 2015).

Ena Hartman (1935–)

HOLLYWOOD TRAILBLAZER ENA HARTMAN had a successful modeling career that led a contract with a national television network—the first African American woman to sign such a contract. Her movie and television appearances in the 1960s and '70s helped pave the way for other African Americans in film and television, especially for black women in "glamour" roles.

According to *Jet* and *Ebony* magazines, Ena Hartman's birth name was Gerthalene Henry. She was born to sharecroppers Daniel and Magnolia Smith on April 1, 1935, in Moscow, Arkansas, a small unincorporated community near Pine Bluff. She was raised by her grandparents, picking cotton and attending a one-room school.

At age thirteen, she moved to Buffalo, New York, to live with her mother. Before graduating from high school, she left school to work in a restaurant to earn enough money to pursue a modeling career in New York City. In 1960, at age twenty-five, she began making the rounds of modeling agencies in Manhattan. After being rejected at one agency, she sat in the lobby to consider her next move. A passing photographer saw her and was impressed with her stunning looks. With his help, Hartman became one of the most successful black fashion models of the era.

Between modeling assignments, she took acting and singing lessons. In 1962, she was brought to the attention of the NBC television network's vice president of talent relations, and she was signed to an NBC contract after performing well in a series of auditions. The five-year talent development contract paid her $12,000 a year. Hartman was the first African American woman to be signed to a national network television contract of this kind.

Hartman took classes in singing, dancing, and acting. Her dramatics coach was Lloyd Richards, the ground-breaking director who had staged the original production of *A Raisin in the Sun* on Broadway in 1959. Hartman was an apt pupil, leading Dave Tebet of NBC to say, "We think very highly of Ena. She has real potential." By 1964, Hartman was appearing in small roles on programs such as *Bonanza*, *The Farmer's Daughter*, and *Profiles in Courage*.

In 1966, she appeared as a crew member in an episode called "The Corbomite Maneuver" on the now-iconic *Star Trek*. After the series pilot, this was the earliest episode of the main series to be filmed. It has become one of the most-watched episodes by *Star Trek* fans, being noted for several elements that became hallmarks of the show, including the first use of the "Space—The Final Frontier" speech as the opening monologue.

That same year, Hartman was tapped to appear in a television movie from NBC-Universal called *Fame Is the Name of the Game* featuring an all-star cast. It was the first TV movie to be picked up as a regular network television series, renamed *The Name of the Game*, on which Hartman appeared in 1968.

Hartman appeared in the hit Hollywood movie *Our Man Flint*, a 1966 spy spoof with James Coburn. She also appeared in such films as *The New Interns* and *Games* with James Caan. In 1967, there were news reports that she and Austrian actor Maximilian Schell would be married, though they did not wed. In 1968, Hartman again made the news in a studio publicity campaign in which she was named the first African American "mayor" of Universal City.

Hartman worked steadily in small roles, alternating between television and movies. TV appearances included *Adam 12*, *Dragnet*, *Ironside*, *It Takes a Thief*, *Police Story*, and *Tarzan*. A noteworthy appearance was in the 1968 television movie *Prescription Murder* starring Peter Falk in his debut as the character of Detective Columbo, which went on to become a long-running series.

Hartman was a finalist for a main role in the 1969 Elvis Presley movie *Change of Habit*, but the part went to Barbara McNair. Another career-changer might have been a movie about the life of actress Dorothy Dandridge, who personally approved having Hartman play her. The film was to co-star Sidney Poitier, but he eventually passed on the project and the movie deal floundered.

She appeared in two films, *Let My Brother Go* and *Memory of an Ice Cream Stick*, before landing the part of a flight attendant in the hit 1970 movie *Airport*. Her final big-screen movie role was 1973's *Terminal Island* with Tom Selleck, in which Hartman—sporting an Afro hairdo—played one of the leads.

In 1970 and 1971, Hartman was a television series regular, playing police dispatcher Katy Grant on *Dan August*, starring Burt Reynolds. After Reynolds won worldwide fame in the 1977 movie *Smokey and the Bandit*, several episodes were edited together after the series ended to produce three *Dan August* TV movies that were broadcast in 1980. Hartman's character of Katy Grant appeared, though the actress was billed as Ena

Hartmann. It would be her final onscreen appearance, after which she retired to West Hollywood.

Film historians note that although Hartman did not rise to stardom, her work paved the way for glamorous, top-tier African American actresses such as Halle Berry.

For more information:

"Ena Hartman." Internet Movie Database. http://www.imdb.com/name/nm0366948/?ref_=nv_sr_1 (accessed December 8, 2015).

"Girl with a TV Dream." *Ebony* (December 1962): 37–44.

Lisanti, Tom. *Glamour Girls of Sixties Hollywood: Seventy-Five Profiles*. Jefferson, NC: McFarland & Company, Inc., 2008.

Barbara Hendricks (1948–)

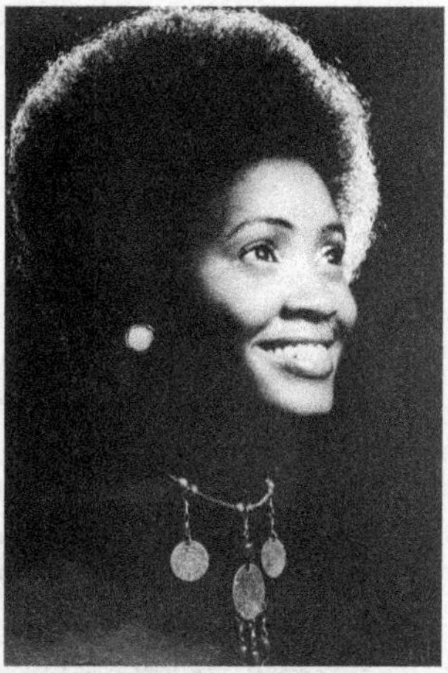

BARBARA HENDRICKS is an internationally renowned operatic soprano and concert singer who is equally at home with grand opera, contemporary standards, and jazz. She is also a leading global figure for her efforts toward peace and human rights.

Barbara Ann Hendricks was born on November 20, 1948, in Stephens, Arkansas, a small town in the south-central part of the state. She entered the world in the rural farmhouse of her maternal grandparents, Johnny and Tumaie Graham. Her mother was Della Mae Hendricks and her father, Malvin Leon Hendricks, was a minister in the Colored Methodist Episcopal (CME) church who supplemented his earnings by working in a restaurant kitchen.

During her childhood, she lived in a number of small towns around Arkansas as her father progressed in the CME church, where she recalls her parents leading the singing. With her sister Geneice and brothers Michael and Malvin Jr., Barbara Hendricks formed a quartet to sing in church. When the quartet disbanded, Barbara became a church soloist.

Barbara's mother became an elementary school teacher, with Barbara entering first grade in 1954 at age five already knowing how to read, write, and count. In 1956, her father was assigned to a church in North Little Rock, so she was living in North Little Rock when the Little Rock desegregation crisis of 1957 erupted. Her parents knew the Little Rock civil rights activist Daisy Bates [SEE ENTRY], and Hendricks was acquainted with some of the six African American girls who became part of the Little Rock Nine. Hendricks was to become very attuned to the civil rights movement.

She finished elementary school in Pine Bluff, especially enjoying music classes. When her father was named presiding elder in central Arkansas, the family moved to Little Rock in 1963 when she was fifteen. Her parents chose for her to attend the all-black Horace Mann High School. There, she became involved with the school choir under the renowned jazz musician Art Porter and was crowned Horace Mann's Homecoming Queen in 1964. She graduated with honors in 1965.

With a scholarship, she enrolled at Lane College in Jackson, Tennessee. Her music teacher encouraged her to study opera and enter an operatic competition in Nebraska, which she won. She transferred to the University of Nebraska as a chemistry major. In 1969, she graduated with a bachelor's degree in mathematics and chemistry.

However, it was in the realm of music, specifically opera, where she thrived. She attended the Aspen Music Festival and School, followed by Juilliard School of Music in New York, where she participated in master classes with soprano Maria Callas. She won a number of vocal competitions in the early 1970s, graduating from Juilliard with a degree in voice.

From that point, she worked steadily with major artistic companies such as the Mini-Met (including a 1974 recording of *Porgy and Bess*); opera companies in San Francisco, Paris, and London; and the Metropolitan Opera in New York City. She appeared at leading opera houses around the world, including the Opéra National de Paris, Covent Garden, and La Scala. In 1998, she sang in a performance of *Turandot* at the Forbidden City in Beijing.

She can be seen in films such as *La Bohème* and *Disengagement*, for which Hendricks also recorded the main theme for the film. Hendricks sang at Switzerland's Montreux Jazz Festival in 1994, followed by performing at major jazz festivals around the world. She has also organized a number of chamber music festivals. In Paris, she created the role of Angel in 2004's world premiere of the operatic adaptation of *Angels in America*. Her voice can be heard on more than fifty recordings for major labels. In 2006, she created a new record label, Arte Verum (Latin for "true art"), in order to retain artistic control.

Hendricks has said her early exposure to the civil rights movement and recollections of such things as "Colored" and "White Only" drinking fountains led to her humanitarian efforts. She has dedicated herself to the plight of refugees, has been a longtime supporter of the United Nations High Commissioner for Refugees (UNHCR), and was named a UN Goodwill Ambassador in 1987. In 2002, she was named an Honorary Lifetime Goodwill Ambassador, the only UNHCR celebrity ambassador so designated.

Some of her humanitarian work includes serving on the Council of the Foundation for the Refugee Education Trust (RET), giving concerts in war-torn cities, and founding the Barbara Hendricks Foundation for Peace and Reconciliation. She sang at a gala for President Bill Clinton's 1993 inauguration, and at the invitation of former UN Secretary-General Kofi Annan, Hendricks performed at Oslo's Nobel Prize ceremony in 2001. When she published her memoir, *Lifting My Voice*, in 2014, Annan—a Nobel Peace Prize laureate—wrote the introduction.

She was the only non-French singer nominated for the French Grammys (winning as Best Performer in the classical music category). She was also named a Commandeur des Arts et Lettres by the government of France, awarded the rank of Chevalier of the Légion d'honneur, given the Prince of Asturias Award for the Arts, given the Lions Clubs International Award, and honored with first prize at the Geneva International Competition and Concours de Paris.

Hendricks married Swedish music manager Martin Engstrom in 1978, living in France and Switzerland. They had two children, Jennie and Sebastian, before divorcing in 1996. In 2003, she married Ulf Englund, with whom she lives in Sweden.

She has said, "I was born curious and have always kept my eyes open, trying to learn as much as I can about the world and in turn about myself."

For more information:

Barbara Hendricks. http://www.barbarahendricks.com (accessed December 8, 2015).

Hendricks, Barbara. *Lifting My Voice: A Memoir*. Chicago: Chicago Review Press, 2014.

Mary Cal Hollis (1952–)

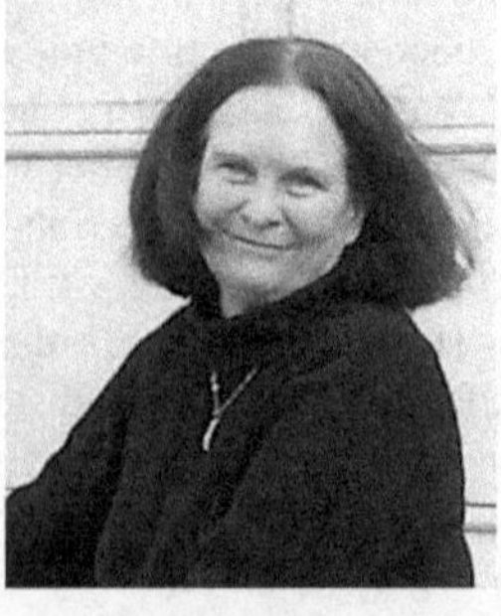

MARY CAL HOLLIS was a candidate for president of the United States in the 1996 election and was the vice-presidential candidate in 2000, both times representing the Socialist Party USA. She has also run for national office on the Green Party ticket.

Mary Cal Hollis was born on January 13, 1952, in Pine Bluff, Arkansas. She was one of four children born to educator Ruth Bylander Hollis and Cal Park Hollis. Hollis attended Pine Bluff High School, graduating in 1970.

In 1970, she entered the University of Arkansas (UA) in Fayetteville, earning a bachelor's degree in special education in 1974. This was followed by a master's degree in specific learning disabilities in 1978, also from UA. She then attended the University of Colorado at Boulder from 1989 to 1991, for studies in multicultural special education.

In Colorado, she served on the board of directors of the San Miguel Power Association from 1981 to 1984. She left the Democratic Party, to which she had belonged, and became active in causes involving world peace, children and families, and environmental issues, finding a platform variously within the Socialist Party, Green Party, and Labor Party. She has said her interest in socialism came from studying the works of Martin Luther King Jr., adding, "I realized I have been socialist all my life."

Beginning in 1994, she served on the Socialist Party USA National Committee, becoming the national co-chair from 1994 through 1998. Working at the party's New York headquarters in 1995, she made an impression on the leadership, ultimately becoming the party's presidential nominee in the upcoming election.

Hollis and her running mate in 1996, Eric Chester, appeared on the ballot in five states: Arkansas, Colorado, Oregon, Vermont, and Wisconsin. Her ticket garnered almost 5,000 votes, which included write-ins from an additional seven states, but was still below .01% of votes counted. By contrast, in that same election, Democrat Bill Clinton defeated Republican Bob Dole with about 47 million to 39 million votes. That election year also included non-mainstream "Third Party" candidates such as Ross Perot running on the Reform ticket and garnering over 8 million votes, or 8.4%. The Green Party's Ralph Nader won 685,000 votes, or .7%.

In the 2000 election, Mary Cal Hollis was again on a national ticket for the Socialists, running as vice-presidential candidate with David McReynolds. They won about 5,600 votes, appearing on the ballot in seven states. Although Hollis expressed interest in seeking the presidential nomination in 2004, she ultimately did not run for the Socialists either as a presidential or vice-presidential candidate. She did, however, run as a vice-presidential candidate for the Green Party in 2004, believing that people can support different organizations rather than being bound by one party's label or ideology.

She has stated that her political position is "anything that puts the interest of people before profits, plain and simple.... The only way to fight is to organize at the grass roots level, and that is, de facto, democratic socialism."

She supports the environmental stance of the Green Party, saying, "I am a member of the Labor Party because I work for a living. I am a member of NOW [National Organization for Women], because I am a woman and I am political." Hollis says she sees disparity of wealth and the concentration of power held by the wealthy as the root of the country's problems, calling programs that benefit the rich to be "wealthfare."

She resides in Boulder, Colorado, where she works as a teacher's aide.

For more information:

Hollis, Mary Cal. "A Third American Revolution." *Synthesis/Regeneration* 12 (Winter 1997). http://www.greens.org/s-r/12/12-06.html (accessed December 8, 2015).

Ross, Jack. *The Socialist Party of America: A Complete History*. Lincoln, NE: Potomac Books, 2015.

Theressa Hoover (1925–2013)

THERESSA HOOVER was the first African American woman to become a top staff executive for the United Methodist Church. She was a mentor to many young women and promoted the leadership of laywomen in the church. She led the Women's Division of the United Methodist Board of Global Ministries from 1968 to 1990, which took her around the nation and world during a time of great change in the Methodist Church.

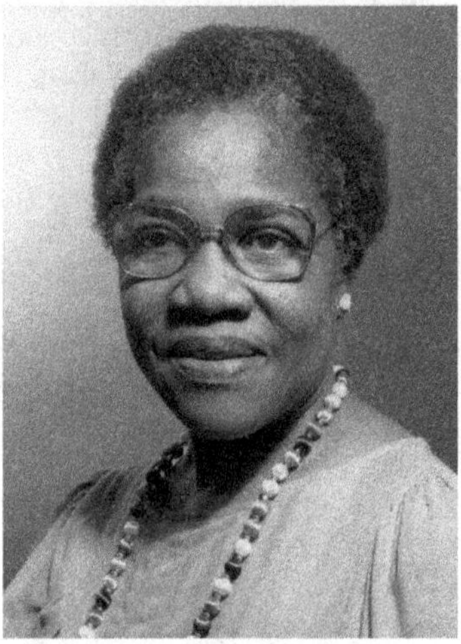

Theressa Hoover was born in Fayetteville, Arkansas, on September 7, 1925, the youngest of five children. Her mother was Rissie Vaughn Hoover, who died when she was about four years old. Her father was James Cortez Hoover, who worked as an orderly at Fayetteville's City Hospital from 1919 until his death thirty-five years later; a wing of the hospital was named in his honor.

Theressa Hoover attended Fayetteville's all-black Henderson and Lincoln Elementary schools, but she could not attend the all-white high school. Her father sent her to live with an aunt in Atlanta, Texas, just across the Arkansas state line, until she graduated from Pruitt High School in 1941.

Returning to Arkansas, Theressa Hoover graduated from Little Rock's Philander Smith College, receiving a bachelor's degree in business administration in 1946. While in college, she served as office secretary at Wesley Chapel and attended the National Methodist Student Conference at the University of Illinois. By her senior year, she was associate director of the Little Rock Methodist Council, a coalition of nineteen black and white Methodist churches doing leadership training and working on social issues. After graduation, she joined the council full time.

Hoover was a progressive who saw the need for interracial fellowship, leadership training, and Christian programs to aid social change and racial harmony. In 1946, with her help, a grant of $25,000 was received from the Women's Division of the General Board of Global Ministries of the Methodist Church to buy a 120-acre turkey farm west of Little Rock.

Meeting rooms and dormitories were built at Camp Aldersgate, named for the place where John Wesley, the founder of Methodism, experienced his spiritual conversion. Camp Aldersgate was dedicated in 1947 as one of the first integrated facilities of its kind in the United States.

In 1948, Hoover joined what was then an all-white staff at the Woman's Division and was a field worker for the Central Jurisdiction of the Methodist Church for ten years. Often, she had to travel alone across the Jim Crow South. Hoover moved to New York City in 1958, where she joined the Department of Christian Social Relations of the Methodist Church. She earned a master's degree in education from New York University's Center for Human Relations in 1962.

In 1968, Hoover was elected associate general secretary of the Women's Division of the United Methodist Church Board of Missions, serving as head of the national policy-making body. Her work took her across all fifty states and to five continents. That same year, as Hoover was elected the top executive of the Women's Division, the Methodist Church merged with the Evangelical United Brethren Church. With the creation of the new United Methodist Church in 1972, Hoover had to undertake a massive reorganization of her division.

Hoover lived in New York City for three decades. She was a supporter of the United Negro College Fund, and she was named one of the most important women in America by *Ladies' Home Journal* in 1971. *TIME* magazine described her as "highly influential" and, in 2004, fourteen years after Hoover's retirement, she was named to *Ebony* magazine's list of the 100 most influential African American women.

A few of the boards on which she served include the Bossey Ecumenical Institute in Celigny, Switzerland; the Methodist Church's Joint Commission on Church Union; the National Council of Churches of Christ, USA; the executive board of the National Council of Negro Women; the National Board of the Young Women's Christian Association (YWCA); and the World Council of Churches.

During her tenure with the national Methodist organization, Hoover wrote a monthly column in *Response* magazine. In 1974, she was a contributor to the anthology *Sexist Religion and Women in the Church: No More Silence* with her article, "Black Women and the Churches: Triple Jeopardy." Hoover described the "triple jeopardy" as being black, female, and Christian. In 1983, she published the book *With Unveiled Face: Centennial Reflections on Women and Men in the Community of the Church.* Her writings often focus on attaining equality for women and people of color within the church and in society.

In 1981, the Theressa Hoover United Methodist Church in Little Rock was chartered. It was one of the denomination's first local churches named for a laywoman. In 1990, to honor her achievements, the Women's Division of the United Methodist Church established the Theressa Hoover Community Service and Global Citizen Fund, awarded to young women for the study of issues relevant to the church community.

Theressa Hoover retired in 1990 at age sixty-five. After spending ten years traveling and speaking, she returned to Fayetteville. Hoover died in Fayetteville on December 21, 2013, at age eighty-eight. A grandniece who was named for Hoover said that Hoover served as a mother and a grandmother to dozens of young women.

For more information:

Bloom, Linda. "Theressa Hoover 'larger than life...gentle as a dove," *UMC Connections*. http://umcconnections.org/2014/01/09/theressa-hoover-larger-lifegentle-dove/ (accessed December 8, 2015).

Hoover, Theressa. *With Unveiled Face: Centennial Reflections on Women and Men in the Community of the Church.* Cincinnati, OH: United Methodist Church, 1983.

Zilphia Horton (1910–1956)

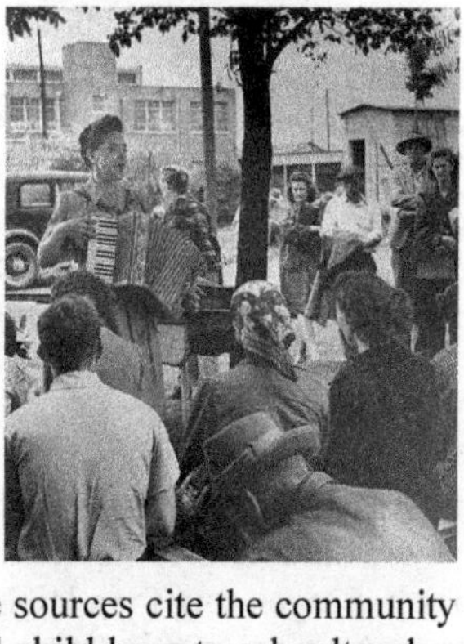

ZILPHIA JOHNSON HORTON was an educator, folklorist, and musician whose work was especially influential during the years of the Great Depression of the 1930s. She is best known for working with her husband, Myles Horton, at Tennessee's Highlander School, as well as for seeking out and preserving traditional folk songs. She adapted songs such as "Keep Your Eyes on the Prize," "This Little Light of Mine," "We Shall Not Be Moved," and, especially, "We Shall Overcome" from traditional hymns into globally recognized anthems.

Zilphia Mae Johnson was born in Paris, Arkansas (some sources cite the community of Spadra instead), on April 14, 1910. She was the second child born to schoolteacher Ora Howard Johnson and Robert Guy Johnson, owner of a local coal mine. Her father's income provided the family with a comfortable lifestyle. Zilphia began taking piano lessons at age five, becoming a talented classical musician.

She studied drama and music at the College of the Ozarks in nearby Clarksville, Arkansas, graduating in 1931. Around this time, Zilphia Johnson attended Paris's Cumberland Presbyterian Church. In 1930, the Reverend Claude Williams became pastor, preaching social justice and concern for the poor. Johnson was influenced by

Williams's message and sought to improve the lives of the poor working class. In 1934, she joined in an attempt to organize workers at her father's coal mine into a miners' union. Ignoring her father's objections, she was disowned by the family.

With the encouragement of friends, in 1935, she attended a workshop at the Highlander Folk School in Monteagle, Tennessee, on the southern Cumberland Plateau. Two months after her arrival, Zilphia Johnson and the school's co-founder, Myles Horton (1905–1990), were married. They had two children, Thorsten and Charis. Myles Horton later helped bring about a partial reconciliation between his wife and her family.

At Highlander, the couple worked together for social justice. Zilphia Horton became the school's cultural director, directing theater productions, leading workshops and youth camps, and organizing community programs. She led the singing at fundraising concerts, picket lines, union meetings, and workshops. She compiled a songbook for the Congress of Industrial Organizations (CIO) to instruct striking workers how to use singing for its power as well as for boosting morale. She inspired thousands at Highlander and at peaceful protests with the joy of making music.

Zilphia Horton valued the region's rich heritage of folk music, protected in the isolation of the mountains. Her goal was both to preserve the songs and to use the simple tunes for social activism. She sent her students to collect folk songs and traditional hymns from around the region. Using her musical training, she adapted the songs into powerful anthems for social causes. She collected hundreds of songs, including "Keep Your Eyes on the Prize," "This Little Light of Mine," and "We Shall Not Be Moved," which were first used for labor protests and later in the civil rights movement that gained momentum in the 1950s.

Horton is best known for her adaptation of the hymn "We Shall Overcome." In 1945, she heard a version with the lyrics "We will overcome" sung on the picket line during a tobacco workers' strike in South Carolina. It became Horton's favorite song. Changing the original lyrics and adding to the song, she put in verses such as "We'll walk hand in hand," and she taught it to musician Pete Seeger, who changed "We will" to "We shall" for its stronger musicality.

Horton was influential in spreading the song throughout the labor and civil rights movements. The song was published in the September 1948 issue of *People's Songs Bulletin*, a publication of the People's Songs organization, which Pete Seeger led. In the bulletin, the song appeared as the contribution of Zilphia Horton, who also wrote about the song in the publication's introduction, saying, "Its strong emotional appeal and simple dignity never fails to hit people."

As Highlander's music director, Zilphia Horton customarily ended meetings each evening by leading audiences in the song. Folk singers in the early 1950s such as Guy Carawan, Ramblin' Jack Elliot, and Frank Hamilton of Pete Seeger's group the Weavers are said to have heard Zilphia Horton sing the song when they visited Highlander.

On April 11, 1956, just before her forty-sixth birthday, Zilphia Horton died in Nashville, Tennessee, of kidney failure. She had accidentally taken a sip from a glass of carbon tetrachloride–based typewriter cleaning fluid, mistaking it for water. She is buried at Summerfield Cemetery in Grundy County, Tennessee.

"We Shall Overcome" continued to be sung at Highlander even after Zilphia Horton's death. Seeger sang for a Highlander audience in 1957 that included Martin Luther King Jr. At his next stop in Kentucky, Dr. King remarked how strongly the song had stayed with him. The song became hugely popular, especially in nonviolent protests both in the United States and abroad. Civil rights leader Julian Bond said, "People tell me that you can go anywhere in the world today and there's somebody singing this song." In 1999, National Public Radio included Horton's version of "We Shall Overcome" on its list of the 100 most important American songs of the twentieth century.

Author Kim Ruehl said, "You've probably never heard the name Zilphia Horton, but you certainly have been touched by her work."

For more information:

Adams, Frank, with Myles Horton. *Unearthing Seeds of Fire: The Idea of Highlander*. Winston-Salem, NC: John F. Blair Publisher, 1975.

Glen, John M. *Highlander: No Ordinary School 1932–1962*. Lexington: University Press of Kentucky, 1988.

Horton, Myles. *The Long Haul: An Autobiography*. New York: Teachers College Press, 1989.

Elizabeth Huckaby (1905–1999)

EDUCATOR ELIZABETH PAISLEY HUCKABY became known for her role in the 1957 desegregation crisis at Little Rock Central High School. Huckaby's book *Crisis at Central High: Little Rock 1957–58* was the basis for a TV movie.

Elizabeth Paisley was born on April 14, 1905, in Hamburg, Arkansas, to Elizabeth Merrel Paisley and Henry Lewis Paisley, who was a Presbyterian minister. Later in life, Elizabeth would credit her parents with raising their five children not to be prejudiced.

After a move to Texas, where Paisley attended grammar school, she returned to Arkansas and attended high school in Fayetteville. She enrolled at the University of Arkansas (UA) in Fayetteville and received a bachelor's degree in education in 1926, after which she taught school in Fort Smith for three years. She then returned to UA for her master's degree in education. In 1930, she was hired to teach English at Little Rock High School, renamed Little Rock Central High School in 1953.

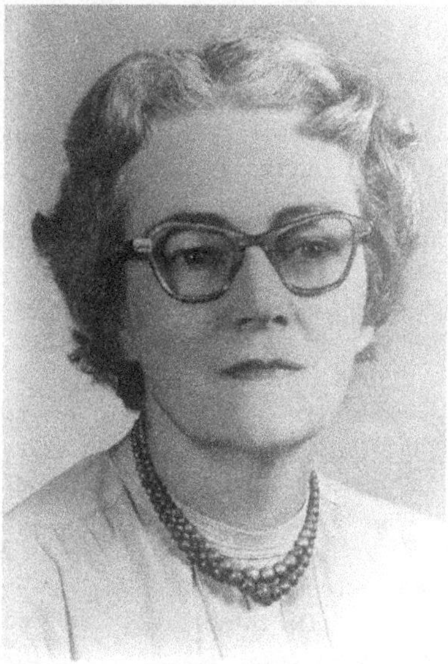

In 1933, she married Glenn Huckaby, a longtime educator in the Little Rock School District. The couple had no children.

Elizabeth Huckaby was a full-time English teacher until 1946, when she was named assistant principal, later called vice principal for girls. Her job was to supervise female students, although she often continued teaching classes, including tenth-grade honors English.

The U.S. Supreme Court ruled in 1954 that the doctrine of racial segregation was unconstitutional. After court action, the Little Rock School District's board admitted nine African American students to Central High for the 1957–58 school year. Arkansas governor Orval Faubus called out the National Guard to prevent their entry. President Dwight Eisenhower then federalized the National Guard and sent the U.S. Army's 101st Airborne Division to ensure the black students' safety.

The African American students became known as the Little Rock Nine, consisting of three boys and six girls. Huckaby's job was to help protect the six black girls. In doing so, she became the target of hostility from segregationists within the school and in the community. During the 1957–58 school year, Huckaby and her fellow educators at Central carried on with their daily classes despite shouting mobs outside, armed soldiers inside, walkouts by white students, and harassment of the black students.

To many people, the most memorable image of the Little Rock crisis is the photograph of a white girl in the mob shrieking at a lone black student, Elizabeth Eckford [SEE ENTRY]. Huckaby said she encouraged Eckford to remain in school in the face of continued harassment.

One of the black students, Melba Pattillo Beals [SEE ENTRY], wrote a memoir, *Warriors Don't Cry*, in which she recalled about fifty boys gathering on the stairs at a school entrance out of sight of the soldiers. The boys shouted racial slurs at the black students as they approached. Beals said, "Vice Principal Huckaby made her presence known at the bottom of the stairs. Tiny, erect, and determined, she stood there all alone between us and our attackers, demanding they leave us alone. One by one she challenged the leaders, calling them by name, telling them to get to class or there would be hell to pay. Whether or not she favored integration, she had a heck of a lot of guts."

At the end of the tumultuous school year, part of Huckaby's job was to help prevent disruptions at commencement, at which one of the African American students was to graduate. Two days before, there had been an incident at the baccalaureate, a religious service for graduating seniors, when a white student spat on a black girl. At graduation, with the FBI scanning for possible snipers, Huckaby and the school nurse sat in chairs at students' eye level to identify any guilty parties amidst rumors that eggs would be tossed at the black graduate. Commencement passed without incident.

The following year, in what would have been the 1958–59 school year, high schools in Little Rock were closed in an attempt to thwart further integration. During what has been called the Lost Year, segregationist legislators and community members targeted Huckaby and others.

In 1959, the Little Rock School Board fired Huckaby and more than forty other educators. With help from community groups such as the Women's Emergency Committee to Open Our Schools (WEC) and Stop This Outrageous Purge (STOP), Huckaby and the others were re-hired. Ten years later, in 1969, Elizabeth Huckaby retired after thirty-nine years of teaching.

Crisis at Central High: Little Rock 1957–58 was published by Louisiana State University Press in 1980. Huckaby's book was the basis for the 1981 TV movie *Crisis at Central High*, in which Huckaby was portrayed by Academy Award–winning actress Joanne Woodward. For her portrayal of Huckaby, Woodward was nominated for an Emmy Award as Outstanding Lead Actress as well as a Golden Globe for Best Performance by an Actress.

Elizabeth Huckaby died in Little Rock on March 18, 1999, at age ninety-three. She was eulogized with an obituary in the *New York Times*, which lauded her for helping to ease the 1957 Little Rock integration crisis. The *Arkansas Gazette* said she was "the object of vilification by the segregationist forces in the 1957 and later school desegregation crises, and conversely a champion of the forces of law and order."

For more information:

"Crisis at Central High." Internet Movie Database. http://www.imdb.com/title/tt0082215/ (accessed December 8, 2015).

Gordy, Sondra. "Through a Heroine's Eyes: Elizabeth Huckaby and the 'Lost Year.'" *Arkansas Historical Quarterly* 67 (Summer 2008): 141–167.

Huckaby, Elizabeth. *Crisis at Central High, Little Rock, 1957–58*. Baton Rouge: Louisiana State University Press, 1980.

Edith Irby Jones (1927–)

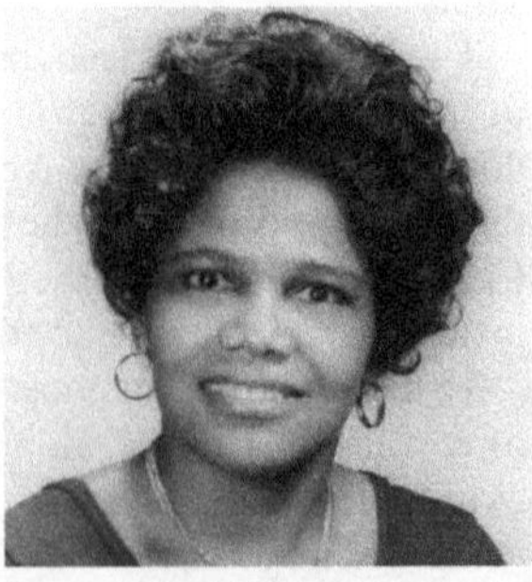

DR. EDITH IRBY JONES is an internationally known physician who has taught and provided healthcare in the United States, Africa, China, Cuba, Haiti, Mexico, and Russia. She provides support for the Dr. Edith Irby Jones Clinic in Haiti, which she helped to build, and the Dr. Edith Irby Jones Emergency Clinic in Mexico. She is active in national healthcare organizations, many of which she helped found. In 1952, she became the first African

American to attend and graduate from the University of Arkansas Medical School.

Edith Mae Irby was born on December 23, 1927, near Conway, Arkansas, to Robert Irby, who was a sharecropper, and Mattie Buice Irby, who was a domestic worker. Her father died in an accident when she was eight, and the family moved to Hot Springs, Arkansas. Her older sister died of typhoid fever at the age of twelve due to her family's lack of access to medical care. When she was seven, Irby suffered from rheumatic fever, which made her joints so painful that she was unable to walk or attend school for a year. She set a goal of a career in medicine to help those who could not afford basic medical care.

Irby graduated as an honor student from the all-black Langston High School in Hot Springs in 1944. With the help of a teacher, she earned a scholarship to the historically black Knoxville College in Tennessee. There, she studied biology, chemistry, and physics. After graduating with a bachelor's degree in 1948, she was accepted at two medical schools in Illinois and at the University of Arkansas Medical School (today's University of Arkansas for Medical Sciences—UAMS) in Little Rock.

She chose to remain in Arkansas, becoming the first African American student accepted at UAMS as well as the first accepted at any previously segregated medical school in the South. Irby joined three other women (all white) in the class of ninety-two students. Her achievement was reported in national publications including *Ebony*, *Life*, *Time*, and the *Washington Post*. *Life* magazine reported that African Americans from across Arkansas had contributed to her medical school fund with dimes and quarters. Langston High School alumni helped pay for her medical school tuition, and an effort sponsored by a black newspaper in Little Rock, the *Arkansas State Press*, paid for her living expenses. In a touching show of support, the medical school's custodians placed fresh flowers on her dining table, as she was not allowed to use the same dining, lodging, or bathroom facilities as white students at UAMS.

Despite the institutional segregation, many of her white classmates chose to eat with her, study with her, and become her friends. A major source of support came from Professor James B. Jones of the University of Arkansas at Pine Bluff, whom Irby met and married while she was a second-year medical student. They had three children.

In 1952, she received her MD degree, becoming the first African American to graduate from UAMS. Jones returned to Hot Springs, where she opened a successful general practice. She also worked with the National Association for the Advancement of Colored People (NAACP) during the civil rights movement, speaking at churches and private homes to urge people to join the struggle for equality.

In 1959, Jones and her family moved to Houston, Texas, where she was the first African American woman resident at Baylor College of Medicine Affiliated Hospitals in Houston. Though she was welcomed at the school, the hospital to which she was assigned segregated her and limited her patient rosters. She completed the last months of her residency at Freedman's Hospital in Washington DC.

Back in Texas, Jones established a successful private practice in internal medicine and gerontology in Houston's inner city. She was a co-founder of Houston's Mercy Hospital, was one of twelve doctors who owned and developed Park Plaza Hospital, was the first female president of the National Medical Association, and became chief of the medical staff at Houston's Riverside General Hospital. Ultimately, she would hold staff privileges at nine Houston-area hospitals, including the Houston Hospital, which was renamed the Edith Irby Jones M.D. Health Care Center in her honor. She also became the only female founding member of the Association of Black Cardiologists.

In 1986, the City of Houston honored her with "Edith Irby Jones Day." She was named Internist of the Year by the American Society of Medicine in 1988, and, in 1998, the former Southeast Memorial Hospital named its ambulatory center in her honor.

Throughout her career, Jones committed herself to treating the poorest people and those most in need of help. She practices in poor neighborhoods and has paid medical school tuition for deserving students. In 1985, she became president of the National Medical Association, which had been established for black doctors who were not allowed to join the American Medical Association. She helped establish and provides support for two clinics that have been named for her: the Dr. Edith Irby Jones Clinic in Vaudreuil, Haiti, and the Dr. Edith Irby Jones Emergency Clinic in Veracruz, Mexico. She has also been active in groups including the American Medical Women's Association.

She continues to practice medicine and to lecture, saying that when she speaks to medical students, she tells them, "If they are really concerned about their fellow man, they will enjoy medicine. If they are going into medicine as a money-making project, then they ought to select something else. Medicine continues to be a service that we render to all."

For more information:

"Arkansas Memories: Interviews from the Pryor Center for Arkansas Oral and Visual History—Edith Irby Jones." *Arkansas Historical Quarterly* 69 (Winter 2010): 387–396.

"Dr. Edith Irby Jones." *To Bear Fruit for Our Race: A History of African-American Physicians in Houston.* http://www.history.uh.edu/cph/tobearfruit/resources_bios_jones.asp (accessed December 8, 2015).

Smith, Jessie Carney, editor. *Notable Black American Women, Book 2.* Farmington Hills, MI: Thomson Gale, 1996.

Willa Saunders Jones (1901–1979)

WILLA SAUNDERS JONES was a nationally prominent religious and cultural leader who wrote, produced, and directed a dramatization of the life of Jesus Christ called the *Chicago Passion Play*. It was produced annually in major churches and ultimately at Chicago's Civic Opera House. She organized the annual event with 150 actors, dancers, and singers for more than a half century. Jones, herself a talented singer and accompanist, recruited talent such as Jerry Butler, Mahalia Jackson, and Dinah Washington and received support from the Reverend Jesse Jackson and Chicago mayor Richard Daley.

Willie (later "Willa") Saunders was born in Little Rock, Arkansas, on February 22, 1901, to Ada Pulliam Saunders and George Washington Saunders. She grew up among a close-knit family who lived nearby. Her grandfather, Joseph Davis, was a charter member and official of the Mosaic Templars of America, a fraternal organization offering insurance services to the African American community.

Willa Saunders's father served as pastor of First Baptist Church-Highland Park, a historically black church that grew under her father's leadership. She also saw her father rise to the leadership of the Home Missions Board of the National Baptist Convention, USA. This was to offer an example to her of the power of a large denominational organization. Despite his position in the church and the esteem in which the family was held by the black community, however, Pastor Saunders's family had little money. When funds were not available for Willa Saunders to learn piano, a neighbor taught her to play by using a piece of cardboard with drawn-on keys colored with charcoal.

Willa Saunders's grandmother was Charlotte Andrews Stephens, a respected black educator who had served as a teacher and principal. Saunders attended Stephens Elementary School, which was named for her grandmother. She witnessed Stephens's work in introducing African Americans to the potential of music and drama in both faith and fundraising.

Willa's father had previously taught at Arkansas Baptist College, a historically black liberal arts college in Little Rock. She enrolled there and graduated with the equivalent of a high school diploma. While at Arkansas Baptist, Willa Saunders experienced the "community sings" that were held at the school on Sunday afternoons. They were arranged by the daughter of the college president, and they demonstrated to Saunders the power of spirituals and faith-based music to appeal to both black and white audiences.

After graduation from Arkansas Baptist, Saunders married her childhood sweetheart, George Washington Jones, who attended Philander Smith College in Little Rock. The couple saved money by living with relatives and holding the kinds of menial jobs available to African Americans at the time—even prominent, educated people. Willa Saunders Jones worked in a laundry until the birth of their first child, George Jr., in January 1921. The couple later had a second son, Charles.

With a goal of being able to afford a house in North Little Rock after the birth of their son, George Jones worked at a lumberyard. In March 1921, a white woman in Little Rock claimed that she had been assaulted by two black men. Though George Jones and a friend, Emanuel West, had been attending a funeral at First Baptist-Highland Park that night, vigilantes accosted them. When the woman identified West as the rapist, George Jones became implicated and was strip-searched. Amid threats of lynching, the Jones family fled from Little Rock. George Jones ultimately returned to Arkansas to act as a witness for West's defense, with the trial ending in a hung jury. West was tried again and sentenced to life in prison, although he was later pardoned.

Starting over in Chicago, far from her beloved family and friends, Willa Saunders Jones became a teacher and community cultural leader in the tradition of the influential African Americans she had known in Little Rock. She began singing with church choirs and played organ for several Baptist churches. In 1933, Jones performed for a large interracial audience at Chicago Orchestra Hall. Through the 1940s and '50s, she directed huge choruses across the country for the National Baptist Convention.

Her national reputation was built on the *Chicago Passion Play*, a production tracing important moments in the life of Christ. She wrote it between 1922 and 1926, when it was first produced. Its annual performances moved to progressively larger venues until 1954 when it reached Chicago's Civic Opera House. There, Jones produced and directed it each year until her death on January 15, 1979, at which point her grandson took over. Her husband, George W. Jones, who had had experience with persecution, played the role of Jesus for more than thirty years until his death in 1965.

There were about 150 cast members, rehearsing under Willa Saunders Jones's direction each year for six months prior to the April performance dates. Jones's vision of faith was to share the story with audiences of all races. She was able to do so for fifty-three years, watching it become a national attraction.

For more information:

Hallstoos, Brian James. "Windy City, Holy Land: Willa Saunders Jones and Black Sacred Music and Drama." http://ir.uiowa.edu/etd/371 (accessed December 8, 2015).

Lewis, Mary C. "The Chicago Passion Play." *Ebony Jr*. (December 1982): 30–31.

"Passion Play: Annual Chicago Presentation of All-Negro Religious Play Proves Big Box Office Draw." *Ebony* (May 1950): 25–28.

Regina Kaplan (1887–1957)

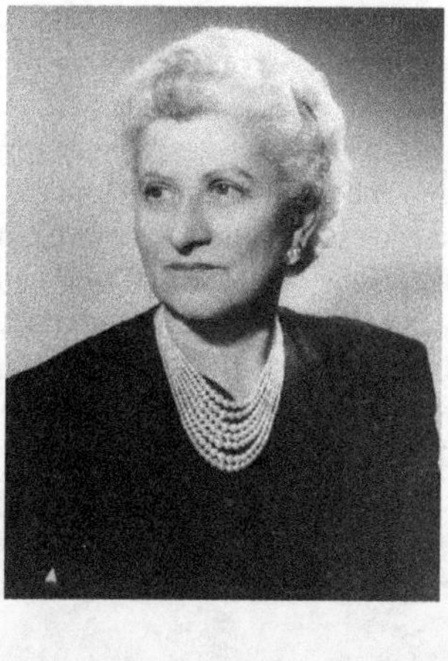

A NURSE, TEACHER, AND HEALTHCARE innovator who was nicknamed "Kappy," Regina Kaplan was the hospital administrator and director of the Nursing School at the Leo N. Levi Memorial Hospital in Hot Springs, Arkansas, for over three decades. She was active in national organizations, was honored by First Lady Eleanor Roosevelt with a brunch at the White House, and gave a speech before Congress. She has been called Arkansas's "Lady with the Lamp."

Regina Kaplan was born on May 12, 1887, in Memphis, Tennessee, the third of five children of German immigrants Adella Traube Kaplan and Gershon

Kaplan. Regina's father had been a schoolteacher in Germany. She always said that she learned "hesed," a Hebrew word for loving-kindness, from her parents.

The family moved to Denver for her mother's health. Unable to afford medical school to become a doctor, Kaplan entered Denver's Mercy Hospital Training School for Nursing at age seventeen. She graduated in 1908 at the top of her class. As was the norm for nursing graduates, Kaplan began work as a private duty nurse after graduation.

With World War I on the horizon, in January 1915, she volunteered for the American Red Cross, which furnished army nurses. However, at under five feet tall and weighing barely ninety pounds, she was rejected by the army. Although she was often affectionately called the "Tiny Dynamo," family members recalled that she remained sensitive about her short stature all her life.

She returned to private practice until she heard of the need for a superintendent in Hot Springs at the new Leo Levi Hospital, which had been founded in 1914. The hospital was created because the Jewish community of Hot Springs recognized the area's unique healing benefits. A large number of Jewish visitors from around the nation came to the Spa City to "take the waters" for their health, and there was a need for a hospital to serve the many poor Jewish people who sought the thermal springs for medical treatment. The non-sectarian Levi Hospital has historically provided services to people regardless of their ability to pay.

On January 16, 1916, the twenty-nine-year-old Kaplan took the reins as Levi Hospital administrator. For most of her career, she lived on site at the hospital. She soon established the Leo Levi School of Nursing as part of the hospital in order to train future nurses and provide a low-cost source of hospital staff. Thirty-five years later, she recalled praying not to fail the trust placed in her, saying, "With His help I would dedicate my life wholly to Levi and the service I hoped to build there." The Levi School of Nursing was the first such institution in the South to admit male students. During World War II, the School of Nursing participated in the U.S. Cadet Nursing Corps Program.

In 1917, Kaplan established a local chapter of the American Red Cross. As part of that program, she taught classes in first aid, home nursing, and nurse's aide training to adults and high school students. She developed a free public health nursing program, hiring the first school nurse for Hot Springs. She was also an early advocate of healthy eating, mandating meatless meals at the hospital twice a week.

Kaplan was a member of the American College of Hospital Administrators and served in numerous national posts, including chairing the National Rehabilitation Association in the State Hospitals in 1928. She was vice president of the American Hospital Association (1945–1946), served as president of the Mid-West Hospital Association, presented papers for the American College of Surgeons, and continued serving the American Red Cross. She was president of the Arkansas Hospital Association (1947–1948) and served on the advisory board of hospitals for the Arkansas State Board of Health from 1949 to 1953.

During this period, she also participated in many local civic activities such as serving on the Hot Springs Community Council and the Federation of Church Women. She was a member of Eastern Star, Hadassah, B'nai B'rith, and Business and Professional Women.

In 1944, she was honored by First Lady Eleanor Roosevelt in Washington DC with a brunch at the White House for her many contributions to nursing. Kaplan also gave a speech on healthcare before Congress. Mrs. Roosevelt presented Kaplan with a copy of *Woodrow Wilson's Life and Letters*, which she personally inscribed to Kaplan.

Kaplan was an early advocate of health insurance through Blue Cross and urged Levi Hospital to participate in the plan. She was one of its Arkansas organizers and served on the original board of trustees of Arkansas Blue Cross Blue Shield. Seeing an increased need for the care of older people, Kaplan founded Lakewood Convalescent Home of Garland County, serving as its president from 1946 to 1953.

On January 16, 1951, exactly thirty-five years after starting work at Levi Hospital, Kaplan retired, though she remained a consultant for the hospital. A city-wide tribute was held, with the mayor of Hot Springs proclaiming "Kaplan Honor Week." Levi Hospital released a tribute volume titled *Hospital Heartbeat: Honoring Regina Kaplan for Thirty-five Years in a Ministry of Service, Jan. 16, 1951*.

The Levi nursing school closed in 1952. In 1953, Kaplan became director of central supply at St. Joseph's Hospital in Hot Springs and was a charter member of the St. Joseph's Hospital Guild.

After being diagnosed with cancer, Kaplan returned to Denver, where she entered the Jewish Hospital. She died on October 8, 1957, with her adopted daughter, Betty, at her side. Before her strength completely failed, Kaplan got up and made her bed every day.

For more information:

Anthony, Isabel Burton, ed. *Garland County, Arkansas: Our History and Heritage*. Hot Springs, AR: Garland County Historical Society, 2009.

Mayer, Susan L. "Regina Kaplan 1887–1957." *Encyclopedia, Jewish Women's Archive*. http://jwa.org/encyclopedia/article/kaplan-regina (accessed December 8, 2015).

Gloria Ray Karlmark (1942–)

GLORIA RAY KARLMARK was a member of the group called the Little Rock Nine, black students who sought to desegregate Little Rock Central High School in 1957. She went on to work as a computer analyst, mathematician, patent attorney, teacher, and writer.

Gloria Cecelia Ray was born in Little Rock on September 26, 1942. She was one of three children and the youngest daughter born to Julia Miller Ray, who was a sociologist employed by the State of Arkansas, and Harvey Ray, who was a founder and agent of what was then called the Agricultural Extension Service for Negroes. Both of Gloria Ray's parents graduated from Tuskegee University in Alabama and valued the power of education.

Gloria Ray attended Little Rock's all-black Horace Mann High School. At age fifteen, she signed up to be one of the first African American students to attend the all-white Little Rock Central High School for her junior year. She later said of herself and the other pioneering black students at Central High, "An important ingredient in what happened 50 years ago was the parents, our nine sets of parents, and their generation that taught us to seek knowledge, to seek skills, and to give to our community, to give back." She said her parents spoke to her about the difficulties she faced if she remained committed to attending Central High School, but she would not back down, reasoning that because her parents paid taxes, she deserved the same education as other Americans.

Though the courts had ordered Little Rock schools to desegregate, a firestorm was unleashed when the nine black students tried to attend Central in September 1957. They faced angry mobs who cursed them, spat on them, and blocked them when they tried to enter Central. The Arkansas governor called in the state's National Guard to prevent their entry, but President Dwight Eisenhower federalized the National Guard and ordered the U.S. Army's 101st Airborne Division to protect the students' lives.

When the black students were finally able to enter school, they faced daily harassment and threats by the white students. Gloria Ray recalled being tormented by one particular white boy who called her names and bumped her several times, once knocking her to the floor. She said that "from the first day, when the soldiers blocked my entrance to the school, I usually say that Gloria Ray, the child, ceased to exist at that moment. It became more a question of a principle. I see there the girl who thought that she would be welcomed to the Central High School and was rejected in a way that was beyond her imagination from the community that she lived in all of her life." Since the Little Rock Nine went to different classes and were separated throughout the day, she recalled that at the end of the day, "we would check to see that we were still nine."

Faubus closed Little Rock's high schools in 1958–59 in an attempt to continue blocking integration, so Mr. and Mrs. Ray moved the family to Kansas City, Missouri. There, Gloria's mother was able to find employment, having been fired from her job in Arkansas for refusing to withdraw her daughter from Central. In 1960, Gloria Ray graduated in Kansas City from an integrated school that also was called Central High.

After high school, she attended Illinois Institute of Technology (IIL), earning a bachelor's degree in chemistry and mathematics. While at IIL, she met and married her Swedish husband, Krister Karlmark, a professor and industrial designer, in 1966. The couple became the parents of two children, Mats and Elin.

Gloria Ray Karlmark worked as a public school teacher and research assistant at the University of Chicago Research Medical Center. In 1970, she and her husband moved to Stockholm, Sweden, where Gloria Karlmark worked as a systems analyst and technical writer for the International Business Machine (IBM) Nordic Laboratory.

She went on to graduate from Sweden's Kungliga Patent & Registreringsverket as a patent attorney, working from 1977 to 1981 in IBM's International Patent Operations. Karlmark founded an international journal of computer applications for businesses called *Computers in Industry*, for which she served as editor-in-chief from 1976 to 1994. She subsequently worked for Philips Telecommunications in the Netherlands as well as Philips International in Belgium, France, Germany, Scotland, and Spain. She and her family reside in Europe.

Among her honors are the Spingarn Medal from the National Association for the Advancement of Colored People (NAACP) and the Congressional Gold Medal, the nation's highest civilian award. In 2005, the Little Rock Nine appeared on a postage stamp issued by the U.S. Postal Service, and the U.S. Mint released a commemorative coin to honor them in 2007.

In 2013, Gloria Ray Karlmark was invited to the U.S. Ambassadorial Residence in Sweden where the American ambassador, Mark Brzezinski, said, "She is living proof of the great strides taken in America's struggle for civil rights and human dignity." Karlmark herself has said her experience in 1957 strengthened her in life, including as a female in a male-dominated engineering school. She said that her strength showed itself "with the soldier standing in front of me with his rifle, saying, 'No, you can't have that good education that they're offering inside that school.' And I said, 'I'll get that education or I'll die for it.'"

For more information:

Bates, Daisy. *The Long Shadow of Little Rock.* Fayetteville: University of Arkansas Press, 1986.

Beals, Melba Pattillo. *Warriors Don't Cry: A Searing Memoir of the Battle to Desegregate Little Rock's Central High School.* New York: Washington Square Books, 1994.

Little Rock Central High School National Historic Site Visitor Center. Little Rock, Arkansas. http://www.nps.gov/chsc (accessed December 8, 2015).

Deena Kastor (1973–)

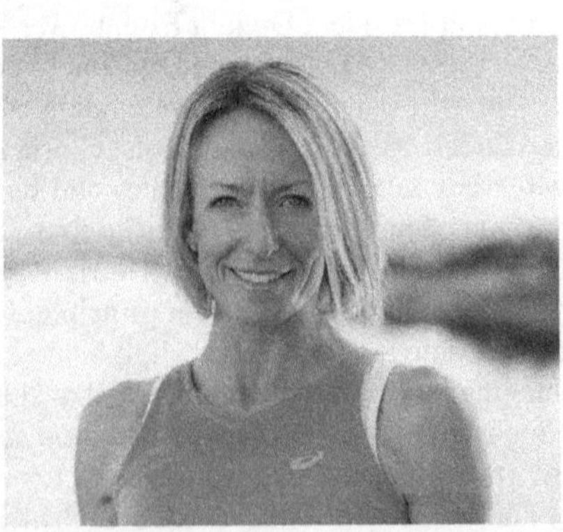

DEENA DROSSIN KASTOR is a long-distance runner who was named All-American at the University of Arkansas (UA) in Fayetteville. She is an Olympic medalist for the twenty-six-mile marathon, holds American records in both the marathon and half marathon, and is the eight-time national cross-country champion. She was named the top women's marathoner in the world by *Track and Field News* magazine. Kastor is renowned for her courage in the face of a freak occurrence during the World Cross-Country Championships in 2000.

Deena Michelle Drossin was born on February 14, 1973, in Waltham, Massachusetts, later moving to Agoura Hills, California. She began long-distance running at age thirteen, breaking the 3,000-meter national record and reigning as the two-time National Cross Country Champion in the Youth Division. She attended Agoura High School, and, in the high school division, became the five-time California State Champion, also winning three California state cross-country titles and two California Interscholastic Federation (CIF) California State Meet titles. She competed in the Foot Locker Cross Country Championships all four years of her high school career, and she ran in both the North American Youth Maccabiah Games and the Pan-American Maccabiah while in high school.

In 1992, she enrolled as an English major at UA. Its renowned track and field program was the most successful athletic program in national collegiate history, with forty-two NCAA national championships. There, she trained with Lance Harter, called the most successful coach in Southeastern Conference (SEC) women's track and field history.

At UA, Deena Drossin was running about fifty-five miles per week. The work culminated in her becoming a four-time SEC champion and repeated All-American. She would go on to be elected to the Arkansas Sports Hall of Honor, in which she was lauded as "one of the most decorated athletes in Arkansas history….The ten-time All-American distance runner was the first Razorback woman in University of Arkansas history to make the U.S. Olympic team as a competitor in 2000, then the first American medalist in 2004."

Drossin graduated from UA in 1996 and then moved to Colorado to train in the thin air of higher elevations. In 2003, she married Andrew Kastor, who also served as her trainer and coach. Their daughter, Piper, was born in 2011. The family subsequently moved to Mammoth Lakes, California, at an altitude of over 8,000 feet.

Among Deena Kastor's career highlights are winning the 2004 Olympic bronze medal in the marathon in Athens, Greece—the first U.S. woman in twenty years to medal in the event. According to her website, she currently holds the American record in the marathon and half marathon, and she has held American records in distances from 5,000 meters to the full marathon.

Kastor has made nineteen U.S. teams, won eighteen U.S. titles, and earned two silver medals at the World Cross-Country Championships. She has won iconic marathons in most of the world's major cities as well as the most prestigious cross-country meets. Her win at the 2005 Chicago Marathon was highlighted in the documentary film *Spirit of the Marathon*. She followed that win by taking first place in the 2006 London marathon. That victory ranked her number one in the world that year. Among subsequent triumphs, in 2014, Kastor set five world masters records in one race during the Philadelphia Half Marathon.

She has accrued numerous medals and championship titles despite several injuries, such as breaking her foot at the five-kilometer mark in the 2008 Beijing Olympics. Many people especially remember the heartbreak and tenacity she displayed after an unusual occurrence at the 2000 World Cross-Country Championships in Portugal. Soon after the start of the race, a bee flew into Kastor's mouth and stung the back of her throat. She stayed with the leaders, but her throat started to swell and close, blocking her air. She blacked out and fell but continued the race after regaining consciousness. She still managed to finish twelfth in the race. She said of the incident, "I felt my throat start to close up, and I didn't think I was getting enough oxygen. I was scared, and I thought about quitting. But you don't want to quit when you've trained so hard and long."

Among her honors are the Jesse Owens Award as the top female U.S. track and field athlete, four-time Runner of the Year, and induction into the National Jewish Sports Hall of Fame. She currently serves as president of the ASICS Mammoth Track Club, works as a motivational speaker, and acts as executive producer of the marathon documentary *BOSTON*.

For more information:

Deena Kastor. http://deenakastor.com (accessed December 8, 2015).

"Deena Kastor." Internet Movie Database. http://www.imdb.com/name/nm2548210 (accessed December 8, 2015).

Urwin, Dave. *Why Don't We All Run Spartathlons? Marathon Memories Featuring Stephen Kiprotich, Deena Kastor, Sage Canaday, Kamiel Maase, Carlos Grisales, Mehmet Terzi, Adam Holland and many more.* Kindle Edition, Amazon Digital Services, 2015.

Janis Kearney (1953–)

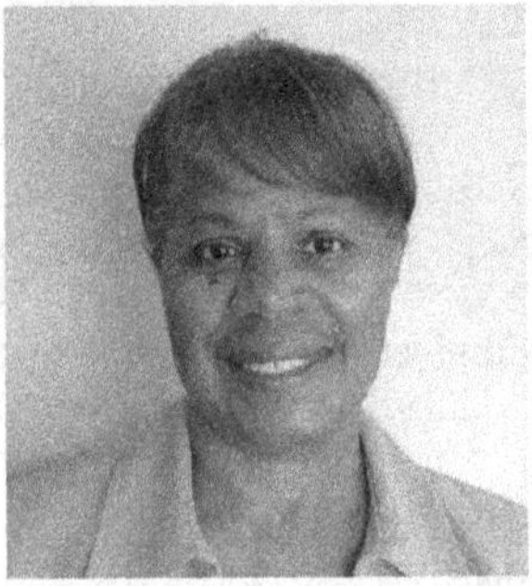

JANIS FAYE KEARNEY is an author, lecturer, and publisher who served as presidential diarist to President Bill Clinton from 1995 to 2001, the first such appointment in presidential history. She was also the publisher of the historic *Arkansas State Press* newspaper. She found herself in the national spotlight during the Independent Counsel investigation of Bill Clinton, though no wrongdoing was found.

Janis Faye Kearney was born on September 29, 1953, in Gould, Arkansas, a small rural town in the southeastern part of the state. She was the fourteenth of nineteen children of sharecropper Thomas James Kearney and homemaker Ethel Curry Kearney, who also worked in the fields.

Starting when she was seven years old, Janis Kearney spent her summers "chopping cotton" (cutting down weeds growing in the cotton rows), and she helped the family pick cotton in the fall. By the time she was nine years old, Janis was helping to care for her younger brothers and sisters as well as cooking for the large family. Evenings were spent learning to read, write, and master arithmetic. When the Kearney children returned to school in the winter after the fall harvest season, they were at the top of their classes. Janis Kearney graduated from Gould High School in 1971.

She then went on to college, as did all but one of her brothers and sisters. During her junior year at the University of Arkansas (UA) in Fayetteville, she got married and had one child. In 1976, she graduated with a bachelor's degree in journalism. She moved to Little Rock to work in state government, also studying for a Master's of Public Administration degree from the University of Arkansas at Little Rock (UALR).

Beginning in 1978, Kearney worked for three years as program manager for the Comprehensive Employment and Training Act (CETA) program, a federal plan to train workers and provide them with job opportunities. She then became director of information for the Migrant Student Records Transfer System (MSRTS), where she spent six years. Kearney oversaw public information for the program, which is responsible for the records of more than 750,000 children nationwide. From its national headquarters in Little Rock, the agency manages education and health data for children of migrant workers as they move from place to place.

In 1987, Kearney joined the historic *Arkansas State Press* as the newspaper's managing editor. Owned and operated by civil rights activist Daisy Bates [SEE ENTRY] since 1941, the *Arkansas State Press* was a statewide weekly newspaper aimed at African Americans. Within three months of Kearney's arrival, Mrs. Bates retired and Kearney bought the company. For the next five years, she served as the newspaper's publisher.

In 1992, Arkansas governor Bill Clinton began a run for U.S. president. He had met Kearney through her family, having taught several of her brothers at the UA School of Law. He also knew Kearney through her role as publisher of the *Arkansas State Press*.

Clinton hired Kearney to serve as director of his campaign's Minority Media Outreach effort. In order to work on the 1992 campaign, Kearney took a sabbatical from the *Arkansas State Press*, appointing her sister to direct operations during her absence.

After Clinton won the 1992 election, Kearney worked in the Little Rock office of the presidential transition team. Following his 1993 inauguration, Kearney was offered a position in the new administration in Washington DC. There, she first worked as a White House media affairs officer, followed by becoming director of public communication for the U.S. Small Business Administration.

In 1995, Kearney was appointed to serve as the personal diarist to the president, the first person to hold such a position. Kearney kept a daily diary of President Clinton's activities, attending top-level meetings, events, and press conferences to document a comprehensive history.

Beginning in 1997, an Independent Counsel investigation of President Clinton resulted in a wide range of inquiries regarding personal and political allegations. Along with others in the administration, Kearney first became involved in a controversy about campaign fundraising. In 1998, she was ordered to testify regarding Clinton's extramarital sexual activities. Her presidential diary was subpoenaed, with no wrongdoing being found.

In 2001, Kearney left Washington after the end of Clinton's second term. With the *Arkansas State Press* having suspended operations in 1998, Kearney moved to Chicago. She commenced a two-year fellowship at Harvard University's W. E. B. Du Bois Institute of African and African American Studies. There, she began writing the Clinton biography *Conversations: William Jefferson Clinton—From Hope to Harlem*. It was published in 2006.

In Chicago, she was named a visiting fellow at Chicago's DePaul University and was appointed Chancellor's Lecturer for Chicago City Colleges. She also wrote a syndicated column, *Politics Is Life*, which appeared in African-American newspapers nationwide.

After establishing Writing Our World (WOW) Press in 2004, she published several books, including *Conversations*. The first installment of her memoir, *Cotton Field of Dreams*, was published in 2004. In 2008, Kearney published her first novel, *Once Upon a Time There Was A Girl: A Murder at Mobile Bay*, the same year she published the second installment of her memoir, *Something to Write Home About: Memories of a Presidential Diarist*.

For more information:

Kearney, Janis F. *Cotton Field of Dreams*. Little Rock, AR: Writing Our World Press, 2004.

_____. *Something to Write Home About: Memories from a Presidential Diarist*. Little Rock, AR: Writing Our World Press, 2008.

Sue Kidd (1933–)

SUE KIDD is a former professional athlete who played in the All-American Girls Professional Baseball League from 1950 through 1954. She attained local fame for playing successfully against all-male baseball teams. A display at the Baseball Hall of Fame honors Kidd and the All-American Girls Professional Baseball League, and she had a small role in the 1992 movie *A League of Their Own*, which depicted experiences like hers on a female professional baseball team.

Glenna Sue Kidd was born on September 2, 1933, in Choctaw, Arkansas, in the north-central part of the state. Called "Sue" by the family, she was one of six children born to homemaker Julia Duncan Kidd and William Marvin Kidd, a farmer and merchant.

Her father was an avid baseball fan who played on a hometown team in addition to running his store and operating the local post office. While his sons had athletic experience playing baseball on their father's team, by the time she was a teenager, Sue Kidd played skillfully enough to compete with her brothers.

She attended high school in the nearby town of Clinton, playing baseball so well that she was permitted to play on the Clinton High School boys' baseball team in 1949. She is best known locally for a game she pitched and won in 1949 at the age of fifteen. She also excelled in basketball and volleyball, and was voted Outstanding Female Athlete all four years of high school.

Her father put together a team of male amateur baseball players from the surrounding area. Kidd is remembered for playing on those teams as well as competing against them. She usually pitched all nine innings of each game, becoming known for her curveball and fastball. After her team defeated the all-male Heber Springs All-Stars, Kidd became a local legend. She then tried out for the All-American Girls Professional Baseball League when the Springfield Sallies traveling team stopped in Arkansas in 1949.

The All-American Girls had been formed in 1942 near the beginning of World War II. During the war, the departure of male players for the armed services along with declining attendance at ballparks led baseball officials to seek an alternative. They therefore recruited young women.

In addition to spring training, the female athletes were required to attend evening charm school classes. The women were not permitted to have short hair or to smoke or drink in public, and were required to wear lipstick at all times. With the novelty of watching talented women play the game (especially in their short skirts), the All-American Girls Professional Baseball League remained active for a time even after the war ended.

In 1949, at age fifteen, Kidd was selected to play in an exhibition game with the Springfield Sallies at Little Rock's Ray Winder Field. She pitched a no-hitter and was added to the team roster. After her high school graduation in 1950, the sixteen-year-old continued pitching for the Sallies.

During the course of her career, she also played for the Muskegon Lassies, Peoria Redwings, Battle Creek Belles, and South Bend Blue Sox. She was particularly successful with South Bend, especially in 1954, during what turned out to be the last season the league would be in existence. After the All-American Girls Professional Baseball League shut down operations, Kidd played for the South Bend Rockettes, a women's basketball team, until 1960. With that team, she won three national championships.

Honoring a promise to her father, Kidd enrolled at Arkansas State Teachers College in Conway (today's University of Central Arkansas). She received a bachelor's degree in physical education with a minor in social studies in 1965, going on to earn a master's degree in physical education in 1966.

Her career took her to Indiana, where she taught middle school and high school physical education for twenty-five years. She was a triple threat, coaching basketball, volleyball, and track and field. After her coaching years ended, she taught elementary school physical education and groomed dogs for enjoyment. Kidd retired in 1989, returning to Choctaw, Arkansas, to help care for her family. She ran a dog-grooming business and helped at an accounting office during tax season.

Kidd continued playing softball until 1975. She also had a small part in the 1992 film *A League of Their Own*, starring Geena Davis and Madonna, which told the story of one of the teams in the women's league. The film spurred renewed interest in the female ball clubs. In the film, she did most of the pitching when they showed the league's original players. Early in the movie, wearing a blue shirt and white ball cap, she is seen pitching in the background when the character played by Geena Davis takes the field.

She was present in 1988 for the opening of "Women in Baseball," a permanent display honoring the All-American Girls Professional Baseball League at the Baseball Hall of Fame in Cooperstown, New York. The exhibit was the first of its kind in the previously all-male Hall of Fame, and it remains a popular attraction. Arkansan Sue Kidd's name is among those engraved permanently on the display's plaque.

For more information:

Sargent, Jim, and Robert Gorman. *The South Bend Blue Sox: A History of the All-American Girls Professional Baseball League Team and Its Players, 1943–1954*. Jefferson, NC: McFarland, 2012.

Sargent, Jim. "Sue Kidd." Society for American Baseball Research at Arizona State University. http://sabr.org/bioproj/person/b91960f1 (accessed December 8, 2015).

Carlotta Walls LaNier (1942–)

CARLOTTA WALLS LaNIER was the youngest member of the Little Rock Nine, known around the world as the first black students to attend the all-white Little Rock Central High School in September 1957. After enduring daily abuse, she became the only female member of the Little Rock Nine to participate in Central's graduation exercises and the first black female graduate of Central High School, even after her home was bombed earlier that year and her father was accused of the crime. She went on to have a thirty-year career as a real estate agent, work in the nonprofit sector, and become president of the Little Rock Nine Foundation, a philanthropic organization.

Carlotta Walls was born on December 18, 1942, in Little Rock, the eldest of three daughters. Her parents were Juanita Cullins Walls, who was a secretary in the Office of Public Housing, and Cartelyou Walls, a brick mason. Carlotta attended Little Rock's all-black Dunbar Junior High School. As an eighth grader, she volunteered to be one of the first African Americans to attend Central High School, which was in her neighborhood. She did so without consulting her parents, which she later said made them proud of her determination. She would enter as a sophomore. Walls was raised to believe in the value of education, and she excelled in her studies. Her desire to attend Central was based on its reputation as an outstanding academic institution. When it was built in the 1920s, it was the nation's largest and most expensive high school facility, and it remains in use today. Carlotta Walls's grandfather had done brick masonry work on Central High.

Like the other girls of the Little Rock Nine, one of her biggest concerns was what to wear on her first day. Like the others, she approached her first day at Central as an opportunity to meet new people. Like the others, she did—in the form of a loud, angry, spitting, cursing white mob opposed to desegregation, blocking the students' way to register. Like the other black students, she was turned away from what would have been her first day of school.

Walls would ultimately donate the dress she wore that day to the Smithsonian's National Museum of African American History and Culture. Though her mother made most of her clothes, Walls's great-uncle had purchased the dress, patterned with numbers and letters, thinking that desegregating Little Rock Central would merit "a store-bought dress."

The Arkansas governor called in the state's National Guard to keep the students from entering on the first day they tried. Subsequently, U.S. president Dwight Eisenhower federalized the National Guard and called in the U.S. Army's 101st Airborne Division to protect the black students. Though the soldiers protected the black students as best they could during the1957–58 school year, they were unable prevent the constant harassment of the youngsters.

Until her graduation, the relentless ordeal continued. The daily abuse by white students was accompanied by persecution of the families of the Little Rock Nine. Members of the Walls family lost their jobs and received death threats, culminating in their home being firebombed. At one point, Carlotta's own father was arrested on suspicion of being responsible. In the face of all this, however, Carlotta Walls said she was determined to receive her diploma: "It validated all I had gone through…all of the problems, all of the bad things that had taken place."

To block desegregation, Little Rock high schools were shut down in the 1958–59 school year, during the time Walls would have been a junior. When they re-opened for the 1959–60 school year, Carlotta Walls returned to Central and walked at graduation in 1960. She was the only young woman among the Little Rock Nine to do so.

After graduating from Central, Walls attended Michigan State University for two years. She then moved with her family to Denver, Colorado, when her father was unable to find a job locally because of Carlotta's role in the Little Rock crisis. In 1968, she earned a bachelor's degree from Colorado State College (now the University of Northern Colorado) in Greeley, Colorado. She began working at the Young Women's Christian Association (YWCA) as a program administrator for teenagers.

Also in 1968, Walls married Ira C. "Ike" LaNier, with whom she would have two children, Whitney and Brooke. In 1977, she founded LaNier and Company, a real estate firm in Denver, where she would work for more than thirty years as a professional real estate broker.

Among her honors are the Spingarn Medal from the National Association for the Advancement of Colored People (NAACP) and the Congressional Gold Medal, the nation's highest civilian award. LaNier received the National Shining Star Award, Pierre Marquette Award, and the Lincoln Leadership Prize. She has served as a trustee for the Iliff School of Theology in Denver and for the University of Northern Colorado. She was named a "Woman of Distinction" by the Girl Scouts, as well as being inducted into the Colorado Women's Hall of Fame and the National Women's Hall of Fame.

In addition, LaNier has served as president of the Little Rock Nine Foundation, a philanthropic organization dedicated to ensuring equal access to education for African Americans.

In 2009, Carlotta Walls LaNier published her memoir, *A Mighty Long Way: My Journey to Justice at Little Rock Central High School*. She said, "It's important for as many of us to talk about what we went through, so that history does not continue to repeat itself."

For more information:

LaNier, Carlotta Walls, and Lisa Frazier Page. *A Mighty Long Way: My Journey to Justice at Little Rock Central High School*. New York: One World/Ballantine, 2009.

Little Rock Central High School National Historic Site Visitor Center. Little Rock, Arkansas. http://www.nps.gov/chsc (accessed December 8, 2015).

Little Rock Nine Foundation. http://www.littlerock9.com (accessed December 8, 2015).

Marjorie Lawrence (1907–1979)

SOPRANO MARJORIE LAWRENCE was a world-renowned opera star whose distinction was elevated by her heroic comeback after being struck by polio at the height of her creative power. She was the subject of an Academy Award–winning film, *Interrupted Melody*, and settled in Hot Springs, Arkansas, where she conducted opera classes and offered public concerts.

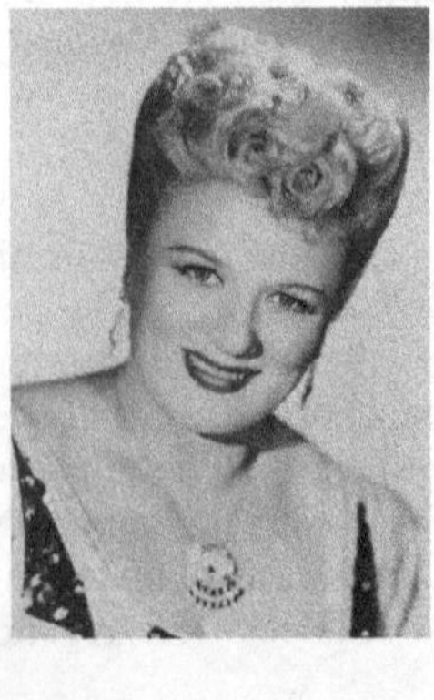

Marjorie Florence Lawrence was born on February 17, 1907, at Deans Marsh, near Melbourne, Australia. She was the fifth of six children born to Elizabeth Smith Lawrence, who was a church organist, and William Lawrence, a farmer who sang in the church choir. After Marjorie's mother died when Marjorie was two years old, she was raised by her grandmother.

Marjorie Lawrence became a soloist in her church choir by the age of ten. She became interested in opera by listening to recordings, and after winning several local singing competitions as a teenager, she left home at age eighteen to study voice in Melbourne. She worked as a live-in housekeeper to pay for lessons under a noted local voice teacher. After winning several voice competitions, she was encouraged to study in Paris by a noted Australian singer, who arranged an audition.

In 1929, Lawrence traveled to Paris, telling herself she would sing at the Paris Opéra one day. Lawrence made her operatic debut in Monte Carlo in 1932. There, she sang in *Tannhauser* by Richard Wagner, going on to become a world-renowned interpreter of Wagner's German operas such as *Die Walküre* and *Götterdämmerung.* She was also celebrated for her work in French and Italian operas. In 1933, Marjorie Lawrence made her debut at the Paris Opéra in Wagner's *Lohengrin*. She also began recording, becoming known to a wider audience. In 1935, she traveled to the United States, where she made her debut with the Metropolitan Opera in New York City singing in acclaimed performances of *Die Walküre* and *Götterdämmerung*.

Lawrence gained fame not only for her voice but for her beauty and glamour. She was said to perform the "Dance of the Seven Veils" in *Salome* more convincingly than most other sopranos. She was invited to sing year after year at the Met through the 1940–41 opera season. She also kept busy on concert tours around the world.

At New York City Hall on March 29, 1941, Lawrence married Dr. Thomas King, a physician. Three months later, she collapsed and found herself unable to stand during a rehearsal in Mexico City. Her husband brought her to Hot Springs, Arkansas, hoping that the healing waters would ease the constant pain. She went by ambulance daily to the Maurice Bathhouse, but the diagnosis was total disability from polio.

The couple bought an estate in Hot Springs they named Harmony Hills, which remained Lawrence's home for the rest of her life. With her husband's help, she slowly recovered the use of her vocal cords. Lawrence struggled through treatment and reached the point where she could sing on the radio as well as performing onstage in a chair or on a special platform. However, she was unable to resume her career at the opera capitals of the world due to World War II, which America entered in 1941, the same year she was stricken by polio.

Despite the wartime danger, she traveled to Australia in 1944. Seated in a chair, she entertained troops and helped raise money for the wounded in benefit concerts. There, the Australian standard "Waltzing Matilda" was repeatedly requested and became her signature song. The Metropolitan Opera in New York declined to have her sing in a wheelchair, but she received a message of support from President Franklin Roosevelt, a fellow polio victim. Lawrence sang "The Star-Spangled Banner" at his 1945 inauguration.

After the end of the war, Lawrence returned to Europe, singing at Buckingham Palace and at a concert in Paris, where she was awarded the cross of France's Légion d'Honneur in 1946. By 1947, she was able to stand while singing.

Though she continued to perform until the early 1950s, Lawrence eventually left the stage to become a teacher. At Harmony Hills in Hot Springs, she taught international students, later accepting students from the University of Arkansas at Little Rock (UALR).

Her bestselling 1949 autobiography, *Interrupted Melody*, became a 1955 motion picture starring Eleanor Parker as Lawrence. Along with Parker's nomination for Best Actress, the film won Academy Awards for best writing, screenplay, and story. The movie's Southern premiere took place at the Malco Theatre in Hot Springs.

In addition to UALR, she also taught at Garland County Community College (now National Park College) in Hot Springs along with Tulane University in New Orleans and Southern Illinois University in Carbondale. She sang with the Arkansas Symphony Orchestra, and at the conclusion of summer workshops at Harmony Hills, she presented her students in concert at the Arlington Hotel.

Lawrence made TV guest appearances and returned for visits to Australia, making her last recording there in 1976, fittingly singing "Waltzing Matilda."

At age seventy-one, Lawrence died of heart failure on January 13, 1979, at St. Vincent's Hospital in Little Rock. She is buried at Greenwood Cemetery in Hot Springs.

She was named a Commander of the Order of the British Empire in 1976, but an extremely significant recognition came when her admirers and students donated the funds to provide wheelchair accessibility for New York's Metropolitan Opera at Lincoln Center.

For more information:

Davis, Richard. *Wotan's Daughter: The Life of Marjorie Lawrence*. Adelaide, Australia: Wakefield Press, 2012.

Lawrence, Marjorie. *Interrupted Melody: The Story of My Life*. New York: Appleton-Century-Crofts, Inc., 1949.

Mary "Brownie" Ledbetter (1932–2010)

MARY WILLIAMS LEDBETTER, KNOWN AS "BROWNIE," was a nationally known civic leader whose causes included civil rights, labor issues, and women's rights, both in the United States and abroad. She was known for her commitment to equality despite cultural, gender, racial, and religious differences, helping adversaries to find common ground. She was a delegate to the National Democratic Convention, was named to the National Commission on Women, was the first political action chair of the National Women's Political Caucus, and served as executive board member of the Women's Environmental Development Organization, working with the United Nations (UN).

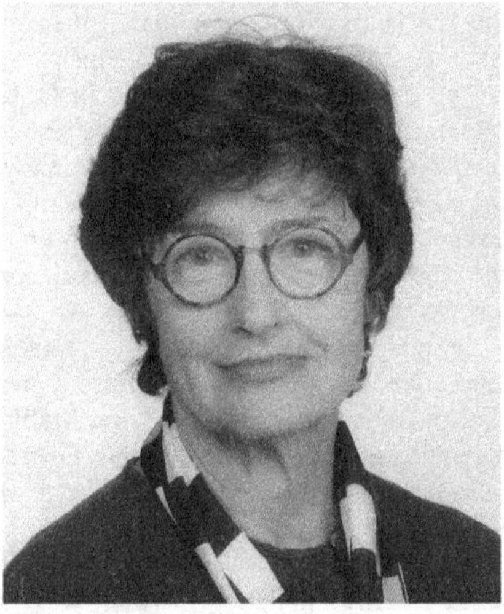

Mary Brown Williams was born in Little Rock, Arkansas, on April 28, 1932. She was the first of four children born to homemaker Helon Brown Williams and dairy farmer/businessman William H. Williams. The family lived at the Tall Timber Jersey Farm. Born with distinctive brown eyes, she was nicknamed "Brownie" from infancy.

Her mother died in 1947, and her father died in 1950 after a lengthy illness. He refers to his illness in a 1948 letter commending the University of Arkansas Medical School for admitting a "Negro" student. After his death, Brownie and her siblings remained at Tall Timber in the care of her aunt and uncle, Frances and Grainger Williams. She graduated in 1950 from Little Rock High School, which was renamed Central High School in 1953 and became the catalyst for Brownie Ledbetter's entry into activism in 1957.

She attended Agnes Scott College in Decatur, Georgia, from 1950 to 1953 but did not finish her degree. On July 26, 1953, she married distinguished attorney Calvin Ledbetter Jr. (1929–2013), a high school classmate. They lived for two years in Germany, where Cal Ledbetter was stationed with the U.S. Army Judge Advocate Corps. The couple returned to Little Rock and had three children: Grainger, Snow, and Jeffery.

After a court order, nine African American students attempted to attend Little Rock Central High School in 1957, but Governor Orval Faubus called in the Arkansas National Guard to prevent them. After U.S. president Dwight Eisenhower called in the U.S. Army to protect the black students, Little Rock high schools were closed the next year in a continued attempt to thwart integration. Brownie Ledbetter's aunt volunteered her to serve on the Women's Emergency Committee to Open Our Schools (WEC).

In 1963, Ledbetter joined the Little Rock Panel of American Women, a nonpartisan forum to encourage open discussions about racial, religious, and cultural divides. Ledbetter moderated the panel's first twenty-five sessions, encouraging women to discuss personal experiences in an effort to bridge the gap between people of different backgrounds and viewpoints. Ledbetter was praised for her ability to help diverse groups of people find common ground and to set shared goals for positive change.

The group became known as the Arkansas Public Policy Panel in 1981, with Ledbetter serving as its volunteer executive director until she retired in 1999. She guided the organization to become involved in issues concerning agriculture, civil rights, corporate accountability, economic development, education, the environment, and government. The group also assisted community leaders, grassroots organizations, and lobbyists, often trained by Ledbetter herself.

She also became involved in the political process, working on at least fifteen political campaigns. In 1967, she was campaign manager for her husband's successful bid for the Arkansas General Assembly, in which he served with distinction from 1967 to 1976. During his term in office, she organized a group of legislative wives to write a weekly newsletter to keep the public informed on legislative actions. She was named a delegate to the 1968 National Democratic Convention and was Arkansas campaign manager for George McGovern in 1972.

Ledbetter was a strong supporter of the Equal Rights Amendment and the women's movement. She was named by President Jimmy Carter to the National Commission on Women, was the first political action chair of the National Women's Political Caucus, and served on the Southern Coalition for Educational Equity, as well as the Arkansas State Advisory Committee to the U.S. Commission on Civil Rights.

She was co-founder and executive board member of the Women's Environmental Development Organization (WEDO), which worked with the UN on women's issues. She was non-governmental organization delegate at UN meetings in New York and UN conferences discussing the environment in Rio de Janeiro, population in Cairo, women's rights in Beijing, and racism/sustainable development in South Africa.

Among many state organizations, she was the founder and president of the Arkansas Fairness Council, board member of the American Civil Liberties Union of Arkansas, and legislative director for the State Federation of Business and Professional Women.

Ledbetter received numerous recognitions, including being named the 1992 American Civil Liberties Union Civil Libertarian of the Year and receiving the Mary Hatwood Futrell Award from the National Education Association in 2005. After retirement in 1999, she continued working on public school issues and served on the board of the Center for the Advancement of Women in New York.

At age seventy-seven, Brownie Ledbetter died at her Little Rock home on March 21, 2010, six months after being diagnosed with a brain tumor. Upon her death, Secretary of State Hillary Rodham Clinton [SEE ENTRY] called Ledbetter a champion "of the right of all Americans to education and opportunity."

In 2010, the Women's Foundation of Arkansas announced the creation of the Brownie Ledbetter Civic Engagement Award to recognize women who display her values and dedication to community building.

For more information:

"Interview with Brownie Ledbetter." February 28, 2007. Audio online at Butler Center Audio Video Collection. http://arstudies.contentdm.oclc.org/cdm/ref/collection/p1532coll1/id/12336 (accessed December 8, 2015).

Lois Lenski (1893–1974)

LOIS LENSKI was a popular author of books for children and young adults. Her works told the story of Arkansas children in the 1940s and '50s in a series of "regionals" for a nationwide audience. She also illustrated her books based on visits to the various locales where she lived among the citizenry, listening to their stories and speech patterns as she sketched. Her writing career spanned a half century, during which she visited

Arkansas for research on several works about the state's children: *Cotton in My Sack*, *Houseboat Girl*, and *We Live by the River*.

Lois Lenski was born in Springfield, Ohio, on October 14, 1893. Her parents were former schoolteacher Marietta Young Lenski and Richard Lenski, a Lutheran clergyman. The family moved to the town of Anna, Ohio, near Springfield, where Rev. Lenski was called to preach.

In Lenski's autobiography, she wrote, "Life in a small town in Ohio before the First World War was simple, sincere and wholesome....I am glad to have been a child in the horse-and-buggy days, and to have known and felt the joys of real peace and security."

Her parents provided books for their five children and were determined that each would go to college. Lenski commuted by train to a high school in Sidney, Ohio, from which she graduated in 1911. She attended Ohio State University, graduating in 1915 with a bachelor's degree in education and a teaching certificate, although she did not wish to become a teacher. After being encouraged by her art professors at Ohio State, Lenski moved to New York City to study at the Art Students League, where she took classes for four years.

While she studied at the Art Students League, she supported herself by taking lettering jobs, doing illustrations, painting greeting cards, and creating drawings for fashion ads. She met art instructor Arthur Sinclair Covey (1877–1960), a noted muralist known for his depictions of industrial workers at their jobs. Lenski became his assistant in painting several murals before traveling to London, England, where she attended Westminster School of Art and was hired by a British publisher to illustrate books.

Returning to the United States, she and widower Arthur Covey married in 1921. She became stepmother to Covey's two young children, Margaret and Laird, and the couple had a son, Stephen, in 1929.

Through the 1920s, Lenski illustrated other people's manuscripts until 1927 when her publisher encouraged her to write and illustrate her own books. Her first, *Skipping Village*, was published in 1927, followed the next year by *A Little Girl of 1900*, based on her own childhood years. She later said her work reflected the theme of a child within a town or environment—a theme which can be traced through all her books.

In 1929, the family moved to a 1790 farmhouse called Greenacres in Harwinton, Connecticut. Based on her son Stephen's early childhood, Lenski began her "Mr. Small" series, which would continue until the 1960s. Inspired by their Connecticut farmhouse, in 1936, Lenski began writing and illustrating historical fiction for young adults with *Phebe Fairchild: Her Book*, which was set in the 1830s. It would be the first of seven well-researched novels for preteens. She wrote that she wished to describe the everyday life of people in a given period. She did this so well she became a multiple Newbery Award winner. She also wrote the "Davy" series and the "Debbie" series, both inspired by her family.

In the 1940s, Lenski's health began to suffer, aggravated by the cold New England winters. After her children were older, she and Covey moved to Florida. She later said that her trips south allowed her to see how children lived in different parts of the country, inspiring her award-winning "Regional Series" in 1943. *Strawberry Girl*, set in Florida, was awarded the 1946 Newbery Medal. Other titles include *Bayou Suzette*, set in Louisiana; *Blue Ridge Billy*; *Corn-Farm Boy*; *Prairie School*; *San Francisco Boy*; and *Texas Tomboy*.

After hearing Lenski read one of her books on the radio, students in northeast Arkansas invited her to visit, which she did in 1947. The resulting book, *Cotton in My Sack*, was inscribed "for my beloved Arkansas cotton children." Local residents pointed out several incidents in the book such as a fire and a tractor accident that were based on true events around Blytheville, Arkansas.

In 1954, Lenski returned to Arkansas to write about children growing up on the Mississippi River, which she depicted in the book *We Live by the River*. Lenski shows a child crossing the huge body of water between Arkansas and Tennessee in a small boat, the family's usual means of transportation, to attend school, go shopping, or visit with friends. Lenski revisited Arkansas with 1957's *Houseboat Girl*.

In 1967, Lenski established the Lois Lenski Covey Foundation, to help advance literacy and foster a love of reading among underserved, at-risk children and young people. She continued to lecture, write, and illustrate, publishing her autobiography in 1972.

Lenski died at her home in Tarpon Springs, Florida, in 1974 at age eighty, having enjoyed a long, prolific, and successful career in which she produced more than one hundred well-loved books. She is buried in Clearwater, Florida, with her tombstone inscribed, "Lois Lenski Covey—Friend of Children."

For more information:

Lenski, Lois. *Journey into Childhood: The Autobiography of Lois Lenski*. New York: J. B. Lippincott Company, 1972.

Lois Lenski Covey Foundation." http://www.loislenskicovey.org/ (accessed December 8, 2015).

Ketty Lester (1934–)

KETTY LESTER is the professional name of the African American singer and actress best known for her chart-topping single "Love Letters," as well as her appearance in the cult classic film *Blacula*. Lester was a regular on the daytime drama *Days of Our Lives* and was especially known for her long-running role on the beloved TV series *Little House on the Prairie*.

Lester was born Revoyda Frierson in Hope, Arkansas, on August 16, 1934 (some sources say 1938). She was one of fifteen children born to a farm family. Her interest and talent for music led to her singing at church and in school choirs. She won a scholarship to San Francisco City College, where she studied music, though her original major was nursing. When she appeared on national TV in 1957, she stated that she was "too dumb" to study nursing and had balked at performing dissection.

In San Francisco, she began singing professionally at the renowned Purple Onion nightclub, under the stage name Ketty Lester. She went on to headline the opening of the Purple Onion in Hollywood, and she sang at clubs such as the Village Vanguard in New York City. She sang in East Coast clubs from Boston to Baltimore, also touring Europe as a singer with the Cab Calloway orchestra.

On December 26, 1957, she appeared as a contestant on the popular television program *You Bet Your Life*, hosted by comedian Groucho Marx. Introduced as Revoyda Frierson, she corrected Groucho on the pronunciation of "FRY-er-son," but she stated that she performed as a nightclub singer under the professional name of Ketty Lester. She said that she was from Arkansas, and after she recounted the story of having to dissect a "dead man" in her college anatomy class, Marx deadpanned, "And the next morning you were back in Little Rock" (this was the year of the Little Rock school desegregation crisis).

After commenting on her striking beauty, Marx asked if she would sing a song. Seemingly unrehearsed, she performed an upbeat version of "You Do Something to Me" with the show's musicians. After an ovation from the audience, Groucho said, "You're going to be one of our top stars before long—very few people can sing that hot."

Through her work at the Purple Onion in Los Angeles, Lester met several record producers. After her first single, 1962's "Queen for a Day," Era Records released her recording of "I'm a Fool to Want You," along with "Love Letters." It was "Love Letters" on the B side that created a sensation, rising to the top of the charts in 1962. Her version of the song was a bigger critical and commercial success than Elvis Presley's similar arrangement would be four years later.

Moving to RCA, she recorded steadily through the 1960s, with singles including "But

Not for Me," "You Can't Lie to a Liar," and an upbeat version of Woody Guthrie's "This Land Is Your Land." "When a Woman Loves a Man" in 1966 was a response to the Percy Sledge hit "When a Man Loves a Woman." Her albums include *Love Letters*, *The Soul of Me*, *When a Woman Loves a Man*, *Ketty Lester in Concert*, and *Where Is Love?*

In 1962, she toured with the Everly Brothers. With her name spelled as "Kitty," she was nominated for a 1963 Grammy as Best Female Pop Vocalist, competing with Peggy Lee, Lena Horne, and Ella Fitzgerald (who won).

While at college, Lester became involved with a theatrical group at the University of California, Berkeley. She put her experience to use in 1964, appearing off-Broadway in the play *Cabin in the Sky*, for which she won a Theatre World Award. It was the start of a longterm acting career, with more than sixty credits listed for her on the Internet Movie Database.

Lester appeared in such feature films as 1968's *Up Tight*, *Uptown Saturday Night* in 1974, and Neil Simon's *Prisoner of Second Avenue* in 1975. However, she may be best known for 1972's cult classic *Blacula*. It was the first horror movie in the genre called "Blaxploitation" (with the word being a mix of "black" and "exploitation"). Lester's other feature films were in addition to appearances on television series including *That Girl*, *Julia*, *Sanford and Son*, *Love American Style*, *Marcus Welby M.D.*, *Streets of San Francisco*, *The Waltons*, *Lou Grant*, *Happy Days*, *Hill Street Blues*, *St. Elsewhere*, *In the Heat of the Night*, *L.A. Law*, and *Courthouse*. Her TV movies include *Louis Armstrong: Chicago Style* and *It's Good to be Alive*, the Roy Campanella story. From 1975 through 1977, Lester portrayed Helen Grant on the daytime drama *Days of Our Lives*. She was especially known as a regular on Michael Landon's *Little House on the Prairie*, playing Hester-Sue Terhune, the teacher at a blind school, from 1978 to 1983.

In 1984, Lester released an album of Christian music, *I Saw Love*, and appeared in movies and television into the 1990s, including the 1994 film *House Party 3* and the TV show *Getting Personal* in 1998.

For more information:

"Ketty Lester." Internet Movie Database. http://www.imdb.com/name/nm0504480 (accessed December 11, 2015).

"The Negro on Broadway." *Ebony* (April 1964).

Kristin Lewis (1975–)

AWARD-WINNING OPERA SINGER KRISTIN LEWIS of Little Rock has performed at leading opera houses in the United States and abroad. Though she specializes in Verdi's operatic heroines, she boasts an extensive repertoire which has gained her an international following. In addition to her musical artistry, she also supports up-and-coming musicians through the Kristin Lewis Foundation.

Kristin Allison Lewis was born in Little Rock, Arkansas, in 1975 to the Reverend Bettye Pearson Lewis, who is active in the United Methodist Church, and Dr. Raphael Lewis, an ex-officio member of the board of trustees of Philander Smith College. In an interview with the *Vienna Review*, Lewis said, "I was very fortunate to have parents who recognized my talents very early and encouraged them."

Lewis has an older sister, Tamara Elizabeth. Following in her sister's footsteps, Kristin Lewis attended the University of Central Arkansas (UCA) in Conway. She studied voice, was a member of the UCA Concert Choir (singing solos on a choir tour to Italy), and performed in UCA's Opera Workshop in such roles as Musetta in *La Bohème* and Lauretta in *Gianni Schicchi*. Lewis participated in the Knoxville Opera Young Artist program and was a three-time finalist in the National Association of Teachers of Singing regional competitions.

In 1999, Lewis received a bachelor's degree in vocal performance from UCA. She would return to her alma mater in 2004 to perform a recital, as well as serving as artist-in-residence in 2009. In 2014, UCA announced the Kristin Lewis Foundation Scholarship for emerging Arkansas vocalists to encourage potential in young singers. The scholarship competition recitals have been held at UCA, with all events free and open to the public.

Lewis also served as a soloist with the choir of Second Presbyterian Church of Little Rock, touring with the group in Eastern Europe. In 1999 and 2001, Lewis won the Mid-South Region Metropolitan Opera National Council auditions and competed in the National Semi-Finals at the Metropolitan Opera in New York City.

She won a scholarship for vocal studies at the University of Tennessee in Knoxville, performing with the Knoxville Opera Studio. Lewis received a master's degree in vocal performance in 2002 before embarking on her international opera career. She made her European operatic debut in 2005 as Donna Elvira in Mozart's *Don Giovanni* at the Opernfestspiele Heidenheim in Germany.

Lewis has established herself as a "lyrico-spinto" or "pushed lyric" soprano, an operatic voice that easily reaches the high notes of a lyric soprano, yet can be "pushed" to achieve dramatic climaxes without strain. Spinto sopranos are expected to handle dynamic changes in the music they perform, commanding a wide vocal range. The lyrico-spinto repertoire includes many roles written by Verdi that are popular with opera audiences. It is in singing Verdi's heroines that Lewis has especially distinguished herself.

One of the world's best-loved operas is Verdi's *Aida*, and Lewis has sung the title role in a number of productions. In 2006, she sang her first *Aida* at the Cairo Opera House, a rare and daunting distinction, with the opera being set in Egypt. Her interpretation of this role has won accolades in such venues as the Teatro San Carlo in Naples, Italy; Berlin State Opera; the Opera Festival in Masada, Israel; Vienna State Opera; and the Savonlinna Opera Festival in Finland.

She performed as the soprano soloist in Verdi's *Requiem* at the Cathedral of Orvieto, Italy, under Maestro Zubin Mehta in 2011 as well as Elisabetta di Valois in Verdi's *Don Carlo*. Her repertoire also includes Amelia in Verdi's *Un Ballo in Maschera*, Leonora in Verdi's *Il Trovatore*, Medora in Verdi's *Il Corsaro*, and Leonora in Verdi's *La Forza del Destino*, along with Maddalena in Giordano's *Andrea Chénier*, Mimi in Puccini's *La Bohème*, Micaela in Bizet's *Carmen*, and Nedda in Leoncavallo's *I Pagliacci*.

A small sampling of her operatic appearances includes performances at Les Chorégies d'Orange in France; the Mariinsky Theatre in St. Petersburg, Russia; Opéra Bastille in Paris, France; the Puccini Festival at Torre del Lago, Italy; Teatro La Fenice in Venice, Italy; and the opera houses of Seoul, South Korea, and Tokyo, Japan.

Lewis has also sung contemporary works such as playing Serena in Gershwin's *Porgy and Bess*. When *Dead Man Walking* by Jake Heggie made its European debut at the Semperoper in Dresden, Germany, Lewis starred as Sister Rose. She has recorded extensively as well, including her *Aida* in 2013, conducted by Daniel Oren. She was presented with the Orazio Tosi Prize from Parma Lirica and was named the Savonlinna Opera Festival's 2010 Artist of the Year.

She resides in Vienna, Austria, where the Red Cross of Vienna named her Ambassador for Humanity. She supports Animal Care Austria in addition to her work with the Kristin Lewis Foundation to encourage the pursuit of musical endeavors at all levels of performance and nurture the appreciation of musical cultures of yesterday and today.

For more information:

Kristin Lewis Foundation. http://www.kristinlewisfoundation.com (accessed December 8, 2015).

Kristin Lewis, Soprano. http://www.kristinlewis.de/ (accessed December 8, 2015).

Mary Lewis (1897–1941)

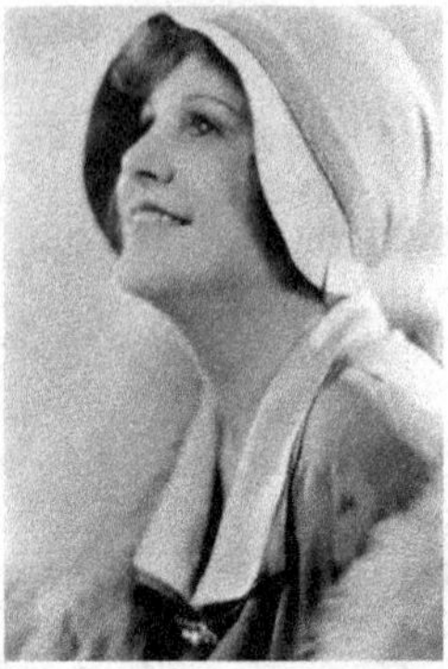

MARY SYBIL KIDD LEWIS, called "The Golden Haired Beauty with the Golden Voice," was nationally renowned in the 1920s and '30s for her extraordinary loveliness and talent as an opera singer. Before earning acclaim as an operatic prima donna, she took center stage as a reigning beauty for the *Ziegfeld Follies* show, a job that may have doomed her to an early death. Her rags-to-riches-to-rags story—from an abusive childhood to the heights of grand opera to an unhappy personal life—was even more poignant than many of the tragic operas she performed.

Mary Sybil Kidd was born on January 29, 1897, in Hot Springs, Arkansas, to Hattie Kidd and Charles Kidd, who died when Mary was about two years old. Her destitute, widowed mother became unable to care for Mary and a baby brother. Her brother was sent to Chicago to live with relatives, while Mary was placed in an orphanage and a series of foster homes.

Her mother remarried, but the family still lived in poverty. Mary took her new stepfather's name, becoming Mary Maynard. Suffering from illness and malnutrition, the child was sometimes given food and clothing by an elderly couple, Rev. William Fitch and Anna Fitch. In 1905, the Fitches brought seven-year-old Mary to live with them. There, she was given musical training along with strict corporal discipline.

In 1906, Rev. Fitch was assigned to a Methodist church in Eureka Springs, Arkansas, where Mary Maynard was praised for her church solos. Two years later, when Fitch was named church pastor in Judsonia, Arkansas, Mary Maynard's singing was again acclaimed. In 1909, Maynard moved with the Fitch family to Little Rock.

In 1912, when she was fifteen years old, Maynard left the Fitch home to live with a friend, fifty-year-old attorney Henry Franklin Auten, a politician and entrepreneur who developed Pulaski Heights as Little Rock's first western suburb. He had taken in other disadvantaged children and, after hearing Maynard sing, believed she could have a career in music. She received vocal training and spent three years at Little Rock High School, her first formal education.

Turning eighteen in 1915, Mary Maynard married J. Keene Lewis of Little Rock but soon left the unhappy marriage to join a traveling vaudeville troupe. Billed as Mary Lewis, she found herself in Hollywood, California, where she sang in vaudeville shows until she strained her voice. She then worked in silent movies as a Christie comedy beauty until her voice healed.

Moving to New York City in 1920, she was just in time for the "Roaring Twenties," when the rise of both technology and publicity would carry her voice and beauty to new heights. In 1921, she was signed by Florenz Ziegfeld to star in the world-famous *Ziegfeld Follies*.

In 1922, the *Follies* show was particularly spectacular, climaxed by an extravaganza in which Lewis wore a stunning costume that became famous. When the stage lights were turned off, all the audience could see was the glow of the dress reflecting Lewis's face as she sang. The dress was lined with the newly discovered radium, which glowed in the dark. It was thought to be miraculous but was later found to be lethal. After about a month, Lewis's health broke down, probably from radiation poisoning. She spent three months in the hospital and would never fully recover.

Lewis then took voice lessons to pursue a career in grand opera. At the Vienna Opera House in 1923, she had her operatic debut starring as Marguerite in *Faust*. Her fame grew when she was signed to perform on the new sound recordings. Returning to the United States, she sang the starring role in *La Bohème* at New York's Metropolitan Opera in 1926. Later that same year, Mary Lewis made a triumphant homecoming to Little

Rock. She was welcomed by the governor, given a key to the city, and proclaimed by the *Arkansas Democrat* to have been given the greatest welcome the state had ever seen.

Returning to the Metropolitan Opera, which would be her home for five years, she married Met leading man Michael Bohnen in 1927. Her fame was so great that the ceremony was performed by the mayor of New York. Bohnen was said to be abusive, likely contributing to his wife's alcoholism. They divorced in 1930 as the Great Depression began to take its toll on theatrical productions.

Lewis made a number of acclaimed recordings of both operatic and popular music. They were played extensively on the radio, a medium that was enjoying the height of its popularity. In 1931, she married Robert Hague, an executive at Standard Oil.

In the 1930s, she appeared at benefits for a number of causes and performed on the radio. In 1936, Lewis was part of a series of nationwide celebrations to honor President Franklin Roosevelt's birthday, with proceeds benefiting people afflicted with polio. She again became a popular performer in the *Ziegfeld Follies*.

When Hague died in 1939, he left Lewis in debt. Her already precarious health went into a decline and she died in New York on December 31, 1941, at age forty-four. There was a funeral in New York City followed by another in Little Rock. Lewis is buried at Pinecrest Memorial Park in Alexander, Arkansas.

Critics have stated that her life left its mark on her work, with her voice taking on an especially soulful quality. One contemporary critic, James Camner, said, "Her fearless singing reflects that of a young woman who though brutally knocked down over and over, always bounced back up, one who never quit striving."

For more information:

Dougan, Michael B. "A Touching Enigma: The Opera Career of Mary Lewis." *Arkansas Historical Quarterly* 36 (Autumn 1977): 258–279.

Zeman, Alice Fitch. *Mary Lewis—The Golden Haired Beauty with the Golden Voice*. Little Rock: Rose Publishing, 2001.

Kay Linaker (1913–2008)

ALTHOUGH ALSO KNOWN PROFESSIONALLY AS KATE PHILLIPS, the actress and screenwriter is listed on the Internet Movie Database as "Kay Linaker," the name by which she was billed in the movies. Considered an exotic beauty, she was a popular film actress who was often cast in "B" or second-tier feature films in the 1930s and '40s such as the Charlie Chan series. She also appeared in top-level "A" movies such as the Academy Award–winning *Kitty Foyle* and the Oscar-nominated *Drums Along the Mohawk*. She was a pioneering female screenwriter for both movies and television who is best remembered for her work on 1958's cult classic *The Blob*, a name she suggested.

Mary Katherine "Kay" Linaker was born on July 19, 1913, in Pine Bluff, Arkansas, to Regina and Charles Linaker. Her father, who owned C. A. Linaker and Company, a wholesaler for Armour Foods, died when Kay was eleven. She was sent at age twelve to the Hillside School in Norwalk, Connecticut, graduating from the private boarding school when she was sixteen.

Her original plan was to attend Wellesley College in Massachusetts, but she contracted polio. The recommended exercise treatments were in New York, where she took night classes at New York University. Having an interest in theater, she studied during the day at the Academy of Dramatic Arts.

After Linaker graduated from New York University, she won acting jobs in supporting roles on Broadway, where she caught the attention of talent scouts looking for screen actors. In Hollywood, she signed an option with Warner Bros. She was not satisfied with some of the conditions of the contract, including the salary, so she crossed out the lines she didn't like and changed them.

The Warner Bros. studio cast Linaker in her first film, *The Murder of Dr. Harrigan*, in

1936. She would go on to appear in more than thirty films, working with major stars from Claudette Colbert to Henry Fonda. A sampling of Linaker's film work includes *The Girl from Mandalay*, *Easy Money*, *Crack-Up*, *Black Aces*, *Buck Benny Rides Again*, *Blood and Sand*, *The Last Warning* (her largest part), *Orchestra Wives*, *War Dogs*, and *Here Come the Waves*. She appeared in critically acclaimed feature films such as *Young Mr. Lincoln*, *Drums Along the Mohawk*, *Laura*, and, notably, 1940's *Kitty Foyle* as a society matron who marries the former husband of Ginger Rogers's character in Rogers's only Academy Award–winning role.

In 1943's *Two Weeks to Live*, she appeared with fellow Arkansans "Lum and Abner" (Chester Lauck and Norris Goff), discovering that all their parents knew each other. Linaker appeared with both Warner Oland and Sidney Toler, the two actors who portrayed Charlie Chan in the popular series. Linaker appeared in *Charlie Chan's Murder Cruise*, *Charlie Chan at Monte Carlo*, *Charlie Chan in Reno*, *Charlie Chan at Treasure Island*, and *Charlie Chan in Rio*.

During World War II, Linaker joined the Red Cross, serving as a hostess at USO clubs run by the U.S. Army. There, she met Howard Phillips of New York, a singer in the U.S. Army Air Forces. She later said Phillips was actually checking on security leaks.

They were married after the war, moved to New Hampshire, and had two children: Bill and Regina. With television entering its golden age in the 1950s, Howard Phillips and Kay Linaker Phillips became a writing team; she was credited at this time as "Kate Phillips." Both had had prior experience as writers, with Linaker writing for the military-sponsored *Voice of America* radio show. Together, they wrote for TV series such as *Bronco*, *Riverboat*, *Whirlybirds*, and *The United States Steel Hour*. Individually, she also wrote for *Lux Video Theatre*.

Her best-known success was the screenplay for the 1958 horror classic *The Blob*. It was originally called *The Molten Meteor*, but Linaker came up with the name *The Blob*. It starred Steve McQueen in his first major role and was a huge success, though both Linaker and McQueen received a payment of only $150.

Her husband Howard became an NBC television executive; he died in 1985. From 1980 to 2006, Linaker taught in the film studies department at New Hampshire's Keene State College. From the 1960s until her death nearly five decades later, she also volunteered as an English teacher and drama coach at Hampshire Country School in Rindge, New Hampshire, a private school for disabled children.

For her work at Keene State College, she earned the distinction of being the oldest college professor in New England when she retired in 2005 at age ninety. Linaker died on April 18, 2008, in Keene at age ninety-four.

In an interview, Linaker looked back at *The Blob*, the low-budget film that went on to earn millions: "Both Steve McQueen and I were to receive $150 plus ten percent of the gross," Linaker said. "Neither one of us got the percentage—and the film (and its remake) have earned millions—but I got an important writing credit, and Steve became a star!"

For more information:

Hevesi, Dennis. "Kate Phillips, Actress Who Christened 'The Blob,' Is Dead at 94." http://www.nytimes.com/2008/04/27/theater/27phillipsobit.html?_r=0 (accessed December 8, 2015).

"Kay Linaker." Internet Movie Database. http://www.imdb.com/name/nm0510989 (accessed December 8, 2015).

Blanche Lincoln (1960–)

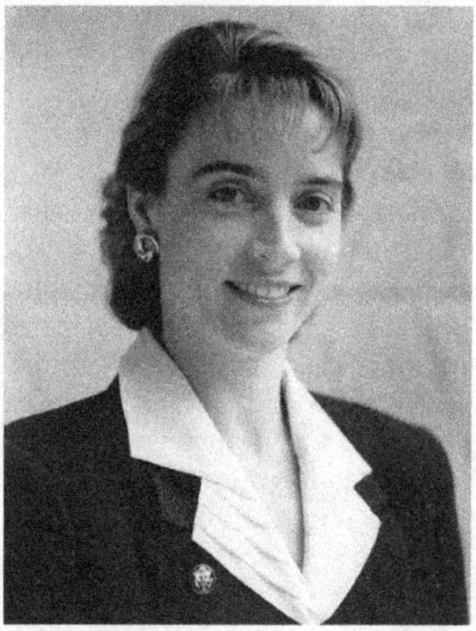

FROM 1999 TO 2011, BLANCHE LAMBERT LINCOLN was a U.S. senator from Arkansas. She is currently the owner of the Lincoln Policy Group, ranked as one of Washington's top lobbying firms. Lincoln was the first woman elected to the U.S. Senate from Arkansas since Hattie Caraway in 1932, and, at age thirty-eight, Lincoln was the youngest woman ever elected to the Senate. She was the first woman and the first Arkansan to chair the Senate Committee on Agriculture, Nutrition and Forestry. In 2004, Lincoln was mentioned as a possible vice-presidential candidate.

Blanche Meyers Lambert was born on September 30, 1960, in Helena, Arkansas, to a seventh-generation Arkansas farm family. Her parents were homemaker Martha Kelly Lambert and farmer Jordan Bennett Lambert Jr. She is the youngest of four children, with siblings including filmmaker Mary Lambert.

Blanche Lambert attended Helena public schools, with her first elective office being president of the Helena Central High School Student Council in 1977–78. After high school graduation in 1978, she briefly attended the University of Arkansas (UA) in Fayetteville before transferring to Randolph-Macon Woman's College in Lynchburg, Virginia. In 1982, she received a bachelor's degree in biology from Randolph-Macon, originally planning to join the nursing profession.

Instead, she moved to Washington DC, where she served as staff assistant to Arkansas's First District congressman Bill Alexander from 1982 to 1984, later working as a lobbyist. In 1992, she returned to Arkansas to challenge Alexander, who had received unfavorable publicity in a House banking scandal.

She won the 1992 congressional election, becoming the first woman to represent Arkansas's First District. In August 1993, she married Dr. Steve Lincoln, who had a medical practice in Fairfax, Virginia. She was re-elected to Congress in 1994, serving through 1997. She did not run in the next congressional election because she was expecting twin boys, Reece and Bennett, who were born in 1996.

After Dale Bumpers announced his retirement from the U.S. Senate in 1998, Lincoln ran for the seat and was elected, becoming the youngest woman ever elected to the Senate. When Lincoln was sworn in, she followed in the footsteps of America's first female senator, Hattie Wyatt Caraway, who served from 1932 to 1944 and was Arkansas's only other woman to serve as senator.

Beginning with her first congressional term, Lincoln called herself a member of the Blue Dog Coalition, a group of moderate Democrats seeking a spirit of bipartisanship and innovative problem-solving. She was a founding co-chair of a group called Third Way, seeking new ways to approach traditional problems. She was re-elected to the Senate from Arkansas in 2004, receiving more than half a million votes, the highest total cast for any senatorial candidate in state history.

In January 2001, she was appointed to the Senate Finance Committee, with only two other women in history serving in that powerful group. She served on the Senate's Agriculture, Nutrition and Forestry Committee; the Rural Health Caucus; the Special Committee on Aging; the Select Committee on Ethics; and the Social Security Task Force. She was founder and chair of the Senate Hunger Caucus, serving Americans who face hunger. Media figures called Lincoln an up-and-coming member of the Senate and an energetic campaigner with an engaging personality. The *Washington Post* named her a possible running mate for John Kerry in the 2004 presidential election.

In her legislative career, Lincoln paid special attention to issues involving working families, veterans, and farmers, reflecting her upbringing in a rural region that has traditionally been mired in poverty. She was an advocate of the Delta Regional Authority, designed to stimulate development in the lower Mississippi Delta.

Her legislative initiatives included repealing the estate tax on family-owned businesses and farms; expanding the Social Security Act to expand coverage to pregnant women; sponsoring a bill to protect children from Internet pornography; creating funding to combat and clean up methamphetamine labs; giving emergency assistance to farmers suffering losses due to natural disasters; and providing temporary Medicaid disaster relief for survivors of Hurricane Katrina.

She was a contributing author for the book *Nine and Counting: The Women of the Senate*, published in 2000. She has served on the boards of University of Arkansas for Medical Sciences Foundation, the March of Dimes, Arkansas Easter Seals, and the American Red Cross. An avid hunter and angler, she was named the National Sportfishing Association's 1996 Woman of the Year.

In the November 2010 mid-term election, Lincoln lost her Senate seat to Republican John Boozman. She had narrowly won the Democratic primary over Lieutenant Governor Bill Halter but was not able to find enough support after failing to satisfy critics on both the left and right wings of the political spectrum.

In January 2011, Entergy Corporation announced that Lincoln would serve on its board of directors. That same year, she became a special policy advisor with the legal firm of Alston & Bird LLP. In 2013, she started her own lobbying firm, the Lincoln Policy Group. The publication *The Hill* put her on its list of the top lobbyists of 2014.

Lincoln has been known for her willingness to seek bipartisan solutions, and she once said, "I am not normally a betting person, but I say that putting your money on the American people is about as close to a sure bet as you are going to get."

For more information:

"Blanche Lambert Lincoln." Biographical Directory of the United States Congress. http://bioguide.congress.gov/scripts/biodisplay.pl?index=l000035 (accessed December 8, 2015).

Mikulski, Barbara, et al. *Nine and Counting: The Women of the Senate.* New York: William Morrow & Co., 2000.

Roberta Martin (1907–1969)

AS A GOSPEL MUSIC ARRANGER, choir director, composer, pianist, and singer, Roberta Martin was a leading gospel figure from the 1930s to the '60s. Martin earned six gold records and made an international impact on gospel music. Her group, the Roberta Martin Singers, launched the careers of many other noted gospel artists. Martin was known for having an impact on the entire gospel music industry not only for her musical compositions but also for her business sense and flair for innovation.

Roberta Evelyn Winston was born in Helena, Arkansas, on February 12, 1907. She was one of six children born to Anna and William Winston, who operated a general store.

By the age of six, Roberta was taking piano lessons from her brother's wife. At around eight years old, she moved with her family to Chicago, where they settled in 1917. They had joined what was called the Great Migration of the early twentieth century, as millions of African Americans left the Jim Crow South for northern urban centers in search of greater opportunity. Chicago was a popular destination, in part for the city's tradition of fostering great music, including gospel.

Roberta Winston attended Chicago's Wendell Phillips High School, where she studied piano and choral directing. Her music teacher encouraged her to attend Northwestern University to pursue her dream of becoming a classical concert pianist. However, when

Roberta began accompanying the Young People's Choir at Ebenezer Baptist Church in 1932, she met Thomas A. Dorsey, the former bluesman who is called the "Father of Gospel Music." She found an artistic home in Dorsey's brand of gospel music, which differed in its dynamism from traditional Christian "folk" spirituals.

She joined the Young People's Choir and began refining her own musical style. Around this time, Roberta Winston married Bill Martin, though the marriage ended in divorce. Under her married name of Roberta Martin, her career in gospel music began its swift ascent in the early 1930s. With the help of Dorsey and Theodore Frye, she organized an ensemble called the Martin-Frye Quartet in 1933.

Adding new members, the renamed Roberta Martin Singers launched in 1936—wearing distinctive "RMS" choir robes. It was the first group to include both male and female singers in a small ensemble format. Martin accompanied the group on piano and also soloed as a vocalist. Meanwhile, Martin was writing and arranging her own music, soon recognizing the need for a publishing outlet. In 1939, she founded Chicago's Roberta Martin Studio of Music, a gospel music publishing house that would distribute not only Martin's compositions but also those of notable gospel figures such as James Cleveland and Dorothy Norwood.

The Roberta Martin Singers had a very successful recording career, becoming known for setting the standard among gospel choirs and mixed groups. "He Knows How Much We Can Bear," recorded in 1941, was an immediate hit, then eclipsed in 1943 by Martin's "Try Jesus, He Satisfies." The composition "Only a Look" became the theme song of the Roberta Martin Singers, always opening their concerts and eliciting a rousing ovation. Martin would go on to earn six gold records, each honoring the sale of more than 500,000 records.

In 1947, Roberta Martin (sometimes called "Bert" by her friends) married James Austin; the couple had one son. However, she retained her stage name of Roberta Martin.

During the course of her career, she composed about seventy gospel songs, arranged and published almost 300 more, and sold thousands of pieces of sheet music. Her most well-known compositions include "Let It Be" in 1950; "I'm Just Waiting on the Lord" in 1953; 1959's "God Is Still on the Throne"; and "Just Jesus and Me" in 1966. The Roberta Martin Singers also made their mark abroad, including a 1963 performance at Gian Carlo Menotti's Spoleto Festival in Italy.

In the 1960s, Roberta Martin was battling cancer. Though she cut back on her performance schedule, she remained as the longtime choir director for Chicago's famed Mount Pisgah Baptist Church. With the Roberta Martin Singers, she recorded her final album *Praise God* in 1968, singing her last song as a vocalist, "I Have Hope."

Martin refused painkilling drugs, believing that God could perform a miracle. At age sixty-one, Roberta Martin died of cancer in Chicago on January 18, 1969. More than 50,000 mourners paid their last respects to Martin during her funeral at Mount Pisgah Baptist Church.

Roberta Martin is buried at Chicago's Burr Oak Cemetery, near the gravesite of gospel star and fellow Arkansan "Sister Rosetta" Tharpe [SEE ENTRY]. In 1998, the U.S. Postal Service issued a commemorative stamp honoring four eminent women of gospel, including Tharpe and Roberta Martin.

In 1981, the Smithsonian Institution held the symposium "Roberta Martin and the Roberta Martin Singers: The Legacy and the Music." The surviving members of the group continue to perform in reunion concerts, and it is said that gospel music fans can instantly recognize a Roberta Martin song.

For more information:

Boyer, Horace Clarence. *How Sweet the Sound: The Golden Age of Gospel*. Urbana: University of Illinois Press, 1995.

Darden, Robert. *People Get Ready!: A New History of Black Gospel Music*. New York: Bloomsbury Academic, 2005.

Heilbut, Tony. *The Gospel Sound: Good News and Bad Times*. New York: Simon & Schuster, 1971.

Deborah Mathis (1953–)

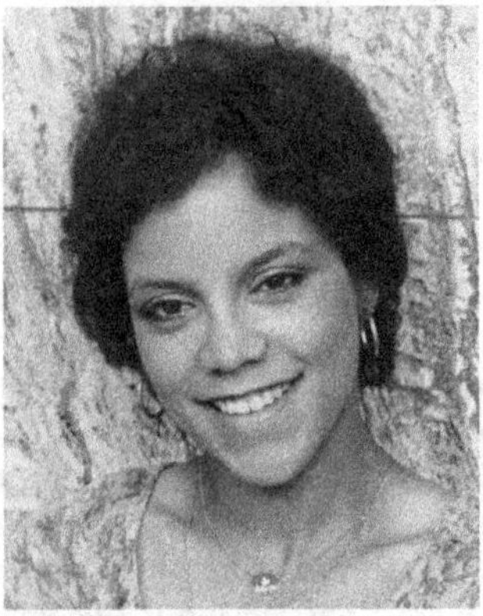

DEBORAH MYERS MATHIS is a reporter and nationally syndicated newspaper columnist whose work has appeared in more than 100 publications across the country. She was a television reporter and anchor in Washington DC, was the only Arkansas reporter to cover the Gulf War, and served as White House correspondent for Gannett News Services. She has frequently appeared as a commentator on such nationally broadcast programs as CNN's *Inside Politics*, *Frontline*, NPR's *All Things Considered*, *Good Morning America*, and *The Oprah Winfrey Show*.

Deborah Myers was born in Little Rock, Arkansas, on August 24, 1953, to educator Rachel Helms Myers, who became assistant superintendent of the Little Rock Public Schools, and the Reverend Lloyd Myers, pastor of Little Rock's Rose of Sharon Baptist Church and later Greater Shiloh Baptist Church in North Little Rock. Deborah Mathis recalled that just after the 1964 Civil Rights Act was passed, Rev. and Mrs. Myers gathered the family to look through clippings from the *Arkansas Gazette* about the struggle to enroll nine black students at Little Rock Central High School in 1957. Mathis said her parents explained "the business of civil rights, the struggles, the risks, the righteousness of it," to the ten-year-old Mathis, adding, "They told me that only the *Arkansas Gazette* had dared to defend it, despite abandonment by advertisers, despite the angry mobs." Mathis would go on to become the first woman and first African American to sit on the editorial board of the Pulitzer Prize–winning *Gazette*.

She attended Little Rock's Gibbs Elementary, Rightsell Elementary, and Westside Junior High, graduating from Central High School in 1971. While there, she became the first female and first African American editor of the school newspaper.

After high school graduation, she began working as a typist at the *Arkansas Democrat* newspaper, moving on to reporting a few months later. She married Bill Mathis, with whom she went on to have three children: Meredith, Allison, and Joseph. The couple later divorced, though Deborah Mathis retained her married name.

Soon after her marriage, she was hired by WTTG-TV in Washington DC. She and her husband lived there from 1974 through 1976, when they returned to Arkansas, having made an agreement to come back to Little Rock when they had a child. She worked for a time at the Winthrop Rockefeller Foundation, and she then became a Little Rock television reporter and anchor. According to the Arkansas Black Hall of Fame, at this time, she also wrote, produced, and narrated two nationally aired documentaries: *Edukashun: The Cost of Failure* (1982) and *Return of the Little Rock Nine* (1987).

After six years in Little Rock TV news, she said she felt a calling to do more purposeful work, and she resigned her television job with no other position on the horizon. Her letter of resignation was shared with a local media columnist, who asked if he could publish it in the newspaper, saying he found it extremely moving. Mathis agreed, and she was besieged with job offers. Mathis joined the staff of the *Arkansas Gazette* in 1988 as an editorial columnist and staff writer. In 1990, she became the *Gazette*'s associate editor.

She traveled to the Middle East to report on the Gulf War in 1991, the only Arkansas journalist to do so, saying that Arkansans made up a larger than usual per-capita number of troops in the conflict. When she returned home to her job at the *Gazette*, she was one of the first to report on another conflict. The "newspaper war" between the *Gazette* and the *Democrat* led to the closing of the 172-year-old *Gazette* when it became part of the *Arkansas Democrat-Gazette* in October 1991.

Mathis joined the staff of the *Clarion-Ledger* in Jackson, Mississippi, as an opinion columnist. Her column was syndicated nationally by Tribune Media Services and was seen in more than eighty newspapers across the country. The Gannett Company, which had owned the *Gazette* prior to its demise, was also the parent company to the *Clarion-Ledger*. When fellow Arkansan Bill Clinton was running for president, Gannett asked Mathis to report from Washington DC. After Clinton's election, Mathis worked as Gannett's White House correspondent beginning in 1993. While continuing to write her syndicated column, she covered the White House until 2000.

Mathis accepted a one-year fellowship at Harvard University's Shorenstein Center on Media, Politics and Public Policy, producing a case study on racial makeup in media discussions of the disputed 2000 presidential election. She then joined the Advancement Project, a civil rights group. As part of her work there, she traveled to Africa to report on the AIDS epidemic. After speaking at a global business conference in Turkey, she moved to that country for a year after her son left for college.

Returning to the Washington DC area, she taught journalism for Northwestern University's Washington branch and became communications director for the Public Justice Foundation.

Her book *Yet a Stranger: Why Black Americans Still Don't Feel at Home* was published in 2002. *What God Can Do: How Faith Changes Lives for the Better* was released in 2005, the same year as *Sole Sisters: The Joys and Pains of Single Black Women.* She continues to write, most recently announcing that she was working on a nonfiction book about a Florida murder case.

For more information:

Deborah Mathis. http://authors.simonandschuster.com/Deborah-Mathis/20109825 (accessed December 8, 2015).

Mathis, Deborah. *Yet a Stranger: Why Black Americans Still Don't Feel at Home.* New York: Grand Central Publishing, 2002.

Susan McDougal (1955–)

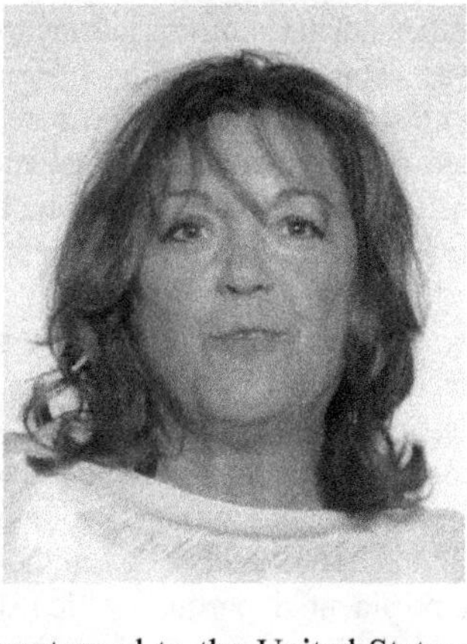

SUSAN HENLEY McDOUGAL became internationally known in the 1990s for refusing to testify before the Office of the Independent Counsel's grand jury during the Whitewater investigation of Bill Clinton. She was one of the few people who served prison time as a result of Whitewater. McDougal was imprisoned for almost two years, being moved from jail to jail, before ultimately being found not guilty and released.

Susan Carol Henley was born in 1955 in Heidelberg, Germany, to James Henley—who was a U.S. Army sergeant from Camden, Arkansas—and Laurette Mathieu Henley, a native of Belgium. When the family returned to the United States, they settled in Camden, where Susan—the middle child of seven—attended the public schools. She entered Ouachita Baptist University (OBU) in Arkadelphia, Arkansas, in the fall of 1972 on a Latin scholarship.

At OBU, she met Jim McDougal, a member of the political science faculty. He invited her to accompany him to political events for Arkansas politicians whom he considered friends. Jim McDougal asked her to organize a group of her fellow OBU students to attend a campaign event for Bill Clinton, who was running for Arkansas attorney general in 1976.

The couple married in 1976, just after her graduation from OBU, with former lieutenant governor Bob Riley presiding. Her husband left OBU after their wedding, and the couple worked together in real estate. In 1978, they partnered with Arkansas attorney general Bill Clinton and wife Hillary Rodham Clinton [SEE ENTRY] to buy approximately 230 acres of undeveloped land on the White River near the town of Flippin, Arkansas, for about $203,000. It was incorporated on June 18, 1979, as the Whitewater Development Corporation.

In 1980, McDougal's husband purchased the Bank of Kingston in Madison County and renamed it Madison Bank & Trust. It failed in 1983. He then purchased Woodruff Savings & Loan in Augusta, Arkansas, which was renamed Madison Guaranty Savings & Loan and moved to Little Rock. In 1983, Maple Creek Farms, a residential development south of Little Rock, was created and wholly owned by Madison Financial Corporation, a real estate development company the couple ran. Jim McDougal created television ads with his wife riding a white horse. They bought local TV advertising space, saturating movies and sporting events. The ads—and Susan McDougal—became well known in central Arkansas.

In 1984, Susan McDougal unsuccessfully ran for election to the Little Rock City Board before separating from her husband and moving to Dallas, Texas. She soon returned to Little Rock, where her husband asked her to sign for a $300,000 Small Business Development loan through former judge David Hale, which she did.

In 1988, she moved to California, where she became a personal assistant to Nancy Mehta, wife of symphony conductor Zubin Mehta. Six months after McDougal left that position in 1992, Nancy Mehta filed charges of forgery against McDougal, who was found not guilty on all counts.

In 1990, the McDougals' divorce was finalized. On August 17, 1995, during the investigations of what came to be called the Whitewater scandal, McDougal and her former husband were charged with bank fraud regarding questionable loans. They were convicted, and Susan McDougal individually was convicted of four felonies: mail fraud, wire fraud, misapplication of funds, and aiding and abetting—charges stemming from her signing for the loan from Hale. Her former husband began cooperating with the Independent Counsel's grand jury, but she refused to testify, believing that its only interest was obtaining damaging information on the Clintons. She also cited a conversation with her mother, who compared their tactics with those of the Nazis, turning friends and family members against each other. McDougal stated that she gladly would have testified under oath in a public courtroom, but she never had that opportunity. She was sent to prison for civil contempt on September 9, 1996.

McDougal spent almost two years in seven jails, including maximum security prisons with violent offenders where she was not even permitted to have books. She was once held for seven weeks in a Plexiglas-enclosed soundproof cell, an experience she described as "hellish." On April 3, 1998, after completing the maximum sentence for contempt, she again refused to testify before the grand jury. In 1999, however, she was found not guilty of obstruction of justice and ordered to be released.

In 2001, on his last day in the White House, President Bill Clinton granted McDougal a presidential pardon, which she learned about on television. In 2003, McDougal published a *New York Times* bestseller, *The Woman Who Wouldn't Talk: Why I Refused to Testify against the Clintons & What I Learned in Jail*.

In June 2011, after completing training, McDougal began working as a chaplain at the University of Arkansas for Medical Sciences (UAMS) in Little Rock. She is also a public speaker, addressing conditions in women's prisons.

"I was frightened in jail," she said. "These were women at the worst time in their lives, yet they embraced me and cared about me. It changed me and made me want to live up to that by offering a personal connection, comfort and caring to those who are in a time of trauma."

For more information:

McDougal, Susan, with Pat Harris. *The Woman Who Wouldn't Talk: Why I Refused to Testify against the Clintons & What I Learned in Jail*. New York: Carroll & Graf Publishers, 2003.

"Mothers in Prison Interview." Arkansas Educational Television Network. May 2001. http://www.aetn.org/programs/mothersinprison/interviews/mcdougal (accessed December 8, 2015).

Mary Medearis (1915–2012)

MARY MEDEARIS was the acclaimed author of the 1942 novel *Big Doc's Girl*, which publisher Liz Smith Russell says holds the distinction of having stayed in print longer than any other work of fiction by an Arkansan.

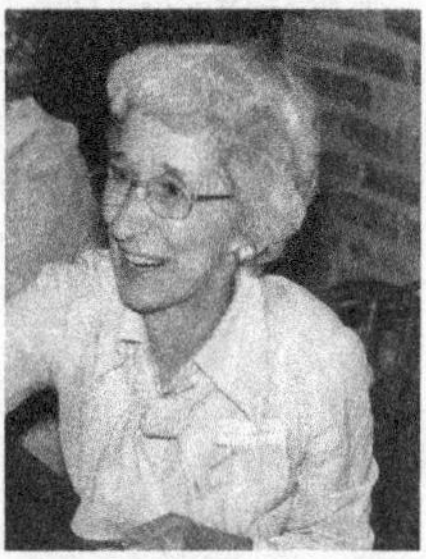

Mary Myrtle Medearis was born in North Little Rock, Arkansas, on May 31, 1915. Her mother, Myrtle Hendricks Medearis, taught piano. Her father, Dr. Robert Summerfield Medearis, practiced medicine in North Little Rock for twenty years and was especially noted for his work during the World War I influenza epidemic. Young Mary inherited both a respect for the medical profession and a love of music. She had a brother, Robert Anderson, and two sisters, Mellie Kate and Ruth Luella.

Medearis graduated from North Little Rock High School in 1933. The following year, in 1934, her father died at their home in North Little Rock after an illness of three weeks. Her mother was also ill, and, although Mary hoped to study music, financial difficulties during the Great Depression intervened. In 1936, an aunt, Mellicent Hendricks Webb, bought Mary Medearis a one-way ticket to New York City to study piano at the Juilliard School. There, Mary lived with a cousin and earned money typing menus and playing piano for a neighborhood café.

Medearis enrolled in a speech class at New York's Columbia University in 1938 because New Yorkers had trouble understanding her Arkansas accent. The speech class was full, but Medearis learned there were openings in a creative writing class, which she was told would help her to verbalize.

When the writing class was assigned to compose an autobiographical short story, Medearis wrote "Death of a Country Doctor" about the loss of her father. The teacher was impressed, entering it in a competition sponsored by *Story* magazine in 1940. "Death of a Country Doctor" won the contest and was printed in the magazine. Noted New York publisher J. B. Lippincott Company offered Medearis a contract to expand the story into a full-length novel. Still thinking of herself as a musician, Medearis bought a piano with the publishing advance.

In 1940, Medearis graduated from Juilliard and married chemist Richard Reeves, who had admired her piano playing and other attributes at lunchtime in the café. They had four children, and settled in Pennsylvania, where Mary Medearis Reeves taught music.

Her novel, published as *Big Doc's Girl* in 1942, told the story from the viewpoint of the teenage Mary Clayborne. Its cast of characters included the father (physician "Big Doc"), a brother called "Little Doc," and two sisters, Mellie Kate and Ruth. Its opening line introduced the author's home state by stating, "The back country of Arkansas is always the same, no matter which fork of the road you follow."

The book was well received by a number of major publications such as the *Los Angeles Times* and the *New York Times Book Review*. It was listed as a *New York Times* bestseller and was included as one of the *Times*'s ten best books published that year. *Redbook* magazine published a condensed version of the novel in September 1942. The book was translated into several languages, including Arabic and Russian, and was adapted as a full-length play.

In 1957, *Big Doc's Girl* was adapted by the New York Theatre Guild for presentation on television's *U.S. Steel Hour*, said by the Internet Movie Database to be a "live drama series that was one of the best TV shows ever shown." It was broadcast by CBS on November 4, 1959, with a cast that included acclaimed actor Gene Hackman at the start of his career.

Medearis frequently visited her home state, becoming fascinated with the historic town of Washington, Arkansas, in the southwestern part of the state. Each summer through 1975, she returned to the town to compile the stories of local residents. After her divorce, she settled permanently in Arkansas and became a charter member of the Hempstead County Historical Society as well as a founding director of the Southwest Arkansas Regional Archives, holding that position for over a decade. In 1976, she authored the book *Washington, Arkansas: History on the Southwest Trail*.

When *Big Doc's Girl* went out of print by its New York publishing company in 1981, Medearis contracted with August House Publishers in Little Rock for a new edition in 1985. That edition remained in print until 1998, was revived in 2006, and remains available in both print and electronic form. Luminous Films, owned by Arkansan Beth Brickell [SEE ENTRY], acquired the rights to make *Big Doc's Girl* into a movie.

Medearis served as writer-in-residence for Ouachita Baptist University in Arkadelphia, Arkansas, from 1993 to 1996. In the autumn of 1996, she went to live in a retirement community for writers and artists at Saratoga Springs, New York, where she died on September 16, 2012, at age ninety-seven.

For more information:

Big Doc. Luminous Films. http://www.luminousfilms.net/bigdoc/index.html (accessed December 8, 2015).

Medearis, Mary. *Big Doc's Girl*. Little Rock, AR: August House, 2006.

Martha Mitchell (1918–1976)

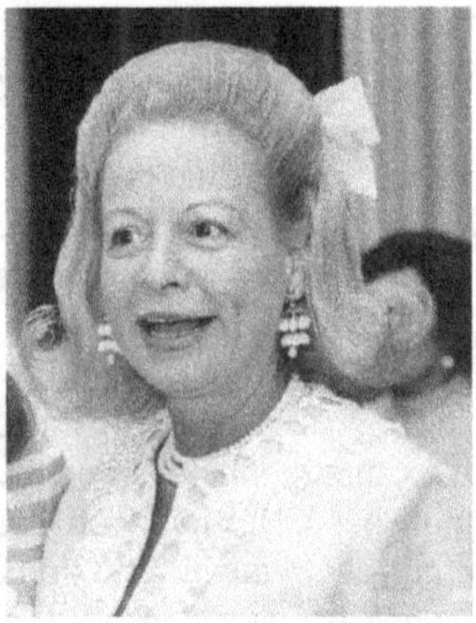

AS THE WIFE OF THE U.S. ATTORNEY GENERAL, Martha Beall Mitchell became known worldwide for her outspokenness and late-night phone calls to reporters during the Watergate scandal that culminated in the resignation of U.S. president Richard Nixon in 1974. Despite attempts to silence her, including what she said may have been injections of cancer-causing sedatives, she felt it was her duty to inform the public of the truth about their government. Nixon was quoted as saying that there would have been no Watergate if it hadn't been for Martha Mitchell.

Martha Elizabeth Beall began life on September 2, 1918, in Pine Bluff, Arkansas. Her mother was speech and drama teacher Arie Ferguson Beall and her father was wealthy cotton broker George Virgil Beall.

In 1936, Martha Beall graduated from Pine Bluff High School, where she was a vivacious, popular student who was said to never be at a loss for words. She attended Stephens College in Columbia, Missouri; the University of Arkansas (UA) in Fayetteville; and the University of Miami, from which she received a bachelor's degree in history in 1942. After finding that she did not enjoy teaching, she returned to Pine Bluff in 1945.

She worked as a secretary at the Pine Bluff Arsenal, accompanying her boss, the commanding general, to Washington DC. There, she met U.S. Army intelligence officer Clyde Jennings Jr. They married in 1946, after which they moved to New York and had a son named Clyde Jay Jennings. The couple divorced in August 1957. In December 1957, she married New York City attorney John Newton Mitchell, with whom she had a daughter, Martha Elizabeth, called "Marty." John Mitchell managed the successful 1968

Nixon presidential campaign and was appointed U.S. attorney general.

By May 1970, national newspaper articles were referring to Martha Mitchell as "the most talked about, talkative woman in Washington." From their apartment in the Watergate East, Martha Mitchell was making documented late-night phone calls to newspapers, legislators, political wives, and congressional staffers—unheard-of behavior for a Cabinet wife. If they did not comply with her requests, she threatened to campaign against them on national TV. In one case, she demanded support for her husband's choice for the U.S. Supreme Court, Clement Haynsworth. In a tape-recorded phone call, she told the *Arkansas Gazette* to "crucify" Senator William Fulbright for voting against another Mitchell-backed nominee, Harold Carswell. She regularly called reporters at all hours of the day and night to share her views on everything from busing to the Vietnam War. She started receiving a large volume of mail, was interviewed by *TIME* magazine in 1970, and ultimately had to hire a press secretary. Martha Mitchell became so well known that only her first name needed to be used in conversations among Washington society.

In 1972, John Mitchell managed Nixon's re-election campaign and became entangled in the Watergate scandal. Martha Mitchell's phone calls then centered on what she believed were the corrupt activities of the Nixon administration, which she felt unfairly made her husband a scapegoat. Her allegations led to her being discredited, especially after the administration "leaked" that she had a problem with alcohol. She then claimed that in order to keep her quiet, she was drugged and imprisoned in a California hotel room, later asserting that the drugs were cancer-causing heavy sedatives. She was shunned by most of her family, except for her son. Nixon would later tell interviewer David Frost that Martha Mitchell was such a distraction to her husband that "no one was minding the store," and, "If it hadn't been for Martha Mitchell, there'd have been no Watergate."

Her husband left her in September 1973, providing no financial support. She worked briefly in local television in 1974. The following year, John Mitchell was convicted of conspiracy, obstruction of justice, and perjury for his role in the Watergate break-in and cover-up, serving nineteen months in prison.

In 1976, Mitchell fell into a coma from the effects of multiple myeloma. At age fifty-seven, she died at Memorial Sloan Kettering Hospital in New York City. She is buried in the Bellwood Cemetery in Pine Bluff. At her funeral, a floral wreath from an anonymous mourner carried a banner saying "Martha Was Right."

Her legacy includes a psychological term, "the Martha Mitchell effect," in which a patient's claims are first thought to be delusions but are later found to be true. Her life has been dramatized in the plays *Dirty Tricks* and *This is Martha Speaking*.

The Pine Bluff birthplace and childhood home of Martha Mitchell was added to the National Register of Historic Places in 1978. It is now the Martha Beall Mitchell Home and Museum. The museum's website says that, when she graduated from high school, these words appeared alongside her picture: "I love its gentle warble, I love its gentle flow, I love to wind my tongue up, And I love to let it go."

For more information:

"Martha Beall Mitchell Birthplace and Childhood Home." http://www.atrol.com/martha/ (accessed December 8, 2015).

McLendon, Winzola. *Martha: The Life of Martha Mitchell*. New York: Random House, 1979.

Raye Montague (1935–)

RAYE JORDAN MONTAGUE, an internationally registered professional engineer, broke through gender and racial barriers to forge a career with the U.S. Navy. She is credited with the first computer-generated draft of a U.S. naval ship. She was the U.S. Navy's first female program manager of ships (PMS 309), holding the civilian equivalent rank of captain. She was nominated by the Secretary of the Navy for the Federal Woman of the Year Award, was a regular presenter to the U.S. Department of Defense's Joint Chiefs of Staff, and was the first woman to serve on the board of directors for the International Numerical Control Society's Department of Defense (DOD) Manufacturing Technology and Advisory Group. She was honored with the U.S. Navy's Meritorious Civilian Service Award and the Society of Manufacturing Engineers Achievement Award.

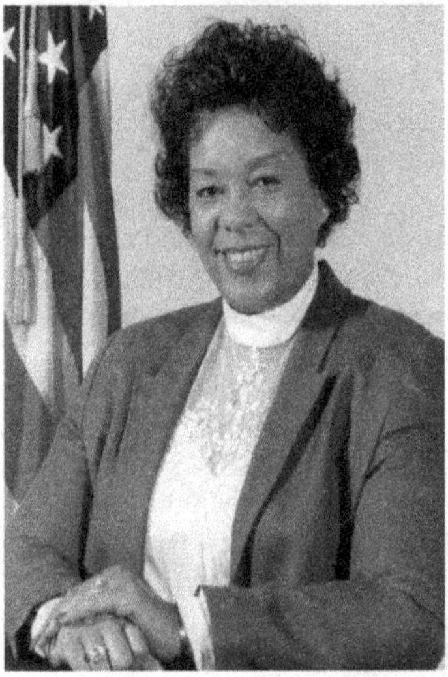

Raye Jean Jordan was born on January 21, 1935, in Little Rock, Arkansas. Her parents were Flossie Graves Jordan and Rayford Jordan. She attended St. Bartholomew School, an all-black Catholic school, before moving to Pine Bluff. In 1952, she graduated from Pine Bluff's all-black Merrill High School. In an interview, she said her mother once told her, "You're female, you're black and you're going to have a segregated school education, so you're going to have three strikes against you. But you can do anything you want to do and you can be anything you want to be, provided you are educated."

She said that, in 1942, when she was seven years old, she saw a German mini-submarine that had been captured off the coast of South Carolina. She was fascinated and asked a man there what a person needed to do to work with naval vessels. He responded that a person would have to be an engineer but that she should not think about such an ambition. "I grew up in an era of segregation and I was told by many people I could not do a lot of things," she said. "When I graduated from high school in 1952, I was not allowed to attend the one school in Arkansas that offered an engineering degree because minorities were not accepted at the time due to segregation." Although she wished to study engineering, she attended Arkansas AM&N (today the University of Arkansas at Pine Bluff) and graduated in 1956 with a bachelor of science degree in business.

After college, she moved to Washington DC and took a position with the U.S. Navy as a digital computer systems operator with the David Taylor Naval Ships Research and Development Center. She later said that having the first name "Raye" was an asset, with employers assuming from her résumé that she was a man. She said, "They looked at my transcript and said '...with a BS degree, you'll know all about computers.' I had never seen a computer because Arkansas did not have computers in 1956."

She taught herself to use computers as her career spanned the development of technology from the world's first commercially available computer (UNIVAC-1 Serial #2) to the age of modern computers. Many of her colleagues had graduated from Ivy League colleges, including some who had worked on the Manhattan Project to develop the atomic bomb. She learned programming codes and taught herself how to design ships.

After becoming a computer systems analyst at the Naval Ship Engineering Center, she revised the first automated system for selecting and printing ship specifications, taking just eighteen hours to produce a rough draft for the new Oliver Hazard Perry (FFG-7) type of frigate, the first ship designed by computer, revolutionizing naval ship design.

She earned the U.S. Navy's Meritorious Civilian Service Award in 1972 and was nominated for Federal Woman of the Year by the Secretary of the Navy. Montague said her life was threatened and she was warned not to accept either award before a white woman; regardless, she accepted the Meritorious Civilian Service Award (although she did not win the second). Montague was the first female professional engineer in the United States to win the Society of Manufacturing Engineers Achievement Award, in 1978, as well as the National Computer Graphics Association Award for the Advancement of Computer Graphics, in 1988.

She rose to become program director for the Naval Sea Systems Command Integrated Design, Manufacturing, and Maintenance Program, as well as becoming division head for the Computer-Aided Design and Computer-Aided Manufacturing (CAD/CAM) program. In 1984, she accepted the newly created position of deputy program manager of the U.S. Navy's Information Systems Improvement Program. Montague worked on the design of the prestigious USS *Dwight D. Eisenhower* (CVN-69) as well as the U.S. Navy's first landing craft helicopter-assault ship (LHA#1) and the SSN-21 *Sea Wolf*, receiving numerous awards in academia, industry, and the military.

Montague retired in 1990 and returned to Little Rock in 2006, where she became active with LifeQuest of Arkansas. She has worked with the University of Arkansas at Little Rock as a speaker in various prisons. Montague is active with the Alpha Kappa Alpha Sorority and with the Arkansas Association of University Women. She is also a member of The Links Inc., an international service organization for professional women of color to mentor youth and adults in environmental science, technology, engineering, mathematics, and the arts.

Montague said, "People put obstacles in your way; however, you must find a way to achieve despite the system."

For more information:

Hutter, David. "Raye Jean Montague Shares Life Story of Overcoming Gender and Racial Barriers." *Pine Bluff Commercial*, April 2, 2015.

"Interview with Raye Montague." January 29, 2009. Little Rock, Arkansas. Audio online at Butler Center for Arkansas Studies. http://arstudies.contentdm.oclc.org/cdm/singleitem/collection/p1532coll1/id/12700/rec/2 (accessed December 8, 2015).

Patsy Montana (1908–1996)

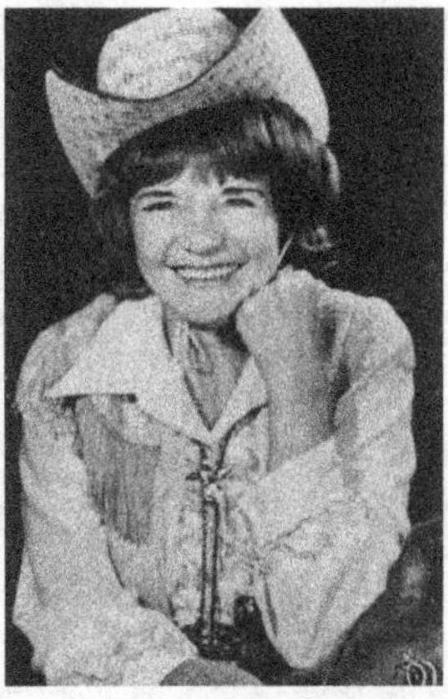

PATSY MONTANA, a pioneering country music singer, was the first female country artist to sell a million records, which she did with her signature song, "I Want to Be a Cowboy's Sweetheart." Known throughout the United States and Europe, she was inducted into the Country Music Hall of Fame and the National Cowgirl Museum and Hall of Fame.

Patsy Montana was born Ruby Blevins on October 30, 1908, in Hot Springs, Arkansas. Her parents were homemaker Victoria Blevins and farmer Augustus Blevins. Ruby was the couple's eleventh child and only daughter. By 1913, her father was working for the postal service. They moved to Hope, Arkansas, where Ruby came to love music through church, listening to local fiddlers, and hearing the songs of country star Jimmie Rodgers.

As a child, she learned to yodel as well as to play guitar and violin. In 1926, she was a violinist with the Hope High School orchestra. In 1928, the Arkansas Inter-School Contest Association awarded Blevins second place in the violin contest. She graduated from Hope High School in 1928, around the same time she added an "e" to spell her name "Rubye."

In 1929, she went with her brother and sister-in-law to Los Angeles. There, she took classes and won first prize in a 1931 talent contest by performing two Jimmie Rodgers songs. She was offered an appearance on the *Hollywood Breakfast Club* radio program, which in turn led to regular work on the radio. At first she was billed as "The Yodeling Cowgirl From San Antone." She was re-christened "Patsy Montana" by singer Stuart Hamblen after performing with the Montana Cowgirls on a radio show Hamblen hosted with silent-screen cowboy star Monte Montana.

After two years in Los Angeles, Patsy Montana returned to Arkansas in 1932. Country singer Jimmie Davis heard her on a radio station in nearby Shreveport. He invited her to sing back-up at his next recording session, during which she recorded several songs of her own.

In 1933, she traveled from the family's Arkansas home to Chicago to enter their large Hope watermelon in the Chicago World's Fair. It is not known if the watermelon won a prize, but the trip allowed Patsy Montana to audition for a record producer who liked her girlish laughter in the middle of the song. He added her as the vocalist to a string band called the Prairie Ramblers. The group became regulars on WLS radio's popular *National Barn Dance*, a country-themed show that began before the Grand Ole Opry began broadcasting shows.

In 1935, she released her composition "I Want to Be a Cowboy's Sweetheart," which would become her signature song. That record made Patsy Montana the first female country recording artist to have a million-seller, especially remarkable during the Great Depression, when there was little money even for food.

Patsy Montana continued performing on *National Barn Dance* until the 1950s, working with stars such as Gene Autry. In 1934, she married Autry's stage manager, Paul Rose. They had two daughters, Beverly and Judy, who later appeared with their mother as the Patsy Montana Trio.

The couple was often separated due to their respective touring schedules. Between 1934 and 1992, Montana made over 7,000 appearances in the United States and Europe. Montana had a distinctive image as a yodeling cowgirl who dressed in western attire complete with holster and gun. Her songs had titles such as "Sweetheart of the Saddle," "She-Buckaroo," "I Wanna Be a Western Cowgirl," and "Rip-Snortin' Two-Gun Gal." Montana also appeared in motion pictures, including 1939's *Colorado Sunset* with Gene Autry. With the coming of World War II in the 1940s, she recorded "Goodnight, Soldier" to boost morale of the troops.

In 1946 and 1947, she had her own ABC network radio show, *Wake Up and Smile*. It featured her signature greeting, "Hi, Pardner! It's Patsy Montana," backed by the sound of horses' hooves. She returned to Arkansas in 1947 to raise her children, but she also did radio shows on KTHS in Hot Springs and appeared on Shreveport's *Louisiana Hayride*.

After the family moved to San Jacinto, California, Montana remained a popular performer as she continued to tour and make records into the 1990s. In 1995, at age eighty-seven, Montana played concerts at Hope and Little Rock. Reports noted that while she appeared frail, she sported a cowboy hat and boots as she heartily sang and yodeled.

At age eighty-eight, Patsy Montana died at her California home on May 3, 1996. She is buried at California's Riverside National Cemetery.

In 1993, she was featured with such stars as Patsy Cline and Dolly Parton in the documentary *The Women of Country*, in which she was cited as an influence in the history of women in country music. Montana's signature song, "I Want to Be a Cowboy's Sweetheart," is heard over the end credits of the acclaimed 1996 movie *Lone Star*, released a month after her death.

For more information:
Bufwack, Mary A., and Robert K. Oermann. *Finding Her Voice: The Saga of Women in Country Music*. New York: Crown Publishers, 1993.
Montana, Patsy, and Jane Frost. *Patsy Montana: The Cowboy's Sweetheart*. Jefferson, NC: McFarland Publishing, 2002.

Charlotte Moorman (1933–1991)

CHARLOTTE MOORMAN was a cellist, performance artist, and advocate of avant-garde music, as the founder of the annual Avant Garde Festival of New York. She has been called the "Jeanne d'Arc of new music," though she is more often remembered as the "Topless Cellist."

Madeline Charlotte Moorman, nicknamed "Mattie" by her family, was born on November 18, 1933, in Little Rock, Arkansas. She was the only child of James Roy "Jerry" Moorman and Vivian Kelly Moorman. She later said that her upbringing was left to her widowed grandmother, Lillie Edna Kelly, who lived with the family. Charlotte's father suffered from tuberculosis and her mother was said to be an alcoholic.

Charlotte began studying cello at age ten, showing great promise. She attended Little Rock High School (renamed Central High School in 1953), during which time she performed with local symphonies. Moorman joined an exclusive all-female high school group called the Southernaires who were the official hostesses for major school events. In the 1950s and '60s, Little Rock's City Beautiful Commission sponsored a beauty pageant called "Miss City Beautiful." The dark-haired Charlotte Moorman was chosen Miss City Beautiful of 1952.

When Moorman graduated from high school in 1951, she was awarded a music scholarship to attend Centenary College in Shreveport, Louisiana. At Centenary, she earned a bachelor's degree in music in 1955. She then earned a master's degree from the University of Texas at Austin and went on to two years of postgraduate studies at New York City's Juilliard School starting in 1957.

While she was in New York, she married a fellow Centenary student, bassist Thomas Coleman, in 1958. Thomas Coleman was granted an annulment in 1963.

At Juilliard, Moorman performed in classical concert orchestras, including the American Symphony Orchestra, with which she would remain until 1967. However, she was becoming drawn to experimental performance art in the 1960s at the encouragement of her friend and roommate, multimedia artist Yoko Ono. Moorman met a number of artists who were considered avant-garde, including John Cage. Moorman worked with a number of performance artists, but her most significant professional partnership was with the Korean-American artist Nam June Paik, who worked with a variety of media and is considered to be the founder of video art.

After Moorman found that, like other female artists of the time, she was excluded from the Fluxus movement of avant-garde performance artists, she founded the annual Avant Garde Festival of New York in 1963. The festival presented experimental music, kinetic art, video art, and "happenings." Twenty-nine-year-old Moorman began coordinating the festivals at various locations around New York until the last one in 1982. In interviews, she said that she disliked the term "avant-garde," preferring "of its time," rather than "ahead of its time." The festivals would include presentations by artists including Cage, Paik, Allen Ginsberg, Ono, and John Lennon, as well as Moorman herself. Moorman often played cello in unique configurations, such as hanging suspended from helium-filled balloons. She also performed Yoko Ono's *Cut Piece*, in which audience members were told to snip pieces from Moorman's dress as she played. In Moorman's performance of *Ice Music*, she played a cello-shaped block of ice in the nude until the ice melted.

Her collaboration with Nam June Paik lasted several decades and focused on fusing art, music, and performance pieces. Paik created many works specifically for Moorman, including *TV Bra for Living Sculpture*, in which two small television sets were attached to Moorman's chest while she played cello.

In February 1967, Moorman became known nationwide for her arrest during a performance of Paik's *Opera Sextronique* at a Times Square–area theater in New York City when she performed on the cello in various states of nudity as required by the score. In the show's program, Paik wrote: "The purge of sex under the excuse of being 'serious' exactly undermines the so-called 'seriousness' of music as a classical art, ranking with literature and painting."

Moorman later told reporters that the New York program had been presented for the previous two years without incident in France, Germany, Denmark, and Sweden. When she came onstage for her second selection before 200 invited audience members, she wore only a long skirt. She was arrested mid-performance by plainclothes New York City police officers and taken to jail without the chance to dress or protect her cello.

Moorman was charged with indecent exposure, although her penalty was later suspended. She gained international attention as the "Topless Cellist" and was fired from the American Symphony Orchestra. Moorman made appearances on TV programs such as *The Tonight Show* with Johnny Carson, being billed as the "Topless Cellist." Many in the avant-garde community disparaged her as an opportunist and sensationalist who had "sold out," although she struggled financially and used her celebrity appearances to promote avant-garde art.

Moorman performed a tenth-anniversary edition of *Opera Sextronique* in 1977 at Carnegie Hall. When she appeared topless except for pasties with spinning propellers, there was a shout of "Up against the wall!" This time, however, the "police" were actually thirty-five performers who were part of the act.

Despite being diagnosed with breast cancer in 1979, Moorman continued performing for twelve more years, treating the pain and subsequent mastectomy as performance art while her health deteriorated. At age fifty-eight, she died in New York City on November 8, 1991, survived by her second husband, Frank Pileggi. Following her death, Paik made a film titled *Topless Cellist* in 1995 about Moorman's life and art.

After her arrest for indecent exposure, Moorman later said, "Imagine me, I grew up in Little Rock, Arkansas, and there I was in New York in handcuffs and overnight in jail."

For more information:

Collins, Glenn. "Charlotte Moorman, 58, Is Dead; A Cellist in Avant-Garde Works." *New York Times*, November 9, 1991 http://www.nytimes.com/1991/11/09/arts/charlotte-moorman-58-is-dead-a-cellist-in-avant-garde-works.html (accessed December 8, 2015).

Rothfus, Joan. *Topless Cellist: The Improbable Life of Charlotte Moorman*. Cambridge, MA: MIT Press, 2014.

Paula Morell (1967–)

PAULA MARTIN MORELL is executive producer and host of *Tales from the South*, an internationally broadcast radio show recorded live each week in Arkansas. The program is heard nationwide on National Public Radio's *NPR Now* as well as on multiple public radio stations around the country and world. Morell is also a noted author, educator, and owner of Temenos Publishing Company.

Paula Martin was born on October 9, 1967, in Pine Bluff, Arkansas, to Paula Kay Hamm Martin and R. A. Martin Jr. The family moved to Little Rock when she was twelve. Paula graduated from Little Rock's Parkview High School in 1986.

After high school, she traveled and lived in such locales as the U.S. Virgin Islands; Breckenridge, Colorado; and Miami, Florida, where she received a bachelor's degree in English from Florida International University. She earned a master's degree in creative writing from the University of New Orleans Creative Writing Workshop before returning to Arkansas in 2002.

Morell, the mother of three children, has taught creative writing for more than twenty years. She has been featured three times as an emerging writer at the International Conference on the Short Story in English, a biennial conference on the short story held in various locations around the world. Her writing workshop, "Invoking the Gifts," is used at arts centers, schools, and drug and alcohol treatment facilities nationwide.

Paula Morell's novel-in-stories, *broken water*, was published to positive reviews in 2006. Her creative nonfiction, poetry, and short stories have appeared in various publications such as *The Double Dealer Redux*, *Foliate Oak*, *New Works Review*, *Outsider Ink*, *Passport Journal*, *Quills and Pixels*, *Short Story Journal*, *Southern Hum*, and *Word Salad*.

In 2005, Morell embarked on two major projects. First, she established a small literary press called Temenos Publishing Company based in the Argenta Arts District of North Little Rock. Temenos, from the ancient Greek word referring to a sacred space, specializes in literary fiction, creative nonfiction, and books of poetry by Arkansas writers.

Within months of that start-up, she then became creator, producer, and host for the radio show *Tales from the South.* On *Tales*, amateur and professional writers read essays about their lives in the South, usually a representative experience, incident, or memory. The programs are recorded in front of a live audience. The thirty-minute programs are aired on KUAR, the Little Rock NPR affiliate. The shows also are distributed to YouTube, Stitcher Smart Radio, Public Radio Exchange, and iTunes, and are broadcast internationally on the World Radio Network (WRN).

The shows were originally recorded at North Little Rock's Starving Artist Café, a restaurant owned by Morell and her then-husband and business partner Jason Morell. After the restaurant closed in 2014, the program has been recorded at various venues around Arkansas.

Tales from the South includes live music by Southern musicians, and it generally features three writers who read a story of about five to eight minutes each. Once a month, the show hosts a special event, the Tin Roof Project, which features a well-known Southerner reading from an original work for about twenty minutes. Guest readers have included artists and politicians as well as authors Kevin Brockmeier, Janis Kearney [SEE ENTRY], Jay Jennings, and Grif Stockley; nationally known gardening and lifestyle expert P. Allen Smith; Broadway star Lawrence Hamilton; screenwriter Graham Gordy of TV's *Rectify*; and film stars Natalie Canerday (*Sling Blade* and *October Sky*) and Judge Reinhold *(Fast Times at Ridgemont High*, *Ruthless People*, and *Beverly Hills Cop)*.

Morell has stated that the series evolved when she was working as an online English professor for Florida's St. Leo University and a colleague asked for her help in getting submissions for a project. When that project did not materialize, Morell was left with a number of stories that had been submitted. She contacted NPR affiliate KUAR, broadcasting from the University of Arkansas at Little Rock, to inquire about using some of the stories on the radio. The basic format for *Tales from the South* soon followed.

Writers must either originally be from the South or currently live in the South, with Morell stating that she wants the stories to promote the "distinct Southern art of story-telling rich in language, detail, and voice."

Tales from the South was a finalist for the annual Stitcher Radio Award. Morell's work on *Tales from the South* was recognized with the Folklife Award, part of the 2013 Arkansas Governor's Arts Awards.

Morell's Temenos Publishing releases an annual anthology titled *Best of Tales from the South*, comprising fifty stories that were featured on the show during the calendar year.

For more information:

Matthews, Jaman. "Tales from the South: True Grits." *Arkansas Times*, April 6, 2011, pp. 14, 17. http://www.arktimes.com/arkansas/tales-from-the-south-true-grits/Content?oid=1626271 (accessed December 8, 2015).

Tales from the South. http://www.talesfromthesouth.com (accessed December 8, 2015).

Carry Nation (1846–1911)

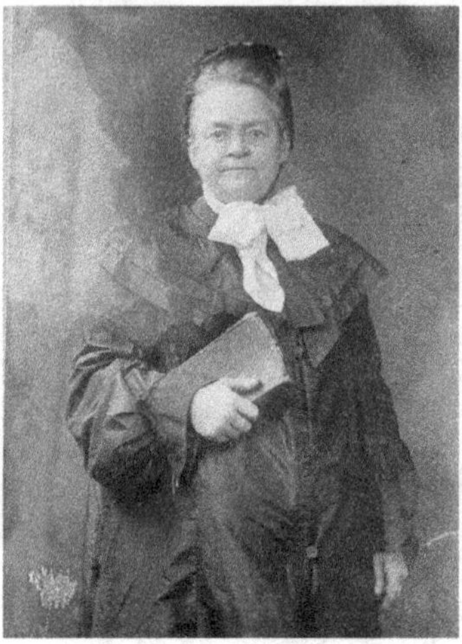

IN THE EARLY TWENTIETH CENTURY, before the coming of Prohibition in the United States, Carry (also spelled "Carrie") Nation violently opposed the sale of alcohol. She claimed that divine inspiration compelled her to destroy taverns—first with rocks and later with a hatchet. She became so well known that signs appeared in innumerable barrooms saying, "All Nations Welcome But Carrie." Her latter years were spent in Eureka Springs, Arkansas, where she made her final public appearance.

Both "Carrie" and "Carry" are considered correct renderings of her name. Some records say "Carrie," which she used at times, although "Carry" was inscribed in the family Bible by her father. Her autobiographical book is titled *The Use and Need of the Life of Carry A. Nation by Carry A. Nation.* She widely promoted that spelling in her temperance campaign, stating it stood for "Carry A Nation for Prohibition."

Carry Amelia Moore was born on November 25, 1846, in Garrard County, Kentucky, to Mary Campbell Moore and plantation owner George Moore. Mary Moore, who gave birth to six children, suffered from mental illness, ultimately thinking she was the Queen of England. Carry grew up under the care of enslaved people owned by her father. The family moved several times due to financial setbacks, with Carry growing up during the Civil War era as a sickly child who did not have much formal education.

In 1867, when she turned twenty-one, she married physician Charles Gloyd. Her parents did not approve. They knew he was an alcoholic, though Carry did not. His drinking problem became apparent after the marriage, and they separated shortly before the birth of their daughter, Charlien, in 1868. Charlien suffered from a mental disability, which Carry felt was caused by her husband's drinking. Gloyd died in 1869, soon after their separation.

With small inheritances from her late husband and father, Carry settled with her daughter in Holden, Missouri. There, she taught school for several years after earning her teaching certificate in 1872 from the Normal Institute in Warrensburg, Missouri.

In 1874, she married her second husband, David Nation, a part-time preacher, newspaper editor, and lawyer. It was not a happy marriage. They moved to Texas in 1877, where Carry eventually became a hotel manager. In 1889, they moved to Medicine Lodge, Kansas, where Carry Nation spoke publicly about the evils of tobacco and alcohol. She started a local branch of the Woman's Christian Temperance Union and began protesting at saloons.

When her peaceful protests had little effect, she prayed for guidance. She said that, in 1900, a voice told her to "Go to Kiowa," a Kansas town, followed by the words, "I'll stand by you." She later said she interpreted this as, "Take something in your hands, and throw at these places in Kiowa and smash them."

At first, she used large rocks to smash the barrooms' supply of liquor while she sang and prayed. After she damaged several Kansas saloons, a tornado hit nearby, which she took as divine approval of her actions. She continued her attacks with rocks until her husband joked that she should use a hatchet instead. She reportedly replied, "That is the most sensible thing you have said since I married you." They divorced in 1901.

Following his advice, she embarked on what she called "hatchetations," and was arrested at least thirty times between 1900 and 1910 in Arkansas, Kansas, Oklahoma, and Missouri, paying her fines from speaking fees and sales of souvenir hatchets. In Arkansas, she was jailed in Little Rock and arrested in Hot Springs, though released when she agreed to make a speech. Although she sometimes had eggs thrown at her, she also gained many admiring followers.

She brought her daughter to Hot Springs after the girl had been committed to an insane asylum in Texas, though they did not take up permanent residence in the city. Josephine Tussaud's Wax Museum in Hot Springs immortalized Nation with a waxen replica, sporting dour attire and her famous hatchet.

Along with appearing in vaudeville, Carry Nation lectured in the United States and Europe, selling photographs of herself and miniature souvenir hatchets. She published a newsletter called *The Smasher's Mail* and a newspaper, *The Hatchet*.

In 1910, saying she wanted a quiet, healthy place to live, she moved to Eureka Springs, buying a large home she called "Hatchet Hall." She took in boarders and offered religious instruction between travels. She reportedly dreamed that she would find a pure water spring in the rock across the street from her home. After blowing up a boulder with dynamite, water began flowing. Today it is called the Carry A. Nation Spring.

During a speech in Eureka Springs on January 13, 1911, she gasped, "I have done what I could," before lapsing into a coma. She died on June 2, 1911, at Evergreen Place Hospital in Kansas, of what doctors said was paresis, or organ failure, though some newspapers hinted at it being a complication of syphilis.

She was buried in an unmarked grave in Belton, Missouri. The Woman's Christian Temperance Union later erected a gravestone on which is inscribed, "Faithful to the Cause, She Hath Done What She Could." She left Hatchet Hall as a home for battered women. Though it has deteriorated, Hatchet Hall still stands in Eureka Springs.

For more information:

Grace, Fran. *Carry A. Nation: Retelling the Life*. Bloomington: Indiana University Press, 2001.

Taylor, Robert Lewis. *Vessel of Wrath: The Life and Times of Carry Nation*. New York: New American Library, Inc., 1966.

K. T. Oslin (1942–)

AWARD-WINNING SINGER AND SONGWRITER Kay Toinette ("K. T.") Oslin is known for a series of chart-topping country hits during the 1980s and early '90s. She was said to embody the spirit of the times with her biggest hit song, "80's Ladies." Achieving fame when she was over forty years old, the former Broadway chorus singer was called an unlikely star whose music is known for its worldly viewpoint as well as its humor. Her first album, *80's Ladies*, made country music history when it rose higher and faster on the charts than the debut work of any previous woman.

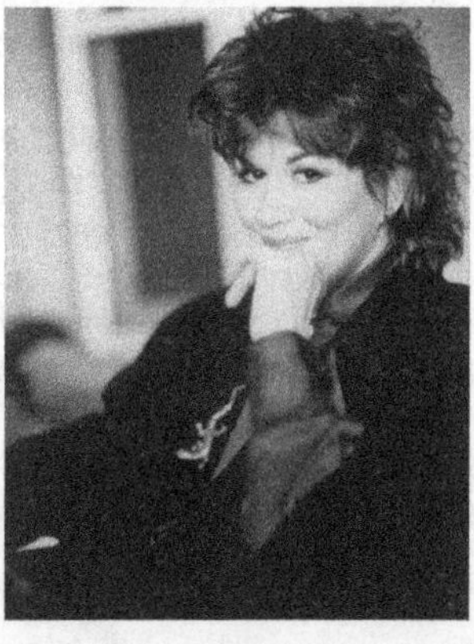

Kay Toinette Oslin was born on May 15, 1942, in Crossett, Arkansas. Her mother, Kathleen, was said to have been an aspiring young country singer whose parents refused to let her go on the road. When Oslin was two, her father, Harold, a foreman at a paper mill, died of leukemia at age thirty-eight. With Oslin's brother, Larry, the family traveled to various places as her mother, a hospital lab technician, sought work to support her family, marrying and divorcing four times along the way. They settled in Houston, Texas, when Oslin was five. She attended high school in Houston, first at Lamar and then at Milby High School, where she graduated with the class of 1960.

She attended East Texas Junior College and Lon Morris College, where she majored in drama as part of the college's noted theater program. She also joined Houston's folk music scene, performing in a folk trio.

After a brief sojourn to Los Angeles, she returned to Houston and performed in musical theater. She found her way to New York after joining the 1965 national touring company of *Hello, Dolly!* Winding up the tour in Manhattan, Oslin was signed to the chorus for the show's Broadway revival. While living in New York during the early 1970s, she also sang advertising jingles, appeared in television commercials, and found chorus work in Broadway musicals such as *Promises Promises* and a revival of *West Side Story*. At this time, she was writing songs that were recorded by others.

In 1981, Elektra Records released two of her singles, "Clean Your Own Tables" and "Younger Men (Are Startin' to Catch My Eye)," on which she was billed as "Kay T. Oslin." She was performing in Nashville, Tennessee, when a producer saw her potential. As "K. T. Oslin," she signed with the RCA Nashville label in 1987.

Her first album with RCA, *80's Ladies*, contained the single of the same name. Both hit the top of the charts, earning Oslin Grammy Awards for Best Female Country Vocal Performance and Song of the Year. Oslin became the first female songwriter to win the Country Music Association Song of the Year award. The follow-up singles from that album, "Do Ya" and "I'll Always Come Back," also hit number one. Her second album, *This Woman*, topped the charts in 1988, with hit singles "Hold Me," "This Woman," and "Hey Bobby."

In the late 1980s, singer/songwriter Oslin won award after award. The Country Music Association awarded her with Song of the Year for "80's Ladies" and named her 1988's Female Vocalist of the Year. Her Grammy Awards include Best Female Country Vocal Performance for "80's Ladies," Best Female Country Vocal Performance for "Hold Me," and 1989's Best Country Song for "Hold Me."

Her subsequent albums were *Love in a Small Town* in 1990, which yielded "Come Next Monday," another number-one hit for Oslin; a greatest-hits album, *Songs from an Aging Sex Bomb*, in 1993; and *My Roots Are Showing* in 1996. The early 2000s saw the release of two albums: *Live Close By, Visit Often* and *Simply.*

Her albums were successful, but Oslin suffered health problems beginning in the mid-1990s that forced her to stop touring. In 1995, Oslin had coronary bypass surgery. She took several acting assignments around this time, including co-starring with Harry Hamlin in the TV movie *Murder So Sweet* (also known as *Poisoned by Love: The Kern County Murders*), as well as the feature film *The Thing Called Love* with Sandra Bullock. She also acted in television shows such as *Evening Shade* with Burt Reynolds, a homespun comedy set in Arkansas.

She has performed onstage sporadically, such as appearing in a 1999 pops concert with the Nashville Symphony and at benefit concerts. Oslin became a popular convention speaker, and she reportedly began writing a memoir. In 2006, she presented a one-woman autobiographical stage play at Nashville's Belmont University.

Oslin presented a concert at Franklin, Tennessee, to celebrate the twenty-fifth anniversary of *80's Ladies*, and performed live onstage in 2014 at the Grand Ole Opry's Ryman Auditorium. Along with re-issues of her original albums, her hits have been spotlighted in Country Legends compilations.

For the most part, Oslin, who has never married, keeps a low profile. In an interview, she said that she asked her management, "Can I quit today and live the way I do, just back away?" Being told she could, Oslin stated, "I said, 'Then I'll do that.'"

For more information:

Dauphin, Chuck. "K. T. Oslin on Her Hiatus from Country Music: 'If This Business

Becomes Not Fun, You're Doomed.'" *Billboard.com*. http://www.billboard.com/articles/columns/country/6590501/kt-oslin-country-hiatus-interview (accessed December 8, 2015).

Twila Paris (1958–)

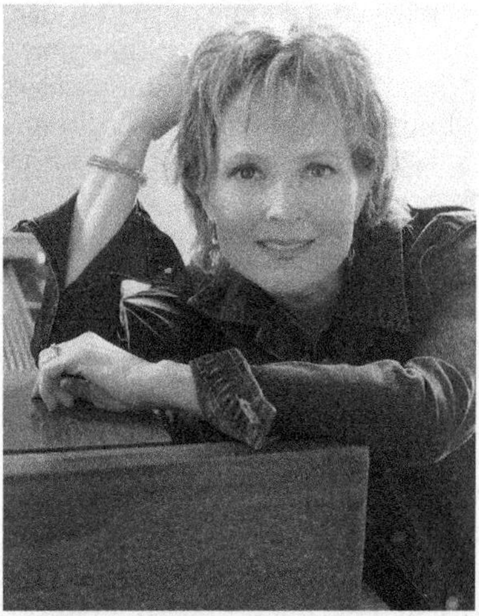

TWILA PARIS OF FAYETTEVILLE, Arkansas, is an award-winning author and musician in the contemporary Christian field who has published and recorded hundreds of songs. Among her best-known compositions are "He Is Exalted," "Lamb of God," "We Bow Down," and "We Will Glorify." To date, Paris has won ten Gospel Music Association Dove Awards and three American Songwriter Awards. She was named the Gospel Music Association's Female Vocalist of the Year three years in a row, and she has been inducted into the Gospel Music Association Hall of Fame. Many of her songs can be found in various church hymnals, both traditional and non-denominational, and are sung in religious observances.

Twila Inez Paris was born on December 28, 1958, in Fort Worth, Texas. She was one of four children born to songwriter Rachel Inez Paris and Oren Paris II, founder of Youth With A Mission ministries and Ecclesia College in Springdale, Arkansas.

Twila Paris was raised in Elm Springs, Arkansas. She was involved in church music since her childhood, composing words and music for songs since she was two years old. She began studying piano in 1965 at age six, the same year she released her first album, *Little Twila Paris*. She was offered a music scholarship to the University of Arkansas (UA) in Fayetteville, but she believed that she was called by God for ministry, attending Youth With A Mission discipleship training instead.

Her first full-length album, *Knowin' You're Around*, was released in 1981, almost immediately bringing the twenty-three-year-old Paris to the forefront of the contemporary Christian praise and worship genre. Since 1981, the singer-songwriter has released one album approximately every one to two years. These include the 1992 album *Sanctuary*, which won the GMA Praise and Worship Album of the Year. Along with greatest-hits albums and compilations, her albums include *Keepin' My Eyes On You*, *The Warrior Is a Child*, *Kingdom Seekers*, *Same Girl*, *For Every Heart*, *It's the Thought*, *Cry for the Desert*, *A Heart that Knows You*, *Beyond a Dream*, *The Time Is Now*, *Where I Stand*, *Perennial: Songs for the Seasons of Life*, *True North*, *House of Worship*, *He Is Exalted: Live Worship*, *Looking Up*, and *Small Sacrifice*. She released *Hymns* in 2014. Her children's album, *Bedtime Prayers: Lullabies & Peaceful Worship*, was released in 2001.

Along with the award-winning album *Sanctuary*, her GMA Dove Awards include Female Vocalist of the Year for 1993, 1994, and 1995; Song of the Year in 1995 for "God is in Control"; Special Event Album of the Year in 1996, 1997, and 1998; and Children's Music Album of the Year for *Bedtime Prayers*. She has also placed more than thirty singles in the top ten of the Adult Contemporary Christian charts.

Though less so in recent years, Paris toured extensively in the 1980s and '90s, at first as an opening act and later headlining her own concert tours as well as joining other artists for the Christian Classics Tour. In 2012, Paris released *God Shed His Grace*, a patriotic-themed album that Paris said was to inspire patriots with themes of God's protection and love, even in difficult times.

Her books echo the themes found in her music, often dealing with the topics of personal worship and praise in devotional life. Among her written works are *Making a Christmas Memory*, *In This Sanctuary: An Invitation To Worship The Savior* (a 1992 volume co-authored with Dr. Robert Webber), *Celebrate the Gift of Jesus Every Day*, *Perennial: Mediations for the Seasons of Life*, and *Bedtime Prayers and Lullabies*.

Paris said she has written Christian music to be accessible to all kinds of Christians. Her works can be found in collections such as the Baptist Hymnal and United Methodist Hymnal as well as in the praise and worship of non-denominational churches.

In 1985, Twila Paris married her manager, Jack Wright of Fayetteville. The couple has worked with Youth With A Mission as well as other Christian ministries. Paris has also been a spokesperson for World Vision, performing benefit concerts for that cause. In 2015, she was inducted into the Gospel Music Hall of Fame.

She and her husband have a son, J. P., home-schooled by Paris. She keeps busy writing and recording, saying, "It continues to be a calling and an honor and a privilege to be able to go and share His Word and sing these songs."

For more information:

Twila Paris. http://www.twilaparis.com (accessed December 8, 2015).

Pauline Pfeiffer (1895–1951)

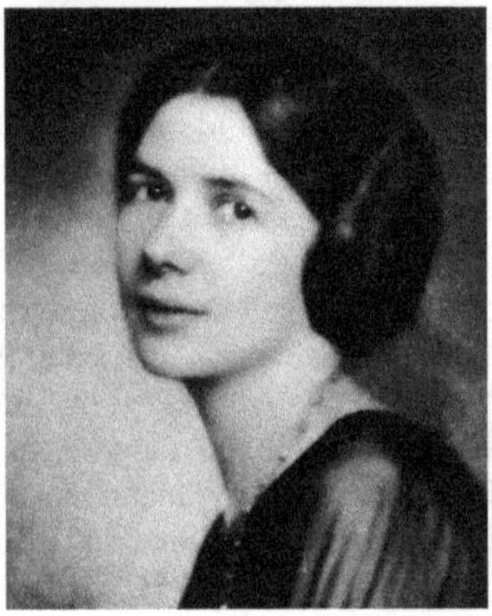

MARRIED TO FAMOUS AUTHOR Ernest Hemingway from 1927 to 1940, journalist Pauline Pfeiffer was the second of his four wives. At her wealthy family's home in Piggott, Arkansas, Hemingway wrote some of the works that would contribute to a 1954 Nobel Laureate in Literature for his contribution to writing. Hemingway himself credited Pauline Pfeiffer as being the best editor with whom he had ever worked. Sometimes called a smart, accomplished woman who made a questionable romantic choice, she is remembered as Hemingway's partner during his most significant creative period.

Pauline Marie Pfeiffer was born in Parkersburg, Iowa, on July 22, 1895. She had a younger sister, Virginia Ruth (called "Jinny"), and brother, Paul Mark. Their parents were Mary Downey Pfeiffer and wealthy businessman Paul Pfeiffer. When Pauline was six years old, she moved with the family to a comfortable home in St. Louis, Missouri, where her father joined the family chemical company. Pauline graduated from the St. Louis Academy of the Visitation in 1913, winning the prize for English. She entered the University of Missouri at Columbia, and she graduated in 1918 from the School of Journalism, the first such school in the nation.

While she was away at college, her family moved to Piggott, Arkansas. Paul Pfeiffer bought thousands of acres of land, overseeing tenant farmers and later going into the lumber business. Paul and Mary Pfeiffer were community leaders in Piggott, living in a spacious home. Pauline visited frequently, though after graduating from college, she set out on her own. She was able to find work as a journalist, starting in Ohio at the *Cleveland Press*, where she worked as a copyeditor. After relocating to Manhattan as a reporter for the *New York Morning Telegraph*, she soon moved to the glossy magazines *Vanity Fair* and *Vogue*.

On assignment for *Vogue*, Pauline Pfeiffer went to Paris in early 1925, accompanied by her sister. Within a month, they met up-and-coming writer Ernest Hemingway and his wife, Hadley. The group became friends, even vacationing together. Soon, an affair between Ernest Hemingway and Pauline Pfeiffer became known to the Paris arts community, including Hemingway's wife.

Hadley and Hemingway divorced in January 1927. Part of the agreement was that

Hemingway and Pfeiffer would separate for a hundred days to confirm that their affair was not a passing fancy. Pauline returned to the Pfeiffer home in Arkansas, during which time Hemingway sent her his manuscripts for editing.

In May 1927, Pauline Pfeiffer married Ernest Hemingway in Paris. As a devout Catholic, she asked Hemingway to convert to Catholicism before the marriage, which he did. The couple left Paris in March of 1928. Pauline was expecting their first child and wished to return to the United States. They arrived in Piggott, where Hemingway met the Pfeiffer family. He often spent time in Piggott hunting quail, but he worked regularly on his writing. A small barn at the Pfeiffer home was converted into his private writing studio, where he worked on the novel *A Farewell to Arms*.

Pauline gave birth to Patrick Hemingway in June 1928 after having a difficult labor and delivery. During this time, Hemingway was writing about the *Farewell to Arms* character Catherine Barkley having a difficult delivery and dying in childbirth. Hemingway found summertime in Arkansas too hot for him to write, departing for cooler climates to work and fish.

During the winter of 1932, he and Pauline came to Piggott for a holiday visit with their children. A second son, Gregory, had been born in 1931. The Hemingway short story "A Day's Wait," concerning the illness of a small boy, was written about this visit. It was published in a 1933 short-story collection, *Winner Take Nothing*, which was Hemingway's third and final collection of stories.

During Pfeiffer's marriage to Hemingway, several of his major works were published, including *A Farewell to Arms* in 1929, *Death in the Afternoon* in 1932, and 1935's *Green Hills of Africa*, an account of a 1933 safari with Pauline. Also during their marriage, the couple acquired two of the most iconic purchases in Hemingway lore: the yacht *Pilar* and a home in Key West, Florida.

In 1936, Hemingway met glamorous journalist Martha Gellhorn at a bar in Key West. At that time, he was completing the novel *To Have and Have Not*. His marriage to Pfeiffer was in conflict, partly due to each favoring opposite sides in the Spanish Civil War (1936–1939). Hemingway and Gellhorn departed to Spain to cover the war, afterward living together in Cuba while Pfeiffer remained in Key West.

Because of her Catholic beliefs, Pauline resisted divorce, but one was ultimately granted in 1940, three weeks before Ernest Hemingway's marriage to Gellhorn and soon after the publication of his *For Whom the Bell Tolls*.

Pauline Pfeiffer spent the rest of her life in Key West, though she often visited Jinny in California. She died there at age fifty-six on October 1, 1951. Her death, attributed to a brain hemorrhage, came after a bitter phone call between her and Hemingway concerning their son Gregory. She is buried in an unmarked grave at Hollywood Memorial Cemetery.

In the 1988 miniseries *Hemingway*, Pfeiffer was portrayed by award-winning actress Marisa Berenson. The Pfeiffer house and barn in Piggott were placed on the National Register of Historic Places in 1982, and the property is today the Hemingway-Pfeiffer Museum and Educational Center.

For more information:

Hawkins, Ruth. *Unbelievable Happiness and Final Sorrow: The Hemingway-Pfeiffer Marriage*. Fayetteville: University of Arkansas Press, 2012.

"Hemingway-Pfeiffer Museum and Educational Center." http://hemingway.astate.edu (accessed December 8, 2015).

Margaret Pittman (1901–1995)

WORLD-RENOWNED SCIENTIST DR. MARGARET PITTMAN was a pioneering researcher in microbiology and the immunology of infectious diseases, becoming instrumental in developing vaccines to prevent cholera, typhoid, and pertussis (also known as whooping cough). She was the first woman to head a major laboratory at the National Institutes of Health (NIH), and she worked with the World Health Organization as an expert on requirements for a cholera vaccine. She wrote more than ninety scientific papers, received the Federal Woman's Award, served as president of the Society of American Bacteriologists, and was president of the Washington Academy of Science.

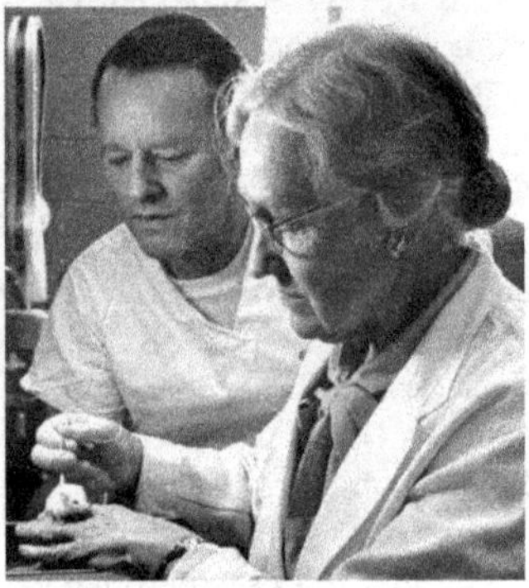

Margaret Pittman was born on January 20, 1901, in Prairie Grove, Arkansas. She was the daughter of Virginia McCormick Pittman and James Pittman, a country doctor. With her sister Helen and brother James, she would often accompany her father in his practice. In 1909, the family moved to the tiny northwestern Arkansas community of Cincinnati, where Margaret sometimes helped with administering anesthesia and vaccinating her father's patients.

In 1919, her father died suddenly after surgery for appendicitis. He had left instructions that all his children would attend Hendrix College in Conway, Arkansas. Margaret's mother worked as a dressmaker, also selling canned fruits and vegetables to help pay tuition at Hendrix. Margaret graduated from Hendrix magna cum laude in 1923, earning a bachelor's degree in biology and mathematics. She was a teacher and principal at Galloway Women's College in Searcy, which would later merge with Hendrix.

Saving as much of her teaching money as possible, she was able to attend the University of Chicago, from which she received a master's degree in bacteriology in 1926. At that time, she was offered a fellowship to pursue a PhD, which she called "an opportunity undreamed of."

Her fellowship allowed her to work as a research scientist at the Rockefeller Institute of Medical Research in New York before receiving her PhD from the University of Chicago in 1929. At the time, bacteriology was a relatively new science. Having lived through the deadly "Spanish flu" pandemic of 1918, Pittman began research centered around infectious diseases such as influenza. In the early twentieth century, such diseases as diphtheria, pneumonia, scarlet fever, typhoid, and whooping cough could be lethal, especially to children. Pittman's research made advances that significantly lowered the death rate. Before she was thirty years old, Pittman earned an international reputation for her work on a vaccine against meningitis associated with influenza, a strain that often resulted in blindness and sometimes death in younger children.

In 1934, Pittman took a job at the New York State Department of Health Laboratories, where she worked on injectable vaccines and antisera, or biologics. With more federal funding available for medical research under the New Deal, Pittman joined the NIH in 1936. With her research partner, she introduced the first statistical method into biologics testing. Her findings led her to champion the concept that a vaccine's effectiveness is related to its potency. Pittman became known for developing standardized methods to test that potency.

The onset of World War II led Pittman to work with blood plasma, as massive amounts were being used to treat the wounded. Transfusions sometimes caused ill effects such as severe fever and chills. Her work involved developing means for ensuring its safety through tests for sterility to protect transfusion recipients, such as keeping donated blood in small vials rather than a mass container.

In 1943, Pittman conducted research at the new NIH Division of Biologics Control in Bethesda, Maryland, near Washington DC. By 1949, Pittman's work had led to setting standards for the pertussis vaccine, both in the United States and globally through the World Health Organization. This resulted in a worldwide decreased mortality rate from the disease.

In 1958, Pittman was named Chief of the Laboratory of Bacterial Products, becoming the first woman to head an NIH laboratory. She held this post until her mandatory retirement in 1971. After retirement, she continued to work as an unpaid researcher with such organizations as the Cholera Research Laboratory in what is today Bangladesh. She served as a consultant to the World Health Organization in formulating requirements for cholera and typhoid vaccines, and she was invited to be a guest scientist in countries including Egypt, Iran, Scotland, and Spain.

In 1986, she was elected to an honorary fellowship in the American Academy of Pediatrics for her efforts in improving the health and welfare of children. In 1994, the Margaret Pittman Lectureship at the NIH was established to honor her accomplishments. Her collected papers are preserved at the NIH's National Library of Medicine in Bethesda, along with an oral history about Pittman at the Office of NIH History.

Ninety-four-year-old Margaret Pittman died on August 19, 1995, of kidney failure and congestive heart failure at Prince George's Hospital Center in Cheverly, Maryland. Her body was returned to Arkansas to be buried at Prairie Grove Cemetery.

Among her honors was the Federal Women's Award in 1970, which stated that "her ability to identify problems, stimulate research and evaluate results [has] made her an unusually effective leader."

For more information:

Dowling, Harry F. *Fighting Infection: Conquests of the Twentieth Century*. Cambridge, MA: Harvard University Press, 1977.

O'Hern, Elizabeth Moot. *Profiles of Pioneer Women Scientists*. New York: Acropolis Books, 1986.

Pittman, Margaret. "A Life with Biological Products." *Annual Review of Microbiology* 44 (1990): 1–25.

Anita Pointer (1948–)

ANITA POINTER IS AN ORIGINAL MEMBER OF THE POINTER SISTERS singing group. Although the family resided in Oakland, California, Anita Pointer lived for several years at her grandparents' home in Prescott, Arkansas, where she attended school. She achieved stardom both with the Pointer Sisters and solo, singing lead vocals on the group's major hits such as "Fire," "Freedom," "Insanity, "I'm So Excited," and "Slow Hand." She still owns land in Prescott.

Anita Marie Pointer was born on January 23, 1948, in Oakland, the fourth child born to Sarah Silas Pointer and the Reverend Elton Pointer. Her parents had six children, four of whom were daughters. Rev. and Mrs. Pointer were both from Arkansas, having married in the town of Prescott. The couple's two sons, Fritz and Aaron, were born in Little Rock, but the family moved to Oakland before the girls were born.

Both of the Pointers were ministers at the West Oakland Church of God in Christ. Each year, they made an annual car trip to visit family in Arkansas, though it was often a "working vacation" related to the ministry. Anita Pointer loved visiting her grandparents in Prescott, a small rural town in the southwestern part of the state. Racially, the town was almost equally split between black and white, with the railroad tracks literally dividing the town in half.

One year, Anita did not want to return home to Oakland. She was allowed to stay in Prescott with her grandparents to attend fifth grade. She then returned to Arkansas for the seventh grade and again for tenth grade. While in Arkansas, she attended Prescott's all-black McRae Elementary, Junior High, and Senior High, named for the Prescott resident who donated the land, not for the northeastern Arkansas town of McRae.

Pointer said that she immediately noticed the differences between Oakland and the racially segregated Prescott, saying, "Going to school in the segregated South is an experience that will bring history to life....Only being allowed to sit in the balcony of the movie theatre, picking up food from the back door of the restaurant because you can't go inside, picking cotton, I did all that and then some."

While at Prescott, Pointer was a member of the McRae High School Band in which she played alto saxophone. While she was growing up, Anita Pointer and her sisters sang gospel in their father's church. However, they soon developed an interest in rhythm and blues, which their parents called "the devil's music." In Arkansas, Pointer was occasionally able to listen to broadcasts from the Grand Ole Opry and surreptitiously experience local "juke joints" (dance halls frequented by African Americans of the era). In Oakland, the Pointer household was a strict one, with dancing, dating, and music outside the church forbidden.

Anita Pointer married at age seventeen. In 1966, she had a daughter, Jada, for whom a Pointer Sisters song was named. The couple divorced, and Jada died in 2003.

Bonnie and June Pointer called themselves "Pointers, A Pair" and began performing as a duo at Bay Area clubs in 1969. With the addition of twenty-one-year-old Anita, who quit her job at a law office to sing bluesy pop music, the Pointer Sisters musical group was born. Their sister Ruth joined the group in 1972. The group sang back-up in clubs and studio sessions for Bay Area acts. After signing a record contract, they wanted to create an original bluesy jazz sound. Also searching for a "look," they recalled the poverty of Prescott's black citizens and their spirited ability to improvise. The Pointer Sisters bought vintage 1940s clothing from thrift shops for their distinctive onstage costumes.

They released their debut album in 1973. Following its success, the Pointer Sisters became the first black female group ever to perform at the Grand Ole Opry in Nashville, where they sang their hit song "Fairytale" in 1974. They said they were serious about country music, stating, "For us, it's no joke....Our folks came from Arkansas and we grew up singing country songs. It's part of us."

The Pointer Sisters won their first Grammy Award in 1975 for Best Country Performance by a Duo or Group. Elvis Presley would later record his own version of "Fairytale," which was co-written by Anita Pointer. In 1986, Anita again made the country charts with "Too Many Times," a duet with Earl Thomas Conley; it rose to the number-two spot.

With the Pointer Sisters, Anita Pointer toured the world, and she appeared on television shows such as *American Bandstand*, *Soul Train*, *The Flip Wilson Show*, *The Carol Burnett Show*, *The Tonight Show*, and *Arsenio Hall*. Her acting roles include the 1976 movie *Car Wash* with Richard Pryor, as well as TV appearances on *Gimme a Break* and *The Love Boat*. Anita Pointer also sang on the all-star recording of "We Are the World," the 1985 single to help famine relief efforts in Africa.

Anita and Ruth Pointer continue to perform. Throughout her stellar career, Anita Pointer has retained her Arkansas roots, saying, "I do feel like home is where the heart is, and my heart feels at home in Arkansas."

For more information:

Pointer Sisters. http://www.thepointersisters.com (accessed December 8, 2015).

Florence Price (1887–1953)

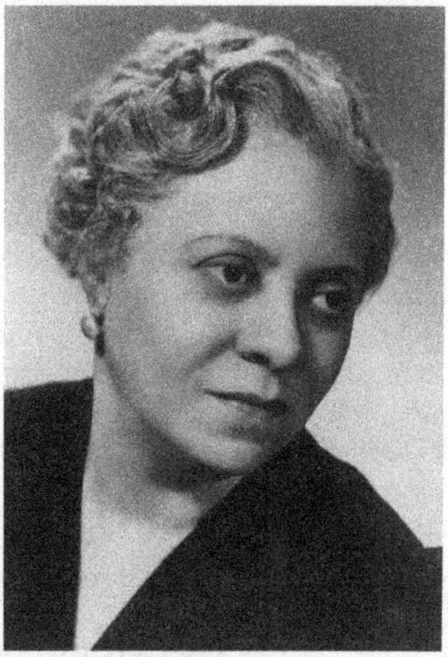

CLASSICAL COMPOSER FLORENCE PRICE was the first African American woman to be nationally recognized for her symphonic works, the first to have a musical composition played by a major American symphony orchestra, and the most widely known black woman composer from the 1930s to the 1950s.

Florence Beatrice Smith was born in Little Rock, Arkansas, on April 9, 1887. She was one of three children. Her mother was Florence Gulliver Smith—who was a musician, teacher, and businesswoman—and her father was Dr. James H. Smith, a dentist, teacher, and inventor. Both of her parents were considered "mulattoes," or African Americans of mixed racial heritage and fair complexions. Until the advent of Jim Crow laws in the 1890s, the family moved in both black and white societies, with Dr. Smith having several white patients and Mrs. Smith able to buy and sell real estate in her own name.

As a child, Florence Beatrice, as she was known, was trained in music by her mother and performed her first piano recital when she was four years old. At age eleven, her first composition was published. She attended Little Rock's all-black Capitol Hill School, from which she graduated at age fourteen as valedictorian in 1903.

Florence Beatrice enrolled in the New England Conservatory of Music in Boston, Massachusetts, a remarkable achievement for a woman of color at the time. At the Conservatory, her compositions so impressed its director, George Whitefield Chadwick, that he took her as a private student, something he did for only the most gifted. She wrote her first string trio and symphony at the conservatory, graduating with honors in 1907 with a diploma in organ and a teaching certificate for piano.

She returned to Arkansas to teach at an all-black school in rural Cotton Plant and at Shorter College in Little Rock. She moved to Atlanta, Georgia, in 1910, to become the head of Clark University's music department, but she came back to Little Rock in 1912 to marry distinguished attorney Thomas Jewell Price. They had two daughters, Florence Louise and Edith Cassandra, as well as a son, Thomas Jr. Their son died young, and Florence Price wrote a song for him called "To My Little Son."

Florence Price opened a music studio in Little Rock, where she offered piano lessons and wrote musical compositions that won national awards. After a number of racial incidents in Little Rock, including a lynching, the Price family moved to Chicago in 1927. There, Florence Price found more opportunity for professional growth. She attended the American Conservatory of Music, Chicago Musical College, and Chicago Teachers' College while becoming a noted Chicago-area music teacher, pianist, and organist. She published four pieces for piano in 1928, the year the major publishing firm of G. Schirmer published Price's work *At the Cotton Gin*. After her marriage ended and she struggled financially to provide for her two daughters, Florence Price also worked as an organist for silent films and composed songs for radio ads.

By 1932, Price was winning national awards for her compositions such as *Piano Sonata in E Minor* and *Symphony in E Minor*. The Chicago Symphony Orchestra performed the premiere of *Symphony in E Minor* in 1933, making Price's work the first composition by an African American woman to be played by a major orchestra.

Florence Price would go on to compose more than 300 works. These ranged from small studies for piano to chamber music, vocal pieces, and popular music for the radio as well as large-scale concertos and symphonies. Her compositions often mixed the classical European styles she had studied with music of the African American culture such as spirituals and African dance rhythms. Some of her songs reflect her Arkansas roots, such as "Arkansas Jitter" and "Dance of the Cotton Blossoms." Her larger pieces such as *Concert Overture on Negro Spirituals* and *Negro Folksongs in Counterpoint* also reflect the black heritage.

Her symphonic work was performed by orchestras in Detroit, Pittsburgh, and Brooklyn, as well as by the Chicago Women's Symphony and European orchestras. Her work was also performed as part of the Century of Progress Exhibition at the 1933 Chicago World's Fair. Price's arrangement of the spiritual "My Soul's Been Anchored in de Lord" was sung in 1939 by opera star Marian Anderson at the iconic concert on the steps of the Lincoln Memorial in Washington DC, broadcast to an international audience. Anderson would later include Price's music in her regular concert repertoire.

Some sources say that despite her teaching credentials, Price had been denied membership into the Arkansas State Music Teachers Association in the 1920s because of her race. However, for her work as a composer, Florence Price was inducted into the prestigious American Society of Composers, Authors, and Publishers (ASCAP) in 1940.

Sixty-six-year-old Florence Price died in Chicago on June 3, 1953, after suffering a stroke while planning a European trip. A Chicago elementary school is named for Price in recognition of her work as a significant American musician and composer.

For more information:

Ammer, Christine. *Unsung: A History of Women in American Music*. Portland, OR: Amadeus Press, 2001.

Brown, Rae Linda. "Lifting the Veil: The Symphonies of Florence B. Price." *Symphonies Nos. 1 and 3 by Florence Price*. Music of the United States of America, Volume 19. Middleton, WI: A-R Editions, 2008.

Lee Purcell

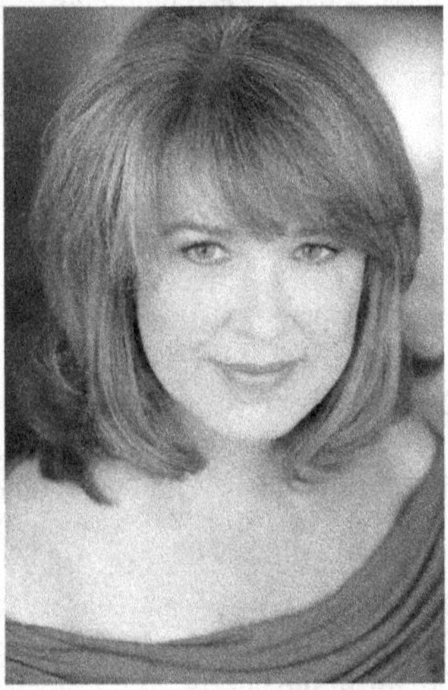

EMMY-NOMINATED ACTRESS, producer, writer, and director Lee Purcell has starred in numerous films, television shows, and stage productions in her ongoing long and successful career. She was personally mentored by legendary movie star Steve McQueen, who said he chose her from about 500 women because she "seemed to jump right out of the screen."

She was born Lee Jeune Williams at the Cherrypoint Marine Corps Air Station, North Carolina. In private life, she is known as Lee Williams-Purcell; professionally, she is known as Lee Purcell. Lee's father, Major Frank D. Williams Jr., was a highly decorated U.S. Marine Corps pilot who was killed while on active duty when Lee was a young child. Lee was then placed into the care of various maternal and paternal relatives until her mother, Ollie L. McKnight Williams, remarried. Ollie's second husband, Don Purcell, was a navy doctor assigned to the U.S. Marine Corps, so they frequently moved to various military bases. At the end of Dr. Purcell's military service, they moved to the small town of Paragould, Arkansas.

Lee began her dance training at the age of three, and from age five, she made frequent television appearances for several years, performing on a Memphis, Tennessee, talent show. She appeared in her first stage operetta at age seven and was performing as a dancer in a traveling troupe by the time she was thirteen, creating her own choreography and costume designs.

After graduating from Paragould High School, Lee left Arkansas to work her way west and later moved to Los Angeles. She was injured in a car accident, so she was unable to dance for a living. She worked selling clothes in a Los Angeles boutique to pay for her education and her expenses, having no familial assistance.

She continued studying acting in Los Angeles and furthered her studies when she moved to London, England. She eventually found work in modeling and commercials to support herself until acting jobs came along. Her big break came when she was personally chosen by Steve McQueen for what would be her first feature film. McQueen selected her to star in his company's production of *Adam at Six A.M.*, with Michael Douglas, and McQueen mentored Lee. Lee has always said McQueen was like the father that she had lost so young.

The model-slim Lee Purcell was told by McQueen that she had to gain 20 pounds to play the role. McQueen showed her exercises and diet to increase her weight, which she did successfully. Interestingly, the exercises from McQueen were those of his personal trainer, the martial arts star Bruce Lee.

She later lived in London for several years, where she continued her drama education, studied French, and extensively traveled in Europe, while commuting to the U.S. for film and television work. She eventually moved back to Los Angeles and has steadily worked all over the world ever since. After her movie debut in *Adam at 6 A.M.*, she starred in feature films *Kids vs. Monsters*, *Mr. Majestyk*, *Big Wednesday*, *Stir Crazy*, *Eddie Macon's Run*, and *Valley Girl*, among many others.

Lee has been nominated for two Emmy Awards for her television work in *Secret Sins of the Father* opposite Beau Bridges and *Long Road Home* opposite Mark Harmon. She portrayed the continuing character of Eleanor Sullivan in the NBC-TV series *Persons Unknown* and the role of State's Attorney Louise St. Laurent (originally written for a male character named Louis) in the CBS-TV series *Due South*. She has appeared often in other TV series, including *Murder, She Wrote*; *The Rockford Files*; *Hawaii Five-O*; *The Waltons*; *Streets of San Francisco*; *Magnum P.I.*; *Matlock*; *Simon & Simon*; *Bonanza*; and *MacGyver*. She has also starred in a number of TV movies/mini-series, including Wes Craven's *Stranger in Our House* (also known as *Summer of Fear*); *Murder in Music City*, opposite Sonny Bono; and *The Gambler*, opposite Kenny Rogers.

Lee is especially noted for portraying Hollywood legends Billie Dove and Olivia de Havilland in the TV movies/mini-series *Howard, the Amazing Mr. Hughes*, opposite Tommy Lee Jones, and *My Wicked, Wicked Ways: The Legend of Errol Flynn*, respectively. She has starred with many popular leading men, including two father-son duos: Kirk and Michael Douglas, and Lloyd and Beau Bridges.

Lee has also been active as a director, producer, and writer, and she co-owned a niche video production company that won a silver medal at the New York Film and TV Festival. She also launched a style website called "BoomerBabes," for baby-boomer women. She was also a performer, co-owner, and co-director of the Green River Ropin' and Recitin' Preservation Society Players, troupe of actors and musicians that performed western literature and music from the 1800s.

Lee Purcell has returned regularly to London as a director, performer, and lecturer, and she travels often to other parts of the world. Her son, Dylan Dunn Purcell, was briefly an actor, appearing with Lee in a few projects. Lee has been involved with many philanthropic groups over the years, including the Special Olympics, Big Brothers, Paralyzed Veterans of America, Heart of a Horse, and Veterans Entertainment Team.

For more information:

Lee Purcell. http://www.leepurcell.com (accessed December 8, 2015).

Lessie Stringfellow Read (1891–1971)

LESSIE STRINGFELLOW READ was a nationally known journalist, newspaper editor, advocate of women's suffrage, and national press chair for the largest women's organization of the early twentieth century. She was on speaking terms with noted figures of her time such as Thomas Edison and John D. Rockefeller, but she is often best known for her colorful connection to spiritualism.

She was born Mabel Staples in Temple, Texas, on January 3, 1891. Her birth parents, William and Lillian Staples, both died from a fever when she was two years old. She was adopted by family friends Alice Johnston Stringfellow, the well-educated daughter of a wealthy Texas physician, and Henry Martyn Stringfellow, a Virginia native who had been posted to Texas in the Civil War. Henry and Alice made their home in Galveston when the war ended. After talking with a man who had grown grapes in Texas before the war, Stringfellow began studying horticulture. He established an orchard and went on to attain wealth and world renown for his pioneering work in the Texas citrus industry.

Henry and Alice Stringfellow had been devastated when their only child, a nineteen-year-old son named Leslie, died from malaria in 1886. Before dying, Leslie promised to contact his mother from beyond. Henry Stringfellow was interested in the then-fashionable field of spiritualism and was a member of the Rosicrucian Order. Though his wife did not originally believe in spiritualism, they sat each evening with a *planchette*, similar to a Ouija board, communicating with their dead son through "spirit writing." As friends of the Staples family, they adopted the orphaned Mabel, with their dead son not only approving but suggesting her name be changed to "Lessie," a childhood pronunciation of "Leslie."

Lessie Stringfellow grew up on her adoptive family's orchard near the Gulf Coast town of Hitchcock, Texas. Her parents taught Lessie at home. They also arranged for a Stanford University professor to tutor her privately in the summers. As a teenager, Lessie contributed articles about local news to the *Houston Chronicle*.

In 1910, when she was nineteen, Lessie married pharmacist James Read. With the Stringfellows, the couple moved to Fayetteville, Arkansas, where Henry Stringfellow died in 1912. The next year, Lessie Read's husband vanished under a cloud of suspicion regarding embezzlement. Nominally married but without its responsibilities, Lessie Stringfellow Read enjoyed moving freely in society without the restrictions placed on a single woman. By 1915, she had become a respectable young matron who was involved in women's organizations, notably founding the local Women's Suffrage Association.

In 1916, she was named national press director for the era's largest international women's organization, the General Federation of Women's Clubs (GFWC), also serving as editor of their *General Federation News*. In 1918, Read coordinated the GFWC's national convention, which was held at Hot Springs, Arkansas.

She directed national press for GFWC conventions until 1926, interacting with notable figures such as Thomas Edison, John D. Rockefeller, and Carrie Chapman Catt, who was president of the American Woman's Suffrage Association. While in Fayetteville to deliver a lecture, Catt stayed in Read's home.

With the onset of World War I, the editor of the Fayetteville newspaper left for the army. Read assumed his position in 1918 and performed so well that when he returned from the war, he refused her offer to resign and took another position with the paper. Read remained as editor for almost thirty years. The work situation was unique, with the newspaper having women as both its owner, Roberta Fulbright [SEE ENTRY], and its only full-time reporter. Read joined Fulbright in a heated clash with the corrupt local sheriff and circuit court judge in 1933. The women used the newspaper to mobilize churches and community organizations in forcing the corrupt officials out of office, never succumbing to frequent threats.

Read remained editor of what would become the *Northwest Arkansas Times* until her retirement in 1945. She continued filing stories with the Associated Press, *Memphis Commercial Appeal*, and *St. Louis Post-Dispatch*. Her articles appeared in national magazines such as *Good Housekeeping* and the *Saturday Evening Post.* She wrote on a wide range of topics from poetry to women's rights, and had a keen interest in history, becoming a founding member of the Arkansas Historical Association in 1942.

In 1926, at the encouragement of "Sherlock Holmes" creator Sir Arthur Conan Doyle, Read helped her mother publish a collection of Leslie Stringfellow's spirit letters, saying it might ease the pain of others mourning loved ones. Quietly, Read sometimes held séances in her home. She lived alone until her health failed in the late 1960s, spending her latter years at the Fayetteville City Hospital. She died on May 28, 1971, at the age of eighty, and is buried at Fayetteville's historic Evergreen Cemetery.

For more information:

Chism, Stephen. *The Afterlife of Leslie Stringfellow: A Nineteenth-Century Southern Family's Experiences with Spiritualism*. Fayetteville: University of Arkansas Press, 2006.

———. "The Very Happiest Tiding: Sir Arthur Conan Doyle's Correspondence with Arkansas Spiritualists." *Arkansas Historical Quarterly* 59 (Autumn 2000): 299–310.

Dillard, Tom W. *Statesmen, Scoundrels, and Eccentrics: A Gallery of Amazing Arkansans*. University of Arkansas Press, 2010.

Jenny Delony Rice (1866–1949)

JENNY DELONY RICE WAS THE FIRST FEMALE ARTIST from Arkansas to rise to international fame as a painter. She was a noted portraitist; her miniature of Britain's Queen Victoria was displayed in New York. In addition to portraits, she worked in the artistic genres of landscape, still life, nature, and scenes of everyday life. Returning periodically from New York and Europe to a studio in Little Rock, she also pioneered art education in Arkansas.

Jenny Eakin Delony was born on May 13, 1866, in Washington, Arkansas, a small community in the southwestern part of the state. Her parents were Elizabeth Pearson Delony and attorney Alchyny Turner Delony, who opened a school at Washington after the Civil War. Jenny Delony was the eldest of three surviving children, having a sister, Daisy, and a brother, Arch. In 1890, the family moved to a home at 616 Rock Street in Little Rock.

After her elementary education, Jenny Delony spent four years at Wesleyan Female Institute, which later became Stuart Hall School in Staunton, Virginia. From 1886 to 1888, Delony studied at the Cincinnati Art Academy, after which she left for Paris, France. There, she studied at Académie Julian followed by Académie Delécluse, and in the studio of noted French painter Paul-Louis Delance.

Delony established her first professional art studio in Little Rock in 1891, painting portraits of distinguished local citizens. That same year, she married businessman Nathaniel Rice of Denver, Colorado, although he died two years after their marriage. She began signing her paintings "Delony Rice."

She studied at the St. Louis School of Art beginning in 1892, followed by a return to Europe around 1895 to study in Venice with Italian painter Stefano Novo. However, she soon found a landmark opportunity in Paris. The École des Beaux-Arts in Paris was known for training many of the greatest artists in Europe for more than three centuries. In 1896, women were admitted for the first time, with Jenny Delony of Arkansas among them. That same year, she was one of the first women allowed to study artistic anatomy at the École de Médecine in Paris.

When she returned to the United States, she studied with American impressionist painter William Merritt Chase in New York, also serving as his personal assistant for over a decade at Shinnecock, a summer school Chase conducted at Southampton, Long

Island, around the turn of the century.

During this period, Delony began her own career as an art educator. She taught art in Virginia between 1893 and 1896. She returned to Arkansas in 1897, where she was the first director of art at the University of Arkansas (UA) in Fayetteville. She was the founder of UA's art department and initiated the state's first baccalaureate art program.

She left Fayetteville in 1900 to establish a studio in New York City. Her miniature of Queen Victoria was exhibited at Tiffany's on New York's Fifth Avenue, providing her work both prominence and prestige. In 1905, her portrait of Hetty Green, who was called the richest woman in America, was run on a full page in the *New York Times*, making Delony as much of a celebrity as her subject.

Delony was a supporter of the women's suffrage movement and was chosen to represent American women as an exhibitor at the International Council of Women's congress at Berlin, Germany, in 1904.

On November 21, 1910, the *New York Times* ran an announcement of the wedding between prominent optician Paul Alexander Meyrowitz and "Mrs. Jennie Delony Rice, a portrait painter," both of New York City. However, the union was not a happy one, and they quietly separated in the early 1920s.

She was a member of organizations such as the American Artists Professional League, Association of Women Painters and Sculptors, National Academy of Design, and National Arts Club. She was one of the first women to exhibit at the National Academy of Design. Her works have been exhibited in Boston, Philadelphia, and New York, and at the Woman's Art Club of New York and the New York Water Color Club. She was represented at national exhibitions such as the World Cotton Centennial Exposition in New Orleans and 1893's famed World's Columbian Exposition in Chicago.

When Delony retired in 1935, she left New York to return to Little Rock, where she lived with her sister Daisy in the family home. There, she established a studio and continued to paint. She died of cancer at age eighty-three on April 1, 1949. She is buried at Little Rock's Oakland Cemetery. Though she signed the name "Delony Rice" on her paintings, her tombstone reads "Jenny D. Meyrowitz."

For more information:

Opitz, Glen B., ed. *Mantle Fielding's Dictionary of American Painters, Sculptors, and Engravers*. Poughkeepsie, NY: Apollo, 1987.

Who's Who in America 1948–1949. Vol. 25. Chicago: A. N. Marquis, 1949.

Sarah Northrup Ridge (1804–1856)

SARAH NORTHRUP RIDGE was at the center of a national scandal when she married Cherokee leader John Ridge. She was part of the forced removal of the Cherokee, culminating in the notorious Trail of Tears, along which thousands died. Settling in Fayetteville, Arkansas, after the murder of her husband, she was instrumental in establishing the town's reputation as an educational center, helping influence the decision to locate the University of Arkansas (UA) in that town.

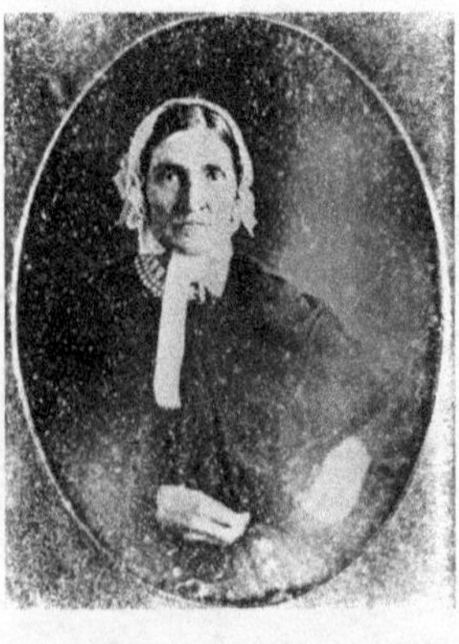

Sarah Bird Northrup was born on December 7, 1804, in Cornwall, Connecticut. Her parents were Lydia Camp Northrup and John Prout Northrup, who was steward of the American Board of Commissioners for Foreign Missions School in Cornwall, which accepted Cherokee students.

The Cherokee, primarily from Georgia, were trying to assimilate into the white population that was steadily encroaching all around them. By the early 1800s, the Cherokee had adopted Christianity and were residing in the same kinds of homes as the whites, raising the same crops and living the same lifestyle. However, when gold was discovered in Georgia in 1828, there was increasing pressure from the State of Georgia and the U.S. government to remove the Cherokee west of the Mississippi.

Cherokee leaders believed that reading and writing English were important in conducting themselves among white government officials. Along with inviting missionaries to live among them to operate schools, they sent Cherokee students to schools such as Cornwall. In 1821, one of the Cherokee students at Cornwall was John Ridge (1802–1839), son of a wealthy Cherokee leader. The eighteen-year-old Ridge had health problems that were aggravated by the cold New England winters. When his condition worsened, he was moved from the dormitory to a room in the Northrup home. There, the handsome Ridge and fourteen-year-old Sarah Bird Northrup fell in love.

Sarah's disapproving family sent her away to live with her grandparents. John Ridge's parents also disapproved, insisting he marry a Cherokee woman. Despite opposition from both families, John Ridge and Sarah Bird Northrup were married in Connecticut on January 27, 1824. It set off a firestorm, with the news spreading around the country. For couples who engaged in such "mixed" marriages, editorials suggested horsewhipping or worse. To avoid being mobbed, John and Sarah Ridge quickly left Connecticut for the Cherokee capital of New Echota, Georgia. They settled on a plantation estate of more than 400 acres, and they had seven children.

John Ridge became an attorney and was a leading member of the Cherokee National Council. Sarah Ridge dressed in silk gowns and oversaw the plantation, which had thirty servants, including enslaved African Americans.

The desire of white Americans for Cherokee lands intensified as word spread about gold in Georgia. In 1838, the U.S. Army began removing the Cherokee at gunpoint west to Indian Territory (today's Oklahoma). The Cherokee became divided into two factions. The Ridge Party, led by John Ridge's family, felt that removal was inevitable. The Ross Party, under the leadership of John Ross, swore to fight removal.

John Ridge was among those who signed the removal treaty. Members of the Ridge Party left their Cherokee homeland for Indian Territory, the onset of what would be called the Trail of Tears, on which thousands of Cherokee died. John and Sarah Ridge, with their children, settled at a place called Honey Creek near the Arkansas border.

John Ridge was assassinated in 1839 for his part in negotiating the loss of Cherokee lands. Sarah Ridge took her children and fled to Fayetteville. She brought with her educator Sophia Sawyer (1792–1854), who had taught the Ridge family and other Cherokee children both in Georgia and at Honey Creek.

In 1839, Sophia Sawyer founded the Fayetteville Female Seminary, where prominent white and Cherokee children were students. The Fayetteville Female Seminary enjoyed an outstanding reputation even after Sawyer's death in 1854. Sawyer's school remained open until 1862, when it was burned during the Civil War. Still, its status was a significant factor in Fayetteville's reputation as a center of superior education. This helped in establishing the state's land grant university, UA, in Fayetteville rather than in a more central, easily accessible part of the state. Sarah Ridge was advised by her friend Sawyer to find solace in hard work following the murder of the husband for whose sake she had been ostracized nationally. Ridge helped at the Sawyer school, which was built near Ridge's home.

Because John Ridge died without a will, Sarah Ridge was compelled to travel from Fayetteville to Indian Territory to sort out his financial affairs for her children. Once she had confirmed her children's security, she returned permanently to Fayetteville. On March 31, 1856, Sarah Northrup Ridge died of pneumonia. She is buried at Fayetteville's Mount Comfort Cemetery.

The Sarah Ridge House remained in the family as long as they lived, after which it passed to a succession of owners. It is the oldest house still standing in Fayetteville, dating back to 1836. According to the Washington County Historical Society, which preserved the home, its original pine flooring and fieldstone fireplaces survived the Civil War and have endured ever since. In 1972, it was listed on the National Register of Historic Places and is an unofficial Trail of Tears landmark to recognize the forced removal of the Cherokee.

For more information:

Poole, Arlen D. "Life of Sarah Bird Northrup Ridge." *Flashback* 57 (Summer 2007): 49–66.

Washington County Historical Society. http://www.washcohistoricalsociety.org (accessed December 8, 2015).

Lottie Shackelford (1941–)

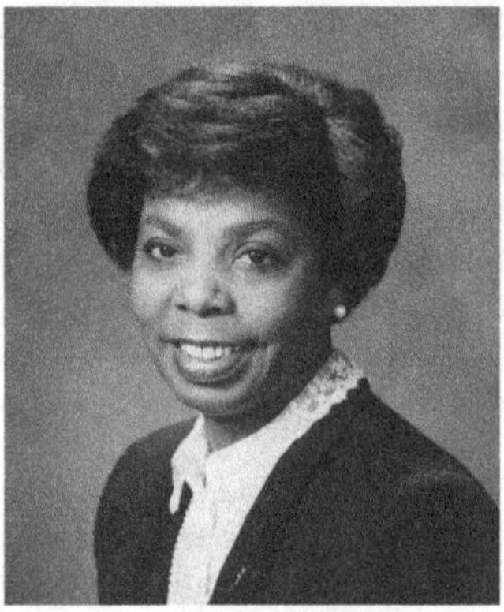

LOTTIE HOLT SHACKELFORD is known for her leadership roles in the national Democratic Party for more than thirty years. She has been a delegate to every Democratic National Convention since 1980, often as a "superdelegate" (a party leader who is seated automatically). Shackelford is the longest-serving national vice chair in the history of the Democratic Party and has served as a fellow at Harvard University's John F. Kennedy School of Government. A member of the Arkansas Black Hall of Fame, she was also the first female mayor of Little Rock, Arkansas.

Lottie Lee Holt was born in Little Rock on April 30, 1941, as one of four children, with a brother, Curtis Jr., and two sisters, Nola and Curtistine. Her mother was Bernice Linzy Holt, who worked in a school cafeteria and for Ottenheimer Manufacturing. Holt's father was Curtis Holt Sr., a truck driver who also worked as a porter and chef for the Union Pacific Railroad.

Lottie Holt attended Little Rock's all-black Horace Mann High School. She graduated in 1958, the same school year of the Little Rock desegregation crisis at the previously all-white Central High School. Lottie Holt developed an interest in science, planning to become a microbiologist. She enrolled in the fall of 1958 at Little Rock's Philander Smith College. That same year, she married Calvin Henry Shackelford Jr. of Little Rock, who was in the U.S. Air Force. They had a son and two daughters before divorcing in 1984.

Lottie Shackelford left college because her father was ill. She returned to Philander Smith when her oldest child was a senior in high school, and she went on to receive a bachelor's degree in business administration with honors in 1979. She was employed at the Urban League of Greater Little Rock; Economic Opportunity Agency of Pulaski County; the Opportunities Industrialization Center, which was formed to promote job opportunities for African Americans; and the University of Arkansas for Medical Sciences as a computer laboratory specialist.

In 1974, she ran for a position on the Little Rock Board of Directors. It was a citywide election, as opposed to the ward system. She finished third in a field of five. Four years later, in 1978, a vacancy opened up on the board, and Shackelford was appointed to finish the two-year term. In 1980, she ran for the seat in her own right and won. Her victory marked the first time a black candidate had won a majority in a citywide race.

She was re-elected three times, with the board electing her the city's first female mayor in 1987. She served in that role until 1991. During that time, Shackelford held leadership positions in the National League of Cities such as the Finance, Administration and Inter-Governmental Relations Committee; Human Development Steering Committee; Budget and Audit Committee Board of Directors; and Advisory Board's Future Forum. She also traveled nationally and internationally to lead trade missions and to deliver papers on economic development, electoral politics, and local government.

Shackelford has been a delegate to every Democratic National Convention since 1980, became vice chair of the Democratic National Committee (DNC) in 1989, and has been repeatedly re-elected to that position. As the longest-serving vice chair in the history of the Democratic Party, she has worked with six different chairmen over two decades. She has served as secretary of the National Association of State Democratic Chairs in addition to various DNC roles such as co-chairing the Platform Committee and serving on the Rules Committee and Resolutions Committee. She was co-chair of the 1988 Democratic National Convention held in Atlanta, Georgia. In 2014, she led the Women's Caucus of the Democratic National Committee.

In 1989, she set out on a six-week lecture tour in Africa, speaking on women in politics. During the 1990s, she was the DNC's vice chair for voter registration and participation, joined political forums in Europe and Asia, and traveled to Balkan and Baltic countries to observe elections in emerging states after the breakup of the Soviet empire.

She has also become a valued asset in presidential politics and as a top-level advisor. She was deputy manager of Bill Clinton's 1992 presidential campaign and was a member of the transition team after Clinton was elected. He appointed her to be the U.S. delegate to the United Nations Commission on the Status of Women held in Vienna, Austria. She was the first black woman to serve on the board of directors of the Overseas Private Investment Corporation (OPIC), an agency that encourages U.S. businesses to invest in developing countries.

In 1994, she became senior executive vice president of Global USA, Inc., an international business facilitator that promotes business opportunities in high-technology industrial sectors. She is a member of civic organizations including the National Association for the Advancement of Colored People (NAACP) and the National Urban League.

Shackelford said, "I was inspired by [Democratic vice-presidential candidate] Geraldine Ferraro, who said you cannot wait and let things happen. You have to plan and strategize and make things happen."

For more information:

"Lottie Shackelford." Global USA, Inc. http://www.globalusainc.com/shackelford (accessed December 8, 2015).

Rains, Judy. "Lottie Shackelford." *Arkansas Gazette*, September 6, 1987, High Profile, pp. 1, 7.

Dorothy Shaver (1893–1959)

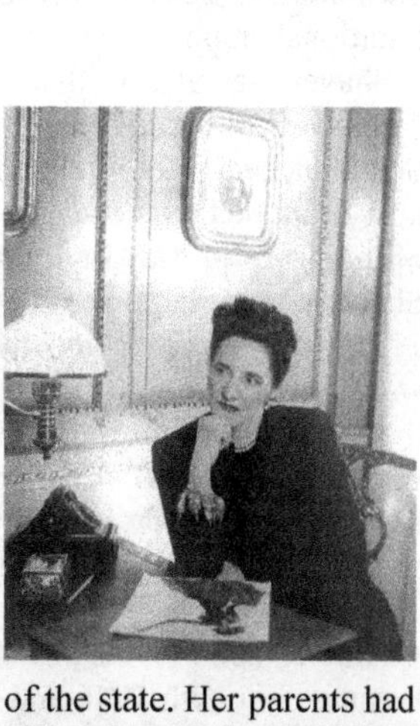

WHEN ARKANSAN DOROTHY SHAVER was named president of the prestigious New York City department store Lord & Taylor in 1945, she became the first woman in the United States to head a multi-million-dollar firm. She was a trailblazer who is credited not only with much of Lord & Taylor's success, but also with upscale retail merchandising in general. The *Encyclopedia of American Women in Business* goes even further by crediting Dorothy Shaver with "both discovering and developing the U.S. fashion industry and creating several new ways for department stores to do business."

Dorothy Shaver was born on July 29, 1893, in Center Point, Arkansas, a rural crossroads in the southwestern part of the state. Her parents had five children—including Dorothy's younger sister, Elsie—raising them to be confident, interesting, and witty. Both parents came from prominent families. Dorothy's mother,

Sallie Borden Shaver, was the daughter of Benjamin Borden, editor of the *Arkansas Gazette*. Dorothy's father, attorney James Shaver, would later serve as district judge.

When Dorothy Shaver was five years old, the family settled in Mena, Arkansas. She graduated as salutatorian from Mena High School in 1910. She enrolled at the University of Arkansas (UA) in Fayetteville, where she studied to become a teacher. Returning home to Mena after two years, she began teaching seventh grade in the Mena Public Schools. In 1914, she was fired after she and three other single female teachers attended a local dance as "unescorted females."

With younger sister Elsie, Dorothy Shaver left Arkansas for Chicago in 1916. There, they both studied art at the University of Chicago. After less than a year, they moved to New York City, which would become their permanent home. Dorothy encouraged the artistic Elsie to create dolls for retail sale, which Dorothy would promote. Elsie produced the "Five Little Shavers," charming handmade creations modeled on popular Kewpie dolls. Dorothy and Elsie opened their own shop, and the dolls proved very popular.

The dolls' success attracted the attention of management from Lord & Taylor, an upscale Manhattan department store. Lord & Taylor is the oldest luxury department store chain in North America, and the first store to locate on New York's Fifth Avenue. Dorothy Shaver was invited to create a store display, which she did by filling Lord & Taylor's Fifth Avenue window with twenty Little Shaver figures. The dolls became a fashion rage with chic young women of Manhattan, who carried them as "mascots." The president of Lord & Taylor was impressed with Dorothy Shaver's marketing savvy. He offered her a position in 1924 in their Comparison Shopper department, with the mission of spying on other stores. Feeling that comparison shopping was ineffective, Shaver reorganized the department to shift its focus toward developing new fashion trends and innovations at Lord & Taylor, distancing itself from competitors.

She proposed coordinating buyers, merchandisers, and advertisers in order to predict, and possibly influence, upcoming trends in fashion. Shifting the emphasis from pricing to promoting quality merchandise, she was also considered the first to cultivate the teenage shopper by appealing to affluent and increasingly fashion-conscious teens. Shaver's innovation, the Red Rose Personal Shopping Service, introduced the concept of the personal shopper. All sales staff were encouraged to offer one-on-one, personalized shopping assistance to in-store customers. In addition, Shaver also introduced the concept of individualized departments or smaller "shops" within the store, in which specialized areas such as bridal, maternity, teens, and petites could be easily accessed. She branded Lord & Taylor as New York's top fashion retailer, departing from the traditional emphasis on Paris fashions by promoting American designers.

Shaver was also brilliant at advertising and marketing. She emphasized storefront window displays, highlighting fashions in fresh new ways in order to attract passersby. She launched extensive ad campaigns to familiarize the public with Lord & Taylor's upscale marketing niche. She also fashioned the Red Rose logo, which became the symbol of the firm. Lord & Taylor set the fashion pace for stylish New Yorkers, and Dorothy Shaver's contribution to the firm's success was rewarded with rapid advancement. In 1931, she became a company vice president, joining the board of directors. In 1937, she was promoted to first vice president. In that position, she authorized what is said to be the first "branch store," opening a full-scale Lord & Taylor department store on suburban Long Island in 1941. This innovation became the model for modern suburban shopping. Dorothy Shaver was named the company president in 1945, becoming the first woman in the United States to head a multi-million-dollar corporation; she held the position until her death.

Among her honors, the Associated Press named Shaver "Outstanding Woman in Business" in both 1946 and 1947. After suffering a stroke, Shaver died at her country home in Tannersville, New York, on June 28, 1959, at age sixty-five. She is buried near her parents in Texarkana, Arkansas.

Like most upscale retail stores, Lord &Taylor continues to follow the standards set by Shaver. Often described as "tall, slender and dressed in a tailored black suit," Dorothy Shaver of Arkansas is known as the "First Lady of Retailing."

For more information:

"Dorothy Shaver (1893–1959): The First Lady of Retailing." *Smithsonian Institution*, 2002.

Keene, Anne E. "Dorothy Shaver." *American National Biography Online*. http://www.anb.org/articles/10/10-02304.html (accessed December 8, 2015).

Krismann, Carol. *Encyclopedia of American Women in Business: M-Z*. Santa Barbara, CA: Greenwood, 2004.

Mary Frances Silitch (1935–)

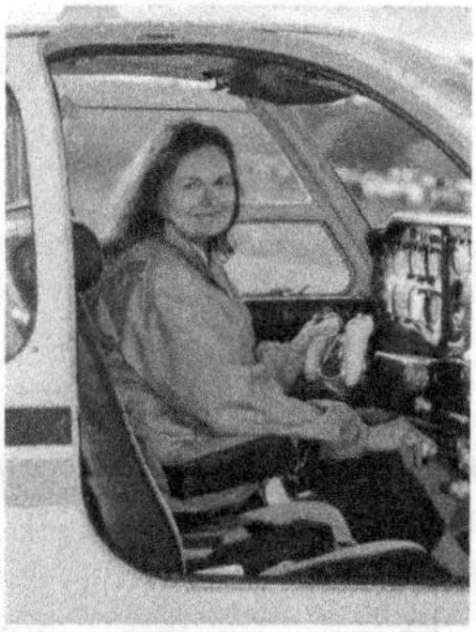

WRITER AND AVIATOR MARY FRANCES SILITCH is the first woman to be editor-in-chief of a national aviation magazine and is the first woman to win the National Business Aviation Association's (NBAA) Platinum Wing Lifetime Achievement Award for Journalism Excellence. She was also named Pilot of the Year by two aviation groups and has been inducted into two aviation halls of fame.

Mary Frances Files was born on November 9, 1935. Though she was born in Little Rock, her family's home was in Parkdale, Arkansas, a small rural community in the southeastern part of the state. Her parents were homemaker Johnnie Caldwell Files and farmer William Thomas Files. She had two sisters, Paula and Susanne.

At age four, Files took her first airplane flight, in an open-cockpit crop-duster over the family farm. She attended schools in Parkdale and in Wilmot, Arkansas, graduating in 1953 from All Saints Episcopal High School in Vicksburg, Mississippi. She went to college at Southwestern (which later became Rhodes College) in Memphis, Tennessee. A freshman English professor praised her work, which led her toward writing. She served as managing editor of the college newspaper, where she was also a columnist. She later said that this gave her good experience in writing for publications in the future. She graduated with a degree in English in 1957 and began working as a secretary at a Memphis real estate law firm that specifically recruited Southwestern students.

She worked there for three years, also enrolling in law school, but left Memphis in 1960 to move to New York City. There, she found work as assistant fiction editor for *Mademoiselle* magazine. She then became an editorial assistant at the *Saturday Evening Post*, and from 1963 to 1965, she was a copyeditor for McGraw-Hill Book Company, all in New York City.

Her career took a turn when a friend told her he was going to work at *Flying* magazine, based in New York. She said, "They were going to teach him to fly. I found a copy on a newsstand and found a few mistakes, so I wrote to the editor and informed them that they needed me too." In 1965, she became the associate editor for *Flying*, billed as the "world's most widely read aviation magazine." She began taking flying lessons and earned her private pilot's license.

While working at *Flying*, she met New York stockbroker Nicholas E. Silitch, who lived on the same street as she did. They were married in 1969 and had two sons.

Mary Frances Silitch later said of her experience at *Flying* magazine, "I broke in a couple of men as managing editor, and suggested that they just make *me* managing editor. The publisher of the magazine told me I couldn't have that job because I was 'a girl.' I was soon asked to be managing editor of *Air Progress*." She took that position, and she moved up to executive editor at *Air Progress* in 1969.

When *Air Progress* moved from New York to California in 1974, she joined the National Pilots Association (NPA) in Washington DC, where she was director of communications, congressional liaison, and editor of *NPA News*. While she later said that gender was not an issue during most of her career, while she worked for NPA, she discovered that a newly hired man she was training received a much higher salary than she did. "I wasn't going to stand for it in my professional life," she said. "I ended up getting a raise."

In 1977, she became director of public relations of the Aircraft Owners and Pilots Association (AOPA) in Washington DC, editing the *AOPA Newsletter* and *AOPA Airport Report* before serving as associate editor of *AOPA Pilot* magazine, executive director of *Seaplane Pilots Association*, and editor of *Water Flying* magazine. In 1982, while she was at AOPA, she earned two Aviation/Space Writers Association national awards for best magazine article.

She also continued adding to her pilot's credentials, earning her multi-engine rating, instrument rating, and seaplane rating. Silitch was recognized with safety commendations from groups including the Federal Aviation Administration and the Seaplane Pilots Association. In 1985, at age fifty, she set a world speed record for light turbine amphibians in a converted Cessna floatplane. Flying at over 180 miles per hour, she took the record from a Russian. Silitch has flown more than 250 kinds of aircraft.

In 1987, Silitch became editor-in-chief of *Private Pilot* magazine, the first woman to attain that position for a major aviation magazine. She went on to become editor-in-chief at *Professional Pilot* magazine as well as contributing editor for *Aviation International News and Convention News*.

In 1993, she was named Pilot of the Year by two chapters of the Ninety-Nines, an international women's aviation group. Silitch has been inducted into the Women in Aviation International Pioneer Hall of Fame and the Arkansas Aviation Hall of Fame.

Silitch and her husband retired to upstate New York, where she still writes for aviation journals. In an interview, Silitch said, "If there is something that you really want to do, you should go for it, and you shouldn't let being a woman, or being this or that, predetermine or limit what you can accomplish."

For more information:

"Honoring Mary Frances Silitch upon her induction into the Women in Aviation International's Pioneer Hall of Fame on March 16, 2013." New York State Senate. http://open.nysenate.gov/legislation/bill/J556-2013

Charlie May Simon (1897–1977)

AUTHOR CHARLIE MAY SIMON is renowned for her children's books, although she also had a successful career writing for adults. An annual award for children's literature is named in her honor. She is generally considered the state's most prolific literary author, with almost thirty published works.

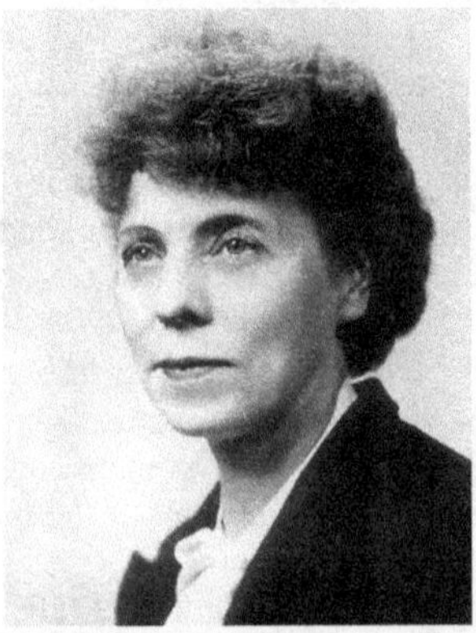

She was born Charlie May Hogue on August 17, 1897. The Hogue family's farm was in a rural area between the town of Monticello and the community of Tillar, Arkansas. Charlie May Hogue was born there in a log cabin, joining an elder sister, Georgia, born in 1895. Charlie May's mother was homemaker Mary Gill Hogue and her father was Charles Wayman Hogue.

When he was about twenty years old, her father had left his home in the Ozarks to attend Little Rock University (now the University of Arkansas at Little Rock), where he worked to trade his Ozark dialect for more standard

English. Becoming a teacher, he went to rural Drew County in the southeastern part of the state, where he met and married Mary Gill. He supported his family by working as a tenant farmer, but he is also known as a teacher and an author. The memoir of his youth, *Back Yonder—An Ozark Chronicle*, was published in 1932. It was well received in such publications as the *New York Times*, which gave it a full-page book review and described it as "a chronicle as engrossing as it is refreshing." It was reissued in 2016.

When Charlie May was three years old, the family moved to Memphis, Tennessee, where she spent her childhood, returning to Arkansas for visits to her grandparents. She received her education in Memphis's public schools and attended the West Tennessee Normal School in Memphis (today's University of Memphis). Hogue's first marriage was to Walter Bernard Lowenstein (1879–1923), almost twenty years her senior and heir to a prominent Memphis family. They lived briefly in California, where Charlie May attended Stanford University. Lowenstein died when Charlie May was twenty-eight years old.

When her first attempt at publishing a novel ended in rejection, she turned her attention to the world of art. Using the inheritance from her late husband, she studied sculpture at the Art Institute of Chicago before moving to Paris, France, to study at the famed Grande Chaumiere. There, she met and married artist Howard Simon, who would become the illustrator of her books. After their 1926 wedding, they returned to the United States, eventually settling in a hilltop cabin called "Possum Trot" in Perry County, not far from Little Rock.

Charlie May Simon's first major work for children was 1934's *Robin on the Mountain.* Published two years after her father's memoir, it was illustrated by Simon's husband. Considered by many to be a classic in children's literature, it concerns an Ozark mountain boy who creates a homestead for himself and his mother after becoming tired of wandering from place to place. The book was an immediate success.

However, the hardscrabble life in Arkansas did not appeal to her husband. Howard Simon returned to Paris, although he continued to illustrate her books. After their 1936 divorce, Charlie May Simon retained the name by which she was known professionally for the rest of her life.

Moving in the same literary circles and admiring each other's writing, Simon's path crossed that of Arkansas Pulitzer Prize–winning poet John Gould Fletcher (1886–1950), who came from a prestigious Little Rock family. In 1936, Simon and Gould were married. They moved in 1941 to a rustic-style home on the bluffs west of Little Rock overlooking the Arkansas River. They named the estate Johnswood, which can today be found on Little Rock's Cantrell Road.

Charlie May Simon's career flourished, and her husband received the 1939 Pulitzer Prize for poetry, the first Southern poet to receive the award. However, John Gould Fletcher soon began suffering from physical and emotional illness, due in part to declining success as a writer. In 1950, Fletcher was found drowned in a pond at Johnswood, an apparent suicide.

Though she continued living at Johnswood, Simon began to travel extensively, with her later works reflecting an expanded world view. She traveled to Africa, where she visited humanitarian Dr. Albert Schweitzer. In 1956, she published *All Men Are Brothers: A Portrait of Albert Schweitzer*. She taught English for a year at the Women's University in Tokyo, Japan, writing 1958's award-winning *A Seed Shall Serve*, the story of Japanese spiritual leader and social reformer Toyohiko Kagawa. Her works range from an acclaimed look at tenant farmers in 1937's *The Sharecropper*, *Art in the New Land* in 1945, *Razorbacks Are Really Hogs!* (1972), and *Christmas Every Friday*, published posthumously in 1981.

The Charlie May Simon Children's Book Award from the Arkansas State Library has been presented annually since 1971. Arkansas schoolchildren in grades four, five, and six vote on the winner. Recipients have included John Grisham (*Theodore Boone, Kid*

Lawyer) and Kate DiCamillo (*Because of Winn-Dixie*).

At age eighty, Charlie May Simon died on March 21, 1977. She is buried next to John Gould Fletcher at Little Rock's Mount Holly Cemetery. Her tombstone reads: "Charlie May Hogue Fletcher—Richer by far are we having each other—Than if each could have alone in the world—Johnswood: By Charlie May Simon."

For more information:

Hagen, Lyman B. *Charlie May Simon*. Jonesboro, AR: Craighead County and Jonesboro Public Library, 1980.

Lampkin, Sheilla. "Drew County's Charlie May Simon – Noted Children's Author." *Memories from the Museum*. http://www.monticellolive.com/drew-countys-charlie-may-simon-noted-childrens-author-whos-who-in-arkansas-memories-from-the-museum/ (accessed December 8, 2015).

Belle Starr (1848–1889)

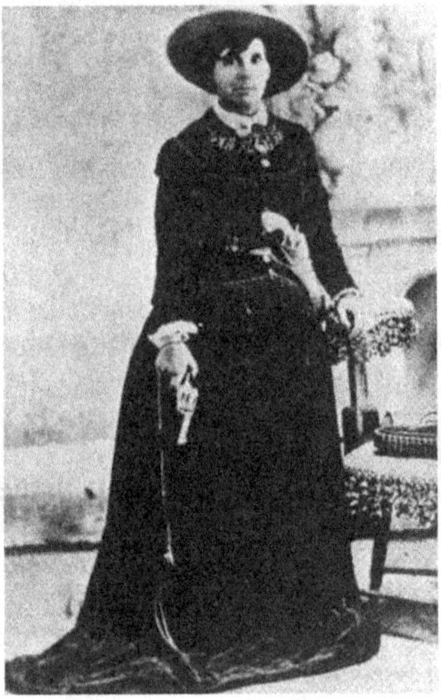

IN THE LATE 1800s, BELLE STARR became nationally known as a notorious female outlaw in America's "Old West." As a resident of Indian Territory, now Oklahoma, she came under the jurisdiction of the equally notorious Judge Isaac Parker, "the Hanging Judge," in Fort Smith, Arkansas, with whom her legend is inextricably linked. Her close friends included the legendary American outlaws Cole Younger and Frank and Jesse James. Her reputation as an outlaw, the novelty of being a female desperado, and her violent, mysterious death led to her being called "The Bandit Queen." When her story was published in dime novels beginning in 1889, her place in the American pantheon was secured.

Belle Starr was born Myra Maybelle Shirley near Carthage, Missouri, on February 5, 1848. Her father was John Shirley, a farmer and innkeeper. Her mother was Elizabeth Hatfield Shirley, who was related to the Hatfield family of the infamous Hatfield-McCoy feud.

The family called her "May" as a child. She attended Carthage Female Academy and enjoyed horseback riding, becoming a better rider than most women of her time. Among her childhood friends in Missouri was Cole Younger, who joined neighbors Frank and Jesse James in robbing trains, stagecoaches, and banks after the Civil War. Fleeing the law, they sometimes hid on the Shirley farm, with the teenage May becoming intrigued by their life of crime.

In 1866, she married another childhood acquaintance, James Reed, the son of a prosperous local farmer. James and Myra Reed had two children: daughter Rosie Lee, called Pearl, and son James Edwin, called Eddie. They moved to Texas, where Myra Reed attracted attention by riding sidesaddle while dressed in a black velvet riding habit and plumed hat, carrying two pistols and with cartridge belts across her hips.

Unsuccessful at farming, her husband joined with the Starr clan, an outlaw Cherokee family in Indian Territory that stole horses, rustled cattle, and bootlegged whiskey. James Reed was accused of robbery in 1874, and Myra Reed was accused of being an accomplice. They fled back to Texas, and James Reed was killed in 1874 while trying to escape from the authorities.

After his death, Myra Reed re-joined the Starr clan and lived in Indian Territory west of Fort Smith. She married Samuel Starr in 1880, at which point she began calling herself

"Belle." She was said to act as a front for bootleggers, harboring fugitives and bribing local officials to look the other way. With Fort Smith having the nearest court of law, Belle Starr came to the attention of Judge Isaac Parker, known as the "Hanging Judge" for his severe sentences.

In 1882, she and Sam Starr were charged in Fort Smith with the theft of two horses. Judge Parker sentenced the Starrs to a year in prison. With it being the first conviction for both, Parker expressed hope that they would "decide to become decent citizens." After she arranged for the care of her children with friends and relatives, Belle and Sam Starr were transported from Fort Smith to Detroit on a railroad prison car, where Belle was the only woman among nineteen other convicts. Belle Starr was a model prisoner and was released within nine months.

After the 1886 death of Sam Starr in a gunfight with a lawman, Belle and one of her late husband's relatives, Jim July Starr, announced their common-law marriage under Cherokee custom. Some sources say Belle decided to do this to maintain ownership of her property on Cherokee land.

At first, she was suspected whenever neighbors' horses and cattle went missing or when it was believed she was harboring criminals, but she was not convicted. She settled into a relatively quiet life, announcing that fugitives were no longer welcome at her home, and was known to help her neighbors when they were ill. She often visited Fort Smith, posing for a famous photograph there. She told the *Fort Smith Elevator* newspaper, "I regard myself as a woman who has seen much of life."

Starr's life ended at age forty when she was shot in the back as she returned to her ranch on February 3, 1889. Though suspects included an outlaw with whom she was feuding, a former lover, her husband, and her son, the killer of Belle Starr was never identified. She is buried on her ranch near today's Eufaula Dam in Oklahoma. Her tombstone is engraved with pictures of a bell, a star, and her horse, as well as a poem by her daughter, Pearl, who lived much of the rest of her life in Fort Smith and Van Buren, Arkansas.

Belle Starr became a legend in popular dime novels, the inexpensive, paper-bound booklets that typically concerned an adventure, melodrama, or romance. The first was 1889's *Belle Starr, the Bandit Queen, or the Female Jesse James* by reporter Richard K. Fox. She later became the subject of feature films such as 1941's *Belle Starr* with Gene Tierney and 1952's *Montana Belle* with Jane Russell. She was also portrayed on numerous TV shows such as *Maverick* and *Dr. Quinn, Medicine Woman*, as well as the 1980 television movie *Belle Starr* with Elizabeth Montgomery. While the facts of her life may have been embellished by legend, she was certainly known in her time as a colorful, notorious female outlaw.

For more information:

Rascoe, Burton. *Belle Starr: The Bandit Queen*. Lincoln, NE: Bison Books, 2004.

Shirley, Glenn. *Belle Starr and Her Times: The Literature, the Facts and the Legends*. Norman: University of Oklahoma Press, 1990.

Steele, Phillip W. *Starr Tracks: Belle and Pearl Starr*. Gretna, LA: Pelican Publishing, 1989.

Mary Steenburgen (1953–)

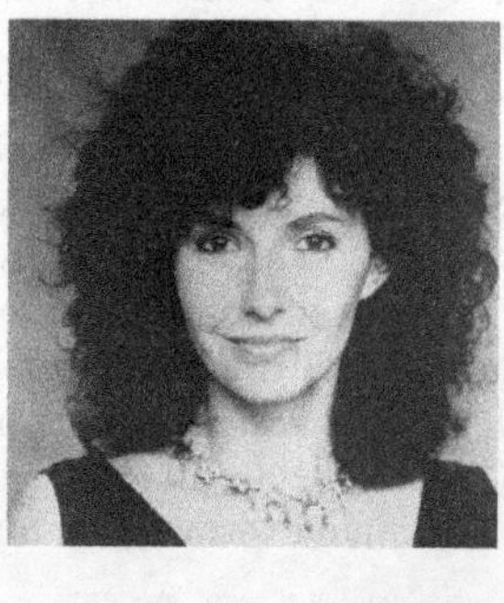

ACADEMY AWARD–WINNING ACTRESS Mary Steenburgen is renowned for her work in movies and television, as well as onstage. As a complete unknown, she was spotted by famous actor Jack Nicholson as she sat in a waiting room with better-known actresses. With about 100 theater, film, and television credits, she received a star on the Hollywood Walk of Fame in 2009.

Mary Nell Steenburgen was born on February 8, 1953,

in Newport, Arkansas. Her mother was school secretary Nellie Wall Steenburgen and her father was Maurice Steenburgen, a Missouri Pacific freight train conductor. With Mary's younger sister, Nancy Lynn, the family moved to North Little Rock when Mary was three years old due to her father's railroad job.

Mary Steenburgen studied dance from an early age, appearing on local television when she was four. She attended Northeast High School in North Little Rock, graduating in 1971. When she was a senior, she appeared as Emily in the play *Our Town*. For her church's youth group, she wrote and directed an adaptation of the musical *Godspell* and also performed in a community theater production of *The Crucible*. In addition, she served as a volunteer at Arkansas Children's Hospital in Little Rock.

She attended Hendrix College in Conway, Arkansas. After her freshman year, she was accepted at the prestigious Neighborhood Playhouse in New York City, moving there at age nineteen. She gained onstage experience by performing regularly at the Manhattan Theatre with the Cracked Tokens, an improvisational comedy group of which she was one of the founders.

In 1978, hearing about an audition for a movie to be directed by Jack Nicholson, she went to the audition, although it was meant for only "name" actresses. While passing through the reception room, Nicholson saw her, gave her a script, and invited her to read. She won the female lead in 1978's *Goin' South*. Steenburgen's work in the movie garnered critical acclaim, earning her a Golden Globe nomination as New Star of the Year.

She also had a starring role in her next project, 1979's *Time After Time*, a film that again generated critical raves for Steenburgen, who won the Saturn Award for Best Actress. In 1980, she married her *Time After Time* co-star, British actor Malcolm McDowell. They had two children, Lilly and Charles, before divorcing in 1989.

She won the Academy Award for best supporting actress in her third film, 1980's *Melvin and Howard*. For her work in *Melvin and Howard*, she also received a Golden Globe Award, Los Angeles Film Critics Association Award, New York Film Critics Circle Award, and National Society of Film Critics Award.

She appeared in a leading role in 1981's highly anticipated *Ragtime*, and she portrayed Marjorie Kinnan Rawlings, author of *The Yearling*, in 1983's well-received movie *Cross Creek*. After that role, she left filmmaking to spend time with her family in England. In 1987, she made her London stage debut at the Old Vic Theatre, co-starring with McDowell in *Holiday*. Her other stage work has included the title role in *Candida* on Broadway in 1993.

She assumed the job of executive producer while also acting in the 1987 film *End of the Line*, which she described as a deeply personal project, as it was the story of cutbacks facing railroads and rail workers such as her father. Her co-star was fellow Arkansan Levon Helm.

Steenburgen has been nominated for major awards recognizing her work in *Ragtime*, *One Magic Christmas*, *Tender Is the Night*, *The Attic: The Hiding of Anne Frank*, *Miss Firecracker*, *Back to the Future Part III*, *Nixon*, *About Sarah*, and *Wish You Were Dead*. She won a Screen Actors Guild Award for outstanding performance by a cast for *The Help*, and a Satellite Award for best supporting actress for the television series *Joan of Arcadia*.

She has also appeared in the movies *Elf*; *Parenthood*; *Philadelphia*; *The Proposal*, with Sandra Bullock; and *What's Eating Gilbert Grape*, with Johnny Depp. In *My Summer Story* (also known as *It Runs in the Family*), sequel to the cult classic *A Christmas Story*, Steenburgen assumed the role of the mother, which was originated by fellow Arkansan Melinda Dillon. Her television work has included *Curb Your Enthusiasm*, *Justified*, *30 Rock*, and *Orange Is the New Black*.

She took time off from her onscreen career to campaign for friend and fellow Arkansan Bill Clinton when he ran for U.S. president in 1992. Steenburgen was a delegate to the

Democratic National Convention, and she became a personal friend to both Bill and Hillary Clinton [SEE ENTRY].

In 1995, a year after working together in the film *Pontiac Moon*, Steenburgen married actor Ted Danson. They starred together in the 1996 television miniseries *Gulliver's Travels* and *Living with the Dead* in 2002, as well as serving as executive producers for their television series *Ink* in 1996–97.

The couple has homes in Los Angeles and Martha's Vineyard, and they also have a residence in Little Rock. Also becoming involved in music and the restaurant business, Steenburgen has been active in the state's nonprofit organizations such as Blackbird Academy of the Arts in Conway as well as Arkansas Children's Hospital and Heifer International, both in Little Rock. She has also supported groups such as the American Oceans Campaign and Amnesty International.

For more information:

"Mary Steenburgen." Internet Movie Database. http://www.imdb.com/name/nm0005460 (accessed December 8, 2015).

Millar, Lindsey. "Mary Does It All." *Arkansas Times*, May 14, 2015, pp. 26, 35.

Lencola Sullivan (1957–)

LENCOLA SULLIVAN IS A TELEVISION PERSONALITY, news anchor, lecturer, and vocalist. She was the first African American to be named Miss Arkansas. As a Miss America finalist, she was the first black woman to win preliminary awards at the pageant and was the first black woman to place among the top five.

Orean Lencola Sullivan was born in Morrilton, Arkansas, on October 29, 1957. She was the oldest of five children born to schoolteacher Macie Sullivan and Richard Sullivan, who was employed by Missouri Pacific Railroad. Lencola Sullivan graduated from Morrilton High School in 1975 and enrolled at the University of Central Arkansas (UCA) in Conway. She majored in speech and theater arts with an emphasis in broadcasting, working as a co-anchor and reporter for the college radio station, KUCA-FM. She graduated with a bachelor's degree in 1980. Sullivan later stated that she paid for her entire college education by winning scholarships from pageants, which also laid the foundation for her professional career.

In 1977, while in college, she began her pageant career. She was named Miss Morrilton 1977, Miss University of Central Arkansas 1978, and Miss White River 1979—the first African American to win those pageants. She was crowned Miss Arkansas in 1980, also being named the Outstanding Talent Winner out of forty-eight contestants. It was the third time she entered the Miss Arkansas Pageant, reportedly impressing the audience with her rendition of the song "St. Louis Blues." She was the first contestant in the history of that pageant to win both the Coleman Talent Award and the Miss Arkansas title.

In 1980, the national spotlight was on Lencola Sullivan when she traveled to Atlantic City for the Miss America Pageant. She won the preliminary swimsuit competition and then made history as the first African American to place in the top five finalists. She finished as fourth runner-up, the highest placement by a black contestant up to that time. (Perhaps due to that visibility, some believe Sullivan was the first black contestant in the Miss America Pageant; however, that distinction went to Miss Iowa Cheryl Browne in 1971, although Browne was not a finalist.) Lencola Sullivan would continue her association with the Miss America Organization through the years as a consultant, emcee, judge, and performer.

Sullivan then served as a news reporter/weathercaster on KARK-TV in Little Rock and KTTV-TV in Austin, Texas. She traveled to Hollywood, where she was cast in a TV pilot show from Dick Clark Productions, though the series was not put into production. She then moved to New York City, making guest appearances on television soap operas in addition to working in TV commercials and industrial films. Her first modeling assignment was in 1984 when she appeared in an ad for Gordon's Distillery. She returned to her home state in 1984 to serve as production secretary for the movie *A Soldier's Story* starring Denzel Washington, which was being filmed in Arkansas.

As a public speaker, she delivered motivational speeches for schools and other groups, an activity she has continued. She has also performed as a vocalist and back-up singer for the Lionel Hampton Orchestra and with Kool and the Gang as well as Stevie Wonder. In 1988, *Jet* magazine reported that Sullivan and Wonder had been dating for six months when he accompanied her to Morrilton to meet her parents. He returned to Morrilton with Sullivan in 1989 for the funeral of her father.

Sullivan sang at both presidential inauguration balls for Bill Clinton, in 1993 and 1997, and has performed for the United Service Organizations, being named to the USO's Board of Governors. In 1994, Sullivan was photographed with Rosa Parks at a birthday party for civil rights leader Daisy Bates [SEE ENTRY].

In 2002, Sullivan married international businessman Roel Verseveldt of The Hague in the Netherlands. Since that time, she has resided there with her husband and two step-daughters. The couple engages in several international business activities. As managing director of the Netherlands American Community Trust, she has helped Dutch companies located in the United States create programs for the improvement of quality of life in their communities.

She has also performed throughout the Netherlands, on Dutch National Television, and at Jazz Club 606 in London. She speaks internationally on corporate social responsibility, diversity, inclusion, leadership skills, multiculturalism, and women's empowerment. She is also a frequent lecturer at Hanze University of Applied Sciences in Groningen in the Netherlands.

In an interview, Sullivan explained why she entered the Miss Arkansas Pageant three times: "The main reason I fought so hard to win the third time was that I thought that I could do something positive for the state." She added, "I'm representing Arkansas first of all, but I think that my experience has encouraged more black women to enter pageants." She said, "It's all a matter of believing in yourself."

For more information:

Lencola Sullivan. http://www.lencolasullivan.com (accessed December 8, 2015).

"Lencola Sullivan." Internet Movie Database http://www.imdb.com/name/nm0838213/ (accessed December 8, 2015).

Louise Thaden (1905–1979)

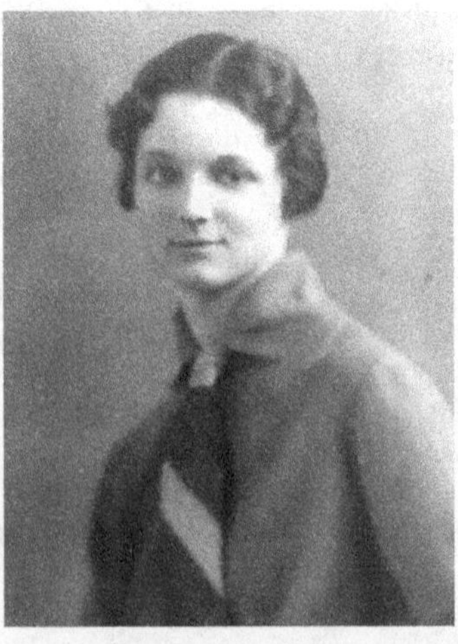

LOUISE McPHETRIDGE THADEN was a pioneering aviator during the 1920s and '30s who held numerous flying records and, along with Amelia Earhart, was one of America's most famous female aviators. Thaden was the first woman to win the Bendix trophy, a transcontinental race in which the formidable Earhart came in fifth. Thaden was born only two years after the Wright Brothers recorded the world's first flight, and she would go down in aviation history less than twenty-five years later.

Iris Louise McPhetridge was born in Bentonville, Arkansas, on November 12, 1905, to homemaker Edna Hobbs McPhetridge and Roy McPhetridge, a traveling salesman. From her father, Louise learned hunting, fishing, and auto mechanics. In 1919, the teenager paid $5 for a ride in a biplane with a barnstormer.

Louise graduated from Bentonville High School at age sixteen. She enrolled at the University of Arkansas (UA) in Fayetteville but was at UA only three years, from 1922 to 1925. She studied journalism and physical education, but she found her calling through a part-time job she had taken in Wichita, Kansas, to help pay for classes.

In Wichita, she met Walter Beech, whose company was the world's largest producer of private aircraft. She was offered a job as a sales agent along with the chance to learn to fly. She earned her pilot's certificate in 1928 as the first female pilot to be licensed by the state of Ohio. Her license was Number 850, signed by Orville Wright. Louise McPhetridge became a sales agent and office manager with the Beech dealership in Oakland, California. There, she met engineer Herbert von Thaden, a former U.S. Army Signal Corps pilot who was working on one of America's first all-metal aircraft, the Thaden T-2. They were married in 1928, and had a son, Bill, and daughter, Pat.

Following Charles Lindbergh's 1927 transatlantic flight, aviation became a national passion, with each new record being highly publicized. Louise Thaden was followed extensively, not only for the novelty of being an attractive woman aviator but also for her achievements. She set the altitude record for women, flying at over 20,000 feet, and set a solo endurance record for women, staying in the air for more than twenty-two hours. In 1929, when she set a women's speed record of 156 mph, she became the only woman ever to hold simultaneous altitude, endurance, and speed records.

Thaden was an associate of pioneering female aviators such as Amelia Earhart and Pancho Barnes, who became her friendly competitors. In 1929, Thaden defeated Earhart and Barnes in the first women's cross-country race, the National Women's Air Derby, also known quaintly as the Powder Puff Derby. Thaden flew the race with her face pressed up to an oxygen pipe to avoid the carbon monoxide poisoning that had killed another flyer. Later that year, ninety-nine female pilots founded the International Organization of Women Pilots, or the Ninety-Nines, for which Louise Thaden would serve in various leadership positions.

In 1932, Thaden and a teammate set a new refueling endurance record. Flying almost 200 hours, they made seventy-eight air-to-air refueling maneuvers in which food, water, oil, and fuel were passed by means of a rope from another aircraft. The pair received national attention, making live radio broadcasts from their plane, which the press called the "The Flying Boudoir"; it is not known what the aircraft of the male competitors were called.

During the Great Depression, Thaden worked with the Bureau of Air Commerce from 1934 to 1935 in creating and marking airfields and aviation landmarks across the nation.

Then came the Bendix Trophy. The cross-country air race was begun in 1931 by industrialist Vincent Bendix, founder of Bendix Corporation, to stimulate interest in building faster, more reliable aircraft. Women were barred from competing until 1936, when they were allowed to race against men. Louise Thaden won, setting a new world record by traveling from New York City to Los Angeles in just under fifteen hours. Remarkably, she flew a Beech biplane, defeating twin-engine planes specifically built for racing. After receiving the winner's trophy, Thaden also took home the women's prize, which had been set aside for the top female competitor on the assumption that a woman would not beat the men. Thaden also received the prestigious Harmon Trophy, aviation's highest honor given to women, as the outstanding U.S. woman pilot for 1936.

In 1937, she became the national secretary of the National Aeronautic Association. After setting two more records for distance and speed in 1937, Thaden received the news that her friend Amelia Earhart was lost over the Pacific. The next year, Thaden retired from professional racing to concentrate on her family. Also in 1938, she published her memoir, *High, Wide and Frightened*, candidly sharing the conflict between her family life and passion for flying. She continued to be active in aviation groups, wrote newspaper and magazine articles about aviation, and flew everything from gliders to jets.

The Bentonville airport was renamed Louise M. Thaden Field in her honor. She was inducted into the Smithsonian Institution's Aviation Hall of Fame as well as the Arkansas Aviation Hall of Fame. At age seventy-four, Thaden died of a heart attack at her home in High Point, North Carolina, on November 9, 1979.

In 1991, Eileen Collins—an astronaut, aviator, and member of the Ninety-Nines, which Louise Thaden had helped to found—carried Thaden's cloth flying helmet on the Space Shuttle to honor the achievements of one of the pioneering women of flight.

For more information:

Mitchell, Charles, and Kirk W. House. *Flying High: Pioneer Women in American Aviation.* Charleston, SC: Arcadia Publishing, 2002.

Thaden, Louise McPhetridge. *High, Wide and Frightened* (1938). Fayetteville: University of Arkansas Press, 2004.

"Sister Rosetta" Tharpe (1915–1973)

SISTER ROSETTA THARPE WAS A MUSICAL PIONEER, performing gospel that was a unique mix of spiritual lyrics combined with what was later called rhythm and blues and then rock and roll. She was the first gospel performer to record for a major record label, gospel's first hit recording star, and one of the earliest musicians to cross over from gospel to secular music. Tharpe has been called the Godmother of Rock & Roll, with one of her recordings credited by some as being the first rock and roll record. Her music was chosen for the National Recording Registry at the Library of Congress, she was inducted into the Blues Hall of Fame, and she was the subject of an *American Masters* documentary on PBS.

She was born Rosetta Nubin on March 20, 1915, in Cotton Plant, Arkansas, a small rural community in the eastern part of the state. Her father was Willis Atkins, who picked cotton and was also a singer. Her mother was Katie Bell Nubin, a singer, mandolin player, and evangelist for the Church of God in Christ. Young Rosetta began singing and playing the guitar at age four. By the time she was six, she was called "Little Rosetta Nubin," joining her mother as a gospel performer in an evangelical troupe traveling across the South.

Her guitar style was influenced by her mother's mandolin playing, and her singing was influenced by popular hymns of the day, such as those by bluesman-turned-gospel-musician Thomas A. Dorsey. In the 1920s, she and her mother settled in Chicago, Illinois, where they performed at local religious concerts and traveled to church conventions around the country. In 1934, at age nineteen, Rosetta married minister Thomas Thorpe. Although the marriage was brief, Rosetta incorporated a version of her married name into her stage name, becoming "Sister Rosetta" Tharpe.

In 1938, Tharpe moved with her mother to New York City. That same year, she was signed to Decca Records and found immediate success. Her songs "Rock Me," "My Man and I," "That's All," and "The Lonesome Road" were the first gospel songs ever recorded by Decca, becoming instant hits for the major label. Tharpe thus became one of the first commercially successful gospel recording artists. These recordings also set the trend for Tharpe's career, alternating between gospel and the bluesy secular music that was attracting a growing white audience.

In late 1938, she was included in John Hammond's black music extravaganza "From Spirituals to Swing" at New York's Carnegie Hall. She performed at Harlem's Cotton Club and recorded with Cab Calloway as well as Lucky Millinder's jazz orchestra, with which "Shout, Sister, Shout" was a hit.

Despite her success, shocked churchgoers were furious at her for combining gospel themes with bluesy jazz arrangements, especially when she did so at nightclubs among scantily clad dancers. Not only was her music itself revolutionary, she also crossed the color line by occasionally performing with the white gospel singing group the

Jordanaires, who would later sing back-up for Elvis Presley. Her popularity was such that during World War II, Tharpe and the Dixie Hummingbirds were the only black gospel acts permitted to record "V-Discs" ("V" for Victory) for U.S. troops overseas.

In 1944, Tharpe's recording of "Strange Things Happening Every Day" became the first gospel song to make the *Billboard* Harlem Hit Parade, later known as the R&B Top Ten. It has been credited by some music historians as being the first rock and roll record.

Tharpe married and divorced a second time, to promoter Fosh Allen, in the 1940s. Her third wedding, to manager Russell Morrison in 1951, attracted 25,000 paying fans to the ceremony at Griffith Stadium in Washington DC, with the nuptials followed by a concert.

In the 1950s, Tharpe returned to religious music but was rebuffed by alienated churchgoers. In 1957, Tharpe left the United States to perform in a European tour, spurring British interest in the blues. In 1964, she toured Europe again as part of the Blues and Gospel Caravan, along with appearing in televised concerts abroad.

She suffered health problems due to diabetes, but she continued to tour and perform even after a 1970 stroke that resulted in speech difficulties and the amputation of her leg. The night before she was scheduled for a recording session, she died in Philadelphia after another stroke on October 9, 1973. She is buried in Philadelphia's Northwood Cemetery. In 2008, a concert was held to raise funds for a marker for her grave.

After her death, there was a resurgence of interest in her work, including a commemorative postage stamp to honor her in 1998, as well as her posthumous induction into the Blues Hall of Fame in 2007. The PBS series *American Masters* chose her story to open its 2013 season.

Numerous musical artists have credited Tharpe with being a major influence on their work. In 1945, Tharpe heard twelve-year-old Little Richard singing before her concert in Macon, Georgia. She invited him to sing onstage, his first public performance outside of church, and paid him for what was his first professional engagement. He later said that her stomping, shouting brand of gospel music made her his favorite singer when he was a child. Fellow Arkansan Johnny Cash also cited Tharpe as a childhood idol when he gave his induction speech at the Rock and Roll Hall of Fame. Many other artists have cited her influence on their work, including Chuck Berry, Aretha Franklin, Isaac Hayes, Jerry Lee Lewis, Elvis Presley, and Tina Turner.

For more information:

Jackson, Jerma. *Singing in My Soul: Black Gospel Music in a Secular Age*. Chapel Hill: University of North Carolina Press, 2000.

Wald, Gayle F. *Shout, Sister, Shout!: The Untold Story of Rock-and-Roll Trailblazer Sister Rosetta Tharpe*. Boston: Beacon Press, 2007.

Blanche Thebom (1915–2010)

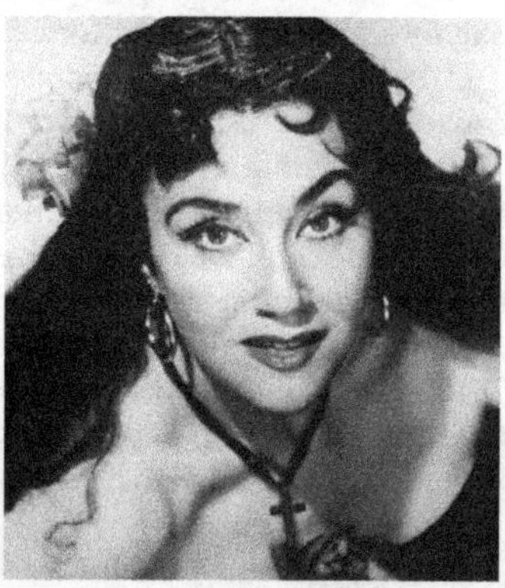

BLANCHE THEBOM WAS A WORLD-RENOWNED operatic soprano, opera director, and educator. With her trademark six-foot-long hair, she was among the first American opera singers to have a highly successful international career, spending more than twenty years with the Metropolitan Opera in New York and appearing in Hollywood feature films. She was praised throughout her career not only for her voice but for her acting skills. Thebom conducted a groundbreaking tour of the Soviet Union at the height of the Cold War. After retirement from the Met, she brought her talents to Arkansas, where she taught and directed opera productions at the University of Arkansas at Little Rock (UALR) for almost a decade.

The daughter of Swedish immigrants, Blanche Thebom was born in Monessen, Pennsylvania, in 1915. (The year is sometimes cited as 1918, though Thebom later said she never bothered to correct it.) She was raised in Canton, Ohio, where she sang in her church choir and also studied ballet, a pursuit she continued until she was in her forties. After attending business college, she worked in Canton as a secretary at an industrial company.

In 1938, she sailed with her parents on a visit to Sweden. Opera star Marian Anderson's vocal coach and accompanist overheard the teenage Thebom singing in the ship's lounge. Impressed with her talent, he arranged for her to study voice in New York and to sign with world-famous manager/impresario Sol Hurok.

After making her professional debut with the Philadelphia Orchestra, Thebom worked steadily for the next three years performing in concerts around the United States. She made her debut with the Metropolitan Opera in 1944 and remained with the prestigious company for twenty-two years, from the 1940s to the 1960s. She was especially noted for her performances in Verdi's *Aida* as well as roles in Wagnerian operas and Mozart's *Così Fan Tutte*. She occasionally stunned audiences by allowing her extremely long hair to drape around her for dramatic effect. Thebom was noted for her attractive appearance as well as her voice. She appeared in Hollywood films such as *Irish Eyes Are Smiling* in 1944 and *The Great Caruso* with Mario Lanza in 1951.

She married Richard Metz in 1951, honeymooning in Iceland as part of Thebom's European tour. They would later divorce, having had no children.

In 1957, at the height of the Cold War between the United States and the Soviet Union, Thebom became the first American to perform at the Bolshoi Theatre in Moscow when Hurok arranged a three-week Russian tour. In Greece, she performed a concert for thousands of people in front of the Parthenon. In 1965, she conducted a New York talk show, *Blanche Thebom Presents...*, which ran for twenty-five episodes. On the program, she interviewed such guests as Marian Anderson, Robert Merrill, Mitch Miller, Roddy McDowell, and Roberta Peters.

After Thebom retired from the Metropolitan Opera in 1967, she continued singing in concerts and recitals. In June 1967, she was named director of the opera division at the Atlanta Municipal Theatre, later founding her own company in Atlanta, the Southern Regional Opera, where she remained until 1973. While in Atlanta, Thebom began working as a voice teacher.

In 1973, she was invited to join the music faculty at UALR, where she taught singing and directed the university's new opera program. Known as "Miss T" to her students, she directed two operatic productions each year. These included *Amahl and the Night Visitors*; *Alice*, Thebom's stage adaptation of *Alice in Wonderland*; *The Astar Experiment*; and *Beret & Per Hanson*. Thebom's final production at UALR was *Cinderella* in 1980. Eleven boxes of Thebom's papers covering her tenure at UALR were bequeathed to Stanford University in California.

In 1980, Thebom was appointed director of the opera program at San Francisco State University. She established her home in San Francisco, co-founding the Opera Arts Training Program of the San Francisco Girls Chorus and serving as chair of the Pacific Region Metropolitan Opera National Council Auditions, along with giving private voice lessons. She continued to be active nationally, serving on the board of the Met from 1970 to 2008 and serving as a judge for the Miss America Pageant.

At age ninety-four, Blanche Thebom died at her home in San Francisco on March 23, 2010. World-famous opera star Roberta Peters eulogized Thebom by saying, "To be next to her when we were onstage was marvelous. Even when I was offstage, I would stand in the wings and listen to her velvety voice....I think she was so happy in her teaching."

For more information:

Serinus, Jason Victor. "In Memoriam: Blanche Thebom (1915–2010)," *San*

Francisco Classical Voice. https://www.sfcv.org/article/in-memoriam-blanche-thebombr1915-2010 (accessed December 8, 2015).

Minnijean Brown Trickey (1941–)

MINNIJEAN BROWN TRICKEY was one of the Little Rock Nine, the first African Americans to enroll at Little Rock's all-white Central High School. Like her fellow black students during the 1957 desegregation crisis, she endured threats, intimidation, and violence each day. She was expelled from Central for reacting to the daily harassment, and she became so well known around the world that she once received a letter in an envelope addressed simply "Minnijean USA," which she says she still has.

Minnijean Brown was born in Little Rock, Arkansas, on September 11, 1941, the oldest of four children born to Willie and Imogene Brown. Her mother worked as a nurse's aide, and her father was a mason and landscaper. As a child, Minnijean went to Little Rock's all-black schools until she heard an announcement asking for students who lived near the all-white Little Rock Central High School to enroll. She signed up to be one of the first black students to enroll at Central.

The black students were told they could not join any clubs, play athletics, sing in choir, or participate in the Christmas program, although Brown had hoped to do these things. Before the first day of class on September 25, 1957, just after her sixteenth birthday, she was primarily concerned with what to wear. Like the other students who made up the Little Rock Nine, Brown was unprepared for the unremitting daily verbal and physical torment they would go through.

As the world watched, troops were sent to Little Rock to protect the young people from angry mobs. The students' names and addresses were published in the newspaper, rocks were thrown through her bedroom window, and people threatened to burn her family's house down, Brown recalled. Each day, her mother gave her the option of staying home, but Brown said her resistance, not courage, kept her going back.

The incident with which Minnijean Brown has been most famously associated followed several occasions when white boys were cheered for throwing hot food on her. In December 1957, she was carrying her tray with a bowl of chili through the cafeteria to the table where the black students ate. White boys pushed chairs in her way and slammed into her as white girls laughed. Brown later said that she dropped the entire tray "accidentally on purpose," earning her a suspension. In February 1958, a group of girls spat on her and hit her with a heavy handbag. After Brown said, "Leave me alone, white trash," she was expelled. She said that after that, a card went around that said "One down, eight to go." She later said that her experience at Central "was not just about us, it was for everyone….It wasn't pleasant, but it had to be done. I don't regret it."

In February 1958, after her expulsion from Central, Brown moved to New York City after receiving a scholarship to the New Lincoln School, a progressive private school in Manhattan. Brown resided with Drs. Kenneth and Mamie Clark [SEE ENTRY], renowned psychologists whose social science research formed the basis for the argument by the National Association for the Advancement of Colored People (NAACP) in the landmark 1954 civil rights case *Brown v. Board of Education*. Minnijean Brown graduated from high school in 1959 and attended Southern Illinois University in Carbondale, where she majored in journalism.

In 1967, Brown married fellow student Roy Trickey, with whom she marched against the draft during the Vietnam War era. When Roy Trickey was called up for the army in 1967, the couple moved to Canada. Minnijean Brown Trickey went on to earn a bachelor's of social work from Laurentian University in Ontario, Canada, and a master's degree in social work from Carleton University in Ontario. They lived in Toronto, and later on a remote farm in northern Ontario. The couple had six children. Minnijean Trickey left her husband in 1985, and they divorced.

Minnijean Brown Trickey continued to be an activist for minority rights. She conducted anti-racism programs and worked with immigrant women. From 1999 to 2001, she served as deputy assistant secretary of the Department of the Interior for Workforce Diversity under the administration of President Bill Clinton. Hoping to spend more time with her family, especially her aging mother, Trickey moved back to Little Rock in 2001, though she later returned to Canada.

Among her honors, Minnijean Brown Trickey has received the Congressional Gold Medal, the International Wolf Award, the NAACP's Spingarn Medal, and the Lifetime Achievement Tribute by the Canadian Race Relations Foundation. A documentary film titled *Journey to Little Rock: The Untold Story of Minnijean Brown Trickey* was produced in 2002 by Canada's North-East Pictures. In 2007, her alma mater, Laurentian University, presented Trickey with an honorary doctor of laws degree.

Continuing to work for such causes as cross-cultural communication, diversity education, environmental issues, youth leadership, gender issues, and social justice advocacy, she has taught social work at the college level and has conducted an interactive traveling program for high school students called *Sojourn to the Past*, visiting historic sites in the civil rights movement.

In 2002, her daughter Spirit Trickey, who attended the University of Arkansas (UA) in Fayetteville, began working at the Central High School National Historic Site across from the school. There, she interpreted the struggle of her mother and the others who desegregated Central.

Speaking of her experience with the Little Rock Nine, Minnijean Brown Trickey said, "It made me really compassionate and made me kind, thoughtful, but also strident in speaking the truth. And saying things as I see them."

For more information:

Jacoway, Elizabeth. "Not Anger but Sorrow: Minnijean Brown Trickey Remembers the Little Rock Crisis." *Arkansas Historical Quarterly* 64 (Spring 2005): 1–26.

Majerol, Veronica. "Minnijean Brown Trickey Looks Back." *Upfront* magazine, *New York Times*, May 16, 2012.

Mabel Jamison Vogel (1905–1994)

MABEL JAMISON "JAMIE" VOGEL was a teacher for Japanese American people incarcerated at the Rohwer Relocation Center in southeastern Arkansas during World War II. She became a national leader after the war in preserving historical items and working for legislation to make up for some of the extensive losses the prisoners experienced. Vogel also wrote and lectured extensively about the Arkansas internment camps, which had been marginalized due to their remote location.

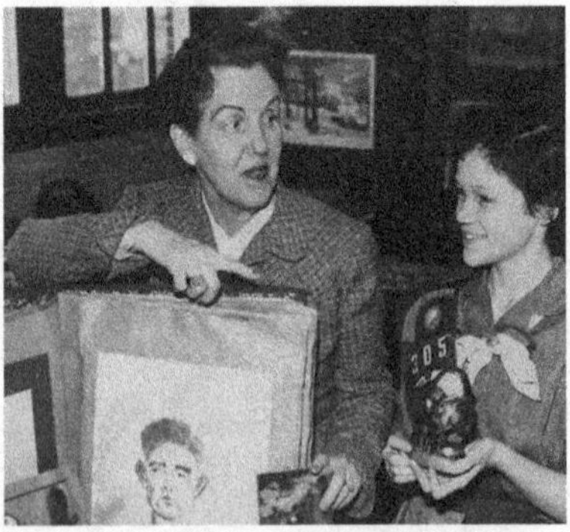

Jamie Vogel showing art created by Japanese Americans at Rohwer to students as part of her education efforts after internment had ended; circa 1950s.

Mabel Rose Jamison was born on September 11, 1905. Although her birthplace was Texas, she spent most of her childhood in Little Rock, Arkansas. She attended college at Arkansas State Teachers College (now the University of Central Arkansas—UCA) in Conway, graduating in 1930. After college, she went to California's Stanford University to study art. She traveled up and down the coast of California to sketch and paint, a rare experience for a young, unmarried woman in the 1930s.

Returning to Arkansas, she became a high school art teacher in Mabelvale, near Little Rock, and taught summer classes in art and music at UCA, as well as teaching for a time at the Normal School of the Ozarks near Harrison, Arkansas. After the United States entered World War II in 1941, she worked at a munitions factory outside Little Rock before accepting an assignment that her family felt fit her adventurous spirit, artistic nature, and compassion for the "underdog."

Jamison, called "Jamie" by her friends, took a job teaching at the Rohwer Relocation Center in rural Desha County, Arkansas, an internment camp for Japanese Americans who had been forcibly moved from their homes on the West Coast. The U.S. government sent Japanese Americans to camps due to fears that they might be a threat to America after the Japanese attack on Pearl Harbor on December 7, 1941.

Rohwer operated from 1942 until late 1945, housing about 8,500 people. Still under construction when the inmates began to arrive, the camp was situated in an uncleared, undrained swamp. In summer, it sweltered in the steamy heat, swarming with mosquitoes. Eventually, the camp would consist of administrative offices, a hospital, school buildings, and communal barracks and sanitary facilities. The camp was contained within a barbed-wire fence, and armed guards were on duty.

Jamison recognized the importance of art for the Japanese American prisoners, allowing them to express their pain in a way that would not be punished by authorities. She purchased art supplies from her meager income.

While visiting Little Rock, she met U.S. Army corporal Herbert Vogel, a Harvard graduate from Brooklyn, New York. He was on his way to an assignment as a guard at a prisoner-of-war (POW) camp for Italian soldiers near Monticello, Arkansas. At a ceremony in her barracks at Rohwer, Jamison and Vogel were married on February 9, 1945, after which Herbert Vogel returned to active duty.

Mabel Jamison Vogel especially championed the artwork of Henry Yuzuru Sugimoto (1900–1990), who had been a noted artist and teacher in San Francisco, California, and Paris, France, before the war. She encouraged his work at the camp, which was painted on sheets, pillowcases, and scrap materials while he was imprisoned. Vogel also helped him after the war when he returned to San Francisco to find that hundreds of pieces of his valuable artwork had disappeared.

When the camps closed after the war, inmates could return to their former place of residence—where their homes and businesses generally no longer existed. Vogel was committed to preserving the work her Rohwer students had produced in the harsh conditions of the camp. She carried trunks full of their art and artifacts with her wherever she moved in order to protect the works. It is said that because of Vogel's efforts, the stories of the people imprisoned at Rohwer were not lost.

She corresponded with former inmates, now scattered across the country after their West Coast homes and businesses were gone. She helped establish a nationwide pipeline for them to support themselves through the sale of art and jewelry they created.

Through Vogel's efforts, art and artifacts from the camp have been housed at the Smithsonian Institution in Washington DC and at the Japanese American National Museum in Los Angeles, California. Although many pieces of art by the students were destroyed in a fire at Rohwer or otherwise lost, replicas and photographs remain to demonstrate the depth of the work by Vogel's Rohwer students. Vogel also recognized the broader scope of the artwork, saying in a letter to the Smithsonian, "I hope more people will realize those things from Rohwer were not so much 'art' as bits of history of young lives in the making during that era."

Vogel became a lecturer and wrote extensively about the experiences at the camp. Her writings have been recognized as valuable historical documents, illuminating both her point of view and that of the internees. Vogel also became an advocate for legislation that eventually acknowledged the injustice of the imprisonment of American citizens, including children who had been born in the United States and knew no other homeland.

Vogel and her husband settled in Cleveland, Ohio, where she returned to the world of art. Herbert Vogel died in 1958, after which Mabel Jamison Vogel moved to Memphis,

Tennessee, in the 1980s to be close to her two sisters. In 1994, Mabel Jamison Vogel died of heart failure in Memphis at age eighty-eight. She is buried next to her husband at Lakewood Park Cemetery in Rocky River, Ohio. The artwork Vogel saved was kept for years by her friend Rosalie Gould of McGehee, Arkansas, and then donated to the Butler Center for Arkansas Studies in 2011.

For more information:

The Art of Living: Japanese American Creative Experience at Rohwer. Butler Center for Arkansas Studies, Little Rock, Arkansas. http://www.butlercenter.org/rohwer/ (accessed December 8, 2015).

Rosalie Santine Gould–Mabel Jamison Vogel Collection. Butler Center for Arkansas Studies. Central Arkansas Library System, Little Rock, Arkansas.

Ziegler, Jan Fielder. *The Schooling of Japanese American Children at Relocation Centers During World War II: Miss Mabel Jamison and Her Teaching of Art at Rohwer, Arkansas*. Lewiston, NY: Mellen Press, 2005.

Thelma Mothershed Wair (1940–)

THELMA MOTHERSHED WAIR BECAME known around the world in 1957 as a member of the Little Rock Nine, the first African American students to attend the all-white Little Rock Central High School. After facing daily harassment from white segregationists, Wair eventually received her high school diploma from Central and went on to have a distinguished career as an educator.

Thelma Jean Mothershed was born in Bloomberg, Texas, on November 29, 1940. She had three sisters and two brothers. Her mother was homemaker Hosanna Claire Moore Mothershed. Her father, Arlevis Leander ("A. L.") Mothershed, became a Veterans Hospital psychiatric aide after the family moved to Little Rock when Thelma was three years old. Of the group that came to be known as the Little Rock Nine, Thelma Mothershed was the only one born outside Little Rock.

Mothershed suffered from a heart ailment since infancy. When she was in elementary school, she had to be tutored at home for three years. She said that from the time she was in junior high, she wanted to become a teacher. Mothershed attended Little Rock's all-black Dunbar Junior High School and Horace Mann High School before volunteering to transfer to the all-white Little Rock Central High. Mothershed later said that when she attended Dunbar and Mann, the teachers would schedule her classes so she would not have to walk long distances or climb a lot of stairs. Her parents expressed concern about her going to Central. The huge six-story building covered two city blocks and held about a hundred classrooms.

Because of her parents' concern, a family conference was held that included Thelma's older sisters, Lois and Grace. Two years earlier, Lois had entered Phillips University in Enid, Oklahoma, to become its first African American student. Grace was one of the first black students to live on campus at the University of Arkansas (UA) in Fayetteville. The family ultimately supported Thelma Mothershed's decision to enroll at Central, with her mother contacting school officials to see if they could arrange Thelma's classes so she would not have to climb so many stairs.

When she registered at Central, sixteen-year-old Thelma Mothershed was an eleventh-grader. At just over five feet tall, she weighed ninety-five pounds. On the day when the students were allowed to tour Central, Thelma suffered a mild heart attack and had to rest in an office. One of the other black students informed their mentor, Daisy Bates [SEE ENTRY], who told Mothershed's parents. They told their daughter she could return to Horace Mann for high school at any time. She never did.

Mrs. Bates recorded that Thelma Mothershed was kicked, shoved, and knocked on her face on the metal stairs. Despite that kind of daily treatment, along with Mothershed's precarious health, she had a near-perfect record of attendance during the 1957–58 school year. Others in the Little Rock Nine have said they were inspired by Mothershed's determination.

In one incident, Mothershed recalls being falsely accused by a white girl who said she had been kicked by Mothershed. More often, she said she was ignored by her fellow students and even some teachers who agreed with the segregationists. One teacher would not touch anything the girl had touched: "If I had a slip to sign, she had me put it on her desk," said Mothershed, "then she would move it with her pencil, sign it, and let me pick it back up."

In 1958–59, which would have been her senior year, Little Rock's high schools were closed in an attempt to thwart desegregation, so Mothershed attended summer school in St. Louis, Missouri, earning the necessary credits for graduation through correspondence courses. In 1960, she received her diploma from Central by mail.

Mothershed went to Southern Illinois University at Carbondale, where she was awarded a bachelor's degree in home economics in 1964. In 1965, she married fellow student Fred Lee Wair from East St. Louis, Illinois; they had a son. After earning a master's degree in guidance and counseling education in 1970, she added an administrative certificate in education from Southern Illinois University at Edwardsville in 1985.

Thelma Mothershed Wair was able to fulfill her dream of becoming a teacher. She taught home economics for twenty-eight years in the East St. Louis school system before retiring in 1994. She has said that when her students would express surprise to learn she was part of history, her response was, "Something historic happens every day."

After her retirement from the public schools, Wair worked at the St. Clair County Jail's Juvenile Detention Center in Illinois and as an instructor of survival skills for women at the American Red Cross Second Chance Shelter for the Homeless.

Among her honors are the Spingarn Medal from the National Association for the Advancement of Colored People (NAACP) and the Congressional Gold Medal, the nation's highest civilian award. She was named Outstanding Role Model by the East St. Louis chapter of the Top Ladies of Distinction. She served for sixteen years as a member of Jack and Jill of America, Inc., an organization to provide children with educational, health, and recreational programs.

Wair has often visited schools to discuss race relations in America. She said, "We've come a long way, baby, but we ain't there yet," quickly adding, "We're *not* there yet. I am a teacher. I don't really speak like that!" She has also said, "I don't mind telling people what my memories are, I don't mind sharing. I think it is good to share with other people so they can know what went on. It gives people a better sense of history."

For more information:

Beals, Melba Pattillo. *Warriors Don't Cry: A Searing Memoir of the Battle to Desegregate Little Rock's Central High School*. New York: Washington Square Books, 1994.

Interview: Thelma Mothershed Wair and Amaree Austin. UALR Public Radio. https://www.youtube.com/watch?v=OjJHEhoZorE (accessed December 8, 2015)

Hazel Walker (1914–1990)

HAZEL WALKER CRUTCHER was a nationally renowned basketball player, beginning as an amateur and later going professional with the All American Red Heads and the Arkansas Travelers, a professional basketball team she founded. She was the only woman known to own, manage, and star for her own pro basketball team. Recognized as one of the greatest players in women's basketball, she was in the top twenty—and the highest-ranking woman—in the CNN/*Sports Illustrated* list of the top fifty athletes from Arkansas in the twentieth century. In 2001, she was inducted into the Women's Basketball Hall of Fame.

Hazel Leona Walker was born on August 8, 1914, to Minnie Chauncey Walker and

Herbert Walker. With her two brothers, Carl and Howard, Hazel was raised on the family farm in the Oak Hill community, near Ashdown, Arkansas. She was a tall, striking young woman of Cherokee descent. She began participating in organized basketball in 1928 as a fourteen-year-old freshman for Ashdown High School. Reaching the height of 5' 9" by the time she was a senior, Walker was a four-year starter, being named All-Conference three times and All-District twice.

In 1932, during her senior year, she led Ashdown to the first Amateur Athletic Union (AAU) state championship for girls. Her team, with several players recovering from measles, lost the championship game by one point. Hazel Walker was elected to the statewide All-Star team as well as being voted most beautiful girl in the tournament.

Walker won a tuition scholarship to play for the "Stenos" team at Tulsa Business College, a two-year school. To help with living expenses, she worked at a soda fountain, limiting her practice time. She led the Stenos to the AAU national championship in 1934 and was named an All-American. Playing on three more championship teams during her fourteen years of AAU competition, she won six national free-throw contests and was named to eleven All-America teams.

After graduation, she became a bookkeeper at the Lion Oil Company in El Dorado, Arkansas. The company sponsored an AAU basketball team, the Oilers, on which Walker starred, leading the team to two championship games. In December 1934, at mid-season, Walker wed Everett Eugene Crutcher, a railroad brakeman. The couple planned to keep their marriage a secret until after the national tournament, because married women were not permitted to work at Lion Oil.

Lion Oil's president, Thomas Harry Barton, ultimately discovered the marriage, but he made an exception for Walker so she could keep playing with the Oilers. When Lion Oil ended its sponsorship of the team in 1936, Walker and her husband moved to Little Rock. There, she played for the Lewis & Norwood Flyers, which lost only eight games in five seasons, earning national championships in 1937, 1940, and 1941.

In 1940, Walker's husband was killed in a railyard accident, leaving her a widow at age twenty-six. She hoped to find consolation in basketball, leading the Flyers to second place in the national tournament, for which Walker was named the tournament's most valuable player. The Flyers team disbanded when its coach joined the armed forces during World War II.

She continued in AAU competition as player and manager for Arkansas Motor Coaches from 1942 through 1944, and as player and promoter for Little Rock's Dr. Pepper Girls from 1944 to 1946. In her fourteen seasons as an amateur, she was named All-American eleven times and won four national championships. She played on four national runner-up teams and appeared in the Final Four an additional three times. Individually, Walker was the six-time national and two-time international free-throw champion, once scoring a record forty-nine of fifty shots.

She moved to the pros in 1946 when she toured the nation with the famed All American Red Heads. Their opponents were mostly men's teams in exhibition games such as those by the Harlem Globetrotters. In 1949, Walker decided to start her own team, Hazel Walker's Arkansas Travelers, becoming the first woman to own a professional basketball team. Her team played serious basketball while still entertaining fans.

Her team appeared at over 200 games a year (triple the NBA schedule at the time), playing only men's teams under men's rules. They traveled from town to town in a nine-passenger station wagon, playing in a different town every night and winning more than eighty percent of their games between 1949 and 1965. At half time, Walker challenged fans to a free-throw competition. She could shoot while standing, kneeling, and sitting. She once stated that in more than 3,000 challenges, she was never defeated.

After almost forty years in basketball, Hazel Walker retired in 1965 at age fifty-one. Her accolades include being named the Associated Press Top Female Athlete of 1940. She was also inducted into the Helms Athletic Hall of Fame, Helms Basketball Hall of

Fame, and Women's Basketball Hall of Fame. In 1959, she was the only woman among the first five inductees into the Arkansas Sports Hall of Fame. In 2000, CNN/*Sports Illustrated* named her the highest-ranking woman on its list of Arkansas's Top Fifty Athletic Figures of the Twentieth Century.

After retirement from basketball, she cared for her parents, gave school basketball clinics, and supported the Special Olympics. At age seventy-six, Walker died in Ashdown on December 18, 1990, after a series of strokes. The tombstone of Hazel Walker Crutcher at the Ashdown Cemetery is inscribed, "The song is ended, but the melody lingers on."

For more information:

Grundy, Pamela, and Susan Shackelford. *Shattering the Glass: The Dazzling History of Women's Basketball Teams from the Turn of the Century to the Present*. New York: The New Press, 2005.

Ikard, Robert. *Just for Fun: The Story of AAU Women's Basketball*. Fayetteville: University of Arkansas Press, 2005.

Alice Walton (1949–)

ALICE WALTON IS A PHILANTHROPIST, businesswoman, and committed patron of the arts. She led the creation of the Crystal Bridges Museum of American Art in Bentonville, Arkansas, which opened in 2011. *TIME* magazine has recognized her as one of the most influential people in the world.

Alice Louise Walton was born on October 7, 1949, in Newport, Arkansas. Her parents were Helen Robson Walton and Samuel Moore "Sam" Walton, the founder of Walmart. She was their fourth child and only daughter.

After the family moved to the small northwestern Arkansas town of Bentonville in 1950, Alice attended local public schools, graduating from Bentonville High School in 1967. She attended Trinity University in San Antonio, Texas, and graduated in 1971 with a bachelor's degree in economics and finance.

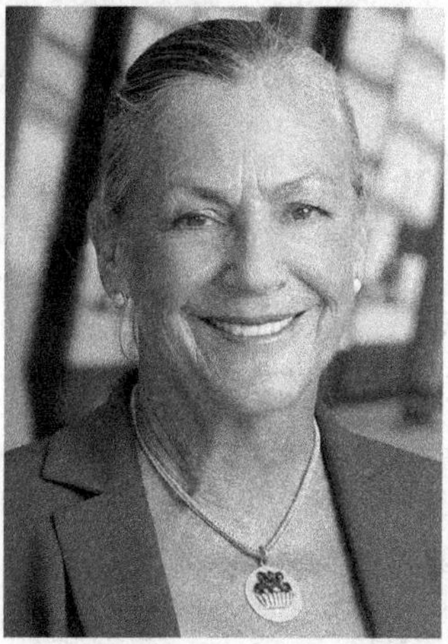

After college, Alice Walton joined Walmart at its Bentonville headquarters as a buyer but found she preferred the field of finance. She began her finance career at First Commerce Corporation and later served as vice chairman and head of investment at Arvest Bank Group. In 1988, she founded the investment bank Llama Company in Fayetteville, Arkansas, serving as president and CEO.

She was the driving force behind the Northwest Arkansas Council, a community development organization that played a major role in developing the Northwest Arkansas Regional Airport. Walton arranged the finances and provided seed capital for construction of the airport, which opened in 1998. For her help as well as support of transportation improvements throughout the region, the Alice L. Walton Terminal Building was named in her honor. In 2001, Walton was inducted into the Arkansas Aviation Hall of Fame.

In the late 1990s, Walton moved to Texas, where she owned the Rocking W Ranch, where cutting horses were bred. In September 2015, sources including *Fortune* magazine announced that she was selling her rural properties.

Walton has been a lifelong art lover. At age ten, she purchased her first piece of art, a Picasso reproduction, from her father's Ben Franklin store. When she was a child, she and her mother would often paint watercolors on family camping trips. As an adult, she nurtured an outstanding private collection.

In November 2011, Crystal Bridges Museum of American Art—founded by Alice Walton—opened in Bentonville. Along with galleries, the museum features spaces for concerts, lectures, and meetings as well as educational venues and library resources. The permanent collection includes works donated by Walton and the Walton Family Foundation, plus gifts and loans from other private collectors. According to the museum, "Crystal Bridges explores the unfolding history of America by collecting and exhibiting outstanding works of art that illuminate our artistic heritage and enrich our understanding and appreciation of our nation and ourselves." On display at the museum are works by noted artists that are not often seen outside major cities, including Asher Brown Durand, Winslow Homer, Edward Hopper, Georgia O'Keeffe, Norman Rockwell, and Andy Warhol. The museum, as well as Walton's vision, earned international accolades.

Walton has distinguished herself in philanthropic activities, including serving on the board of the Walton Family Foundation. She has served on the boards of the University of Arkansas for Medical Sciences and the University of Arkansas Graduate Business School. The Alice L. Walton Chair in Finance at the University of Arkansas (UA) in Fayetteville has a stated mission of pursuing educational excellence on a national and international level.

In 2012, *TIME* magazine named Alice Walton to the *TIME* 100, the publication's annual list of the top 100 most influential people in the world. She has been named Arkansas's Tourism Person of the Year, and she was inducted into the Arkansas Women's Hall of Fame in 2015.

It was Walton's vision that led to the creation of Camp War Eagle, a summer camp in northwestern Arkansas that brings together children of different backgrounds who might not otherwise have the opportunity to participate. Many campers attend at no cost, based on household income as well as performance in school and service to the community.

In his 1992 autobiography *Made in America*, Sam Walton remarked that, of his children, Alice was "the most like me—a maverick."

For more information:

Alice Walton. http://www.alicewalton.org (accessed December 8, 2015)

Helen Walton (1919–2007)

HELEN ROBSON WALTON WAS A NOTED PHILANTHROPIST. Her husband, Walmart founder Samuel Moore "Sam" Walton, said that she was one of his best advisors. When she was ranked as one of the world's wealthiest women, she described herself as "volunteer to community, state and nation." Along with making large charitable donations in areas such as education, the arts, and organizations for families and children, she was the first woman to be named chairwoman of the Presbyterian Church (USA) Foundation.

Helen Alice Robson was born on December 3, 1919, in Claremore, Oklahoma. She was the daughter of homemaker Hazel Carr Robson and banker/rancher Leland Stanford "L. S." Robson. Helen Robson had three brothers and a sister. The family lived modestly, with Mrs. Robson remembered for bringing large pots of vegetable soup to the Claremore elementary school so children would not go hungry during the Great Depression.

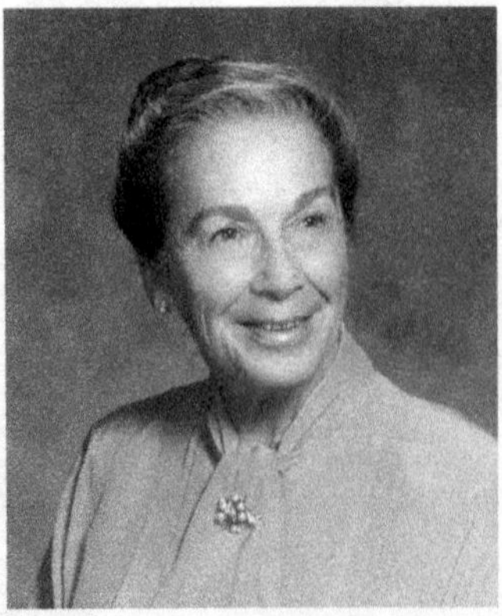

Her parents emphasized the importance of a strong work ethic, honesty, and integrity, as well as giving back to the community. To learn the value of money, Helen Robson was given her own checking account at age thirteen. After high school in Claremore, Helen Robson entered Christian College in Columbia, Missouri, in 1937. Two years later, she transferred to the University of Oklahoma in Norman. She graduated with a bachelor's degree in economics and finance in 1941. She returned to live with her parents in Claremore, where she worked for her father and kept the books for his ranch.

In 1942, she met fellow Oklahoman Sam Walton, who arrived in Claremore from Des Moines, Iowa, where he had been working at a J. C. Penney store. He enlisted in the U.S. Army during World War II and was working in Oklahoma for the Du Pont Corporation while waiting to be called up for active duty. Within weeks of meeting, they were engaged, and they married on February 14, 1943. The couple had four children: sons Samuel Robson (Rob), John, and Jim, and daughter Alice Walton [SEE ENTRY].

After Sam Walton fulfilled his military obligations in World War II, the newlyweds moved to the small town of Newport, Arkansas, in 1945. With a loan of $25,000 from Helen's father, Sam Walton opened a Ben Franklin "five-and-dime store." The couple became active in church, civic, and community groups but was forced to leave Newport when Sam Walton's lease on the Ben Franklin store was not renewed. After visiting Bentonville, Arkansas, with Helen's father, Sam Walton opened Walton's 5¢ and 10¢ on the town square with assistance from Mr. Robson in obtaining the building. Sam Walton opened the first Walmart in the nearby town of Rogers, Arkansas, in 1962. As other stores followed, the chain grew into the largest retailer in the world, but it kept its headquarters in Bentonville, where Sam and Helen Walton resided.

As they had been in Newport, Helen Walton and her husband were active in church, civic, and community groups. The family often went camping, where Helen Walton indulged her love of painting by creating watercolors. Local residents described her as friendly with a good business sense. She was happy living in Bentonville, close to the Oklahoma border, which made it convenient to visit family in Claremore. She was instrumental in determining Walmart's business strategy of focusing on small towns. Sam Walton stated that he considered his wife one of his best business advisors and credited her with encouraging him to offer a profit-sharing plan for Walmart employees.

In 1985, Sam and Helen Walton began the Walton International Scholarship Program, which funds scholarships for students in Central America and Mexico to attend college in Arkansas. The Waltons were also early supporters of the Single Parent Scholarship Fund of Benton County in Arkansas, and they created a scholarship program for Walmart employees and their dependents.

After Sam Walton died in 1992, Helen Walton became even more involved in philanthropy. She presided over the Walton Family Foundation when it made a $300 million gift to the University of Arkansas (UA) in Fayetteville in 2002, which followed an earlier $50 million donation to found the Sam M. Walton School of Business, constituting the largest gift ever made to a public university in the United States. She also donated $500,000 to endow a chair in marketing strategy at her alma mater, the University of Oklahoma. She donated $20 million to the University of the Ozarks in Clarksville, Arkansas, where she chaired the board of trustees and served as honorary lifetime chairwoman. Other philanthropies included the Walton Arts Center in Fayetteville and the Helen R. Walton Children's Enrichment Center in Bentonville, a nonprofit childcare center.

On April 19, 2007, after a lengthy illness, Helen Robson Walton died at age eighty-seven.

For more information:

Trimble, Vance H. *Sam Walton, Founder of Wal-Mart: The Inside Story of America's Richest Man*. New York: Dutton, 1990.

Walton, Sam, and John Huey. *Sam Walton: Made In America*. New York: Bantam, 1993.

Donna Axum Whitworth (1942–)

IN 1964, DONNA AXUM WHITWORTH became the first Miss Arkansas to win the title of Miss America, remaining the only Miss Arkansas to do so for two decades until the crown was won by Elizabeth Ward Gracen [SEE ENTRY] in 1982. Whitworth is an author, speaker, and television personality. She has served on the President's Advisory Committee on the Arts for the John F. Kennedy Center for the Performing Arts and the National Committee for the Performing Arts as well as becoming the first Miss America to be elected to the Miss America Organization's board of directors.

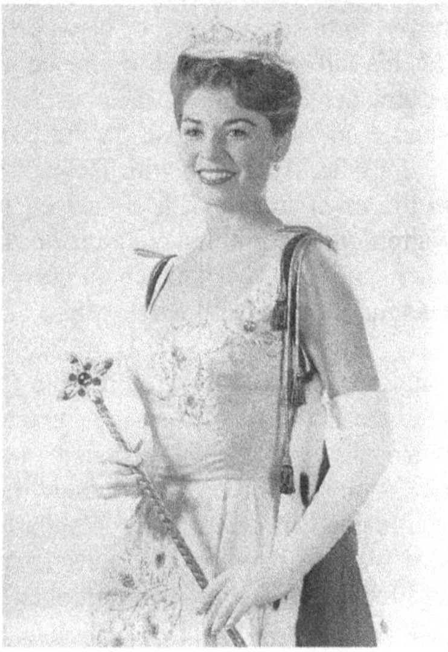

Donna Axum was born in 1942 in El Dorado, Arkansas, to homemaker Idelle Wheat Axum and banker Hurley Benson Axum. She said she began entering beauty pageants because she had an inferiority complex when she was young for being too thin and not having a "figure." She was determined to work at improving herself and enhancing her feeling of self-worth. In 1958, as a high school senior in El Dorado, she won her first title, Miss Union County, when she was sixteen.

While attending the University of Arkansas in Fayetteville (UA), her sorority, Delta Delta Delta, nominated her for Miss University of Arkansas. She finished as second runner-up. During her student years at UA, she worked summers in her father's bank to earn money to buy her pageant wardrobe. She was a founding member of the UARKettes singing group and worked to improve her figure, talent, and personality. She entered and won the Arkansas Forestry Queen competition.

In 1963, during the summer before her senior year at UA, she entered the Miss Arkansas Pageant. She won the swimsuit and talent competitions. At the final ballot, there was a tie for first place, but Axum had two more points in the talent portion and was awarded the title. This victory took her to Atlantic City, New Jersey, for the Miss America Pageant.

For the talent portion, emcee Bert Parks introduced Axum's aria from the opera *La Bohème* as an "interpretation I think you'll find a little bit different." About a third of the way into the three-minute spot, she interrupted her impeccable soprano rendition to say, "Ah, heck," adding that she preferred Paris in the springtime to *La Bohème*'s wintry setting, launching into an upbeat jazzy version of "I Love Paris." During the number, she displayed comedic talent by tussling with her fur piece as if it were still alive. After Parks announced her victory, she was crowned Miss America 1964 after one small glitch: her attendants placed the Miss America sash upside down.

Using her Miss America scholarship, she returned to UA to complete her bachelor's degree in speech and drama in 1966. She then became a graduate teaching assistant there before receiving a master's degree in speech and drama in 1969. In her studies, she emphasized television and public speaking, a background that served her well as she embarked on her career. She taught speech at Texas Tech University in Lubbock and Blinn College in Brenham, Texas. She presented seminars on beauty and women's issues, and she appeared on television shows such as KATV's *Good Morning Arkansas*. In the 1970s, she produced and co-hosted a noontime TV show in Austin, Texas.

She ultimately settled in Fort Worth, Texas. She served on the boards of the Fort Worth Symphony, the Van Cliburn Foundation, and the Texas Christian University College of

Fine Arts Board of Visitors. She has chaired the Texas Cultural Trust, a branch of the Texas Commission on the Arts, and she was a founder of Texas Women for the Arts. She served on the advisory board of the Southwestern Baptist Theological Seminary, working in the areas of development and women's ministries.

Her alma mater named her a University of Arkansas Distinguished Alumna in 1988, and she joined the Fulbright College of Arts and Sciences Distinguished Alumni Academy in 2000. She served on UA's National Development Council and established an endowed scholarship fund for needy UA students who graduate from Arkansas high schools. She served on UA's steering committee for its Campaign for the Twenty-First Century, founding the Women and Philanthropy Committee. Her sorority's national organization named her one of the "Top 100 Tri Deltas in the First 100 Years."

In 1994, she was appointed to the President's Advisory Committee on the Arts for the John F. Kennedy Center for the Performing Arts in Washington DC, and she also served on the National Committee for the Performing Arts.

Axum married Michael Alan Buckley and had one child, Lisa. After divorcing Buckley, she married Gus Franklin Mutscher, who served as speaker of the Texas House of Representatives; they later divorced. In 1984, she married attorney Jennings Bryan Whitworth, former executive vice president of the ConocoPhillips energy corporation. She and Whitworth reside in Fort Worth.

She is author of the books *The Outer You...The Inner You* and *How to Be and Look Your Best Everyday: A Comprehensive Guide from a Former Miss America*. In 2004, she became the first Miss America to be elected to the Miss America Organization's board of directors.

For more information:

Bivans, Ann-Marie. *Miss America: In Pursuit of the Crown: The Complete Guide to the Miss America Pageant*. Sandy, OR: Mastermedia Publishing, 1991.

Donna Axum Whitworth Papers. Special Collections. University of Arkansas Libraries, Fayetteville, Arkansas.

Lucinda Williams (1953–)

MULTIPLE GRAMMY AWARD WINNER LUCINDA WILLIAMS is a critically acclaimed singer and songwriter in genres including blues, country, folk, and rock as well as in "alternative-country." Along with her own concert appearances, she has toured with such luminaries as the Allman Brothers, Bob Dylan, and Tom Petty. She won a 1993 songwriting Grammy Award for "Passionate Kisses," which was a hit recording by Mary Chapin Carpenter. In 2001, *TIME* magazine called Williams "America's best songwriter."

Lucinda Williams was born on January 26, 1953, in Lake Charles, Louisiana, the daughter of poet and literature professor Miller Williams and his first wife, pianist Lucille Day. After her parents divorced in the 1960s, Miller Williams assumed custody of Lucinda and her younger brother and sister. Following the path of her father's work, the family lived in Mexico as well as Baton Rouge and New Orleans in Louisiana, and Jackson and Vicksburg in Mississippi. Lucinda Williams displayed a talent for music, writing songs and playing guitar at age twelve. With a friend who played banjo, she performed a concert in Mexico City at age seventeen.

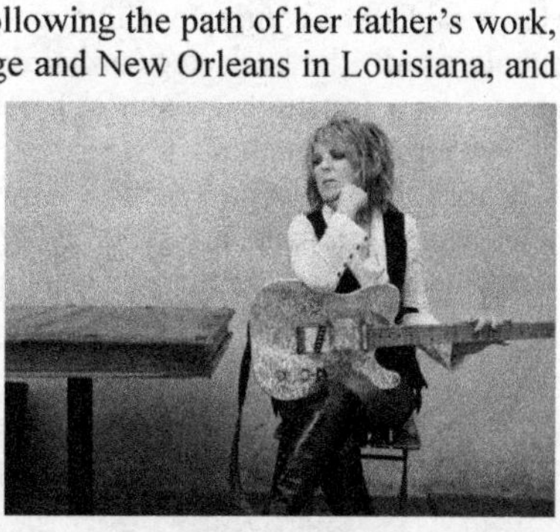

In 1969, when Lucinda was in the tenth grade, she was suspended from high school on various occasions, including for refusing to pledge allegiance to the flag. For her education, her father gave her a reading list of 100 great books.

They moved to Fayetteville, Arkansas, in 1971 when Miller Williams began teaching at the University of Arkansas (UA).

Without a high school diploma, Lucinda Williams passed a college-entrance examination and was accepted at UA. She left after one semester to pursue a career in music, living in cities with active folk music scenes in the early 1970s such as New Orleans, Austin, and Houston. She played in bars and coffeehouses, eventually arriving in New York's Greenwich Village.

Calling herself by the one-name sobriquet "Lucinda," in 1979, she recorded a simple album of traditional country-blues, *Ramblin' on My Mind.* Her second album was recorded in 1980. Titled *Happy Woman Blues*, it contained her original pop country tunes for which she was accompanied by a full band and credited as Lucinda Williams.

Moving to Los Angeles, California, in the early 1980s, she performed with rock bands and developed a cult following and garnered critical acclaim. In 1988, her album *Lucinda Williams* established her as a top-tier musician. It also received praise from the Grammy Awards, earning Williams a 1993 songwriting Grammy for Mary Chapin Carpenter's hit version of "Passionate Kisses" off the album.

Williams was signed by RCA records, but she walked out when her songs were mixed in such a way as to be overly radio-friendly. After signing with a small independent label, she was able to release those songs the way she intended on 1992's *Sweet Old World* album. Reviews noted that the songs essentially involved themes of love, death, longing, and survival. The album yielded songs such as "The Night's Too Long," which was recorded by Patty Loveless, and "Changed the Locks," which was recorded by Tom Petty. *Sweet Old World* was voted the eleventh-best album of 1992 in a poll of critics by New York's *Village Voice*.

Subsequent albums included 1998's *Car Wheels on a Gravel Road*, which won a Grammy Award for Best Contemporary Folk Album. It was followed by *Essence* in 2001; *World Without Tears* in 2003; 2005's *Live @ The Fillmore*; *West* in 2007; *Little Honey* in 2008; *Blessed* in 2011; 2014's *Down Where the Spirit Meets the Bone*; and *The Ghosts of Highway 20* in 2016.

She has guest-starred with numerous artists, including Elvis Costello, Steve Cropper, David Crosby, Rodney Crowell, Steve Earle, Ramblin' Jack Elliott, Jimmie Dale Gilmore, Nanci Griffith, Little Milton, Willie Nelson, the North Mississippi Allstars, John Prine, P. F. Sloan, Chip Taylor, Jimmy Webb, and Tony Joe White. In addition, she performed in low-key concert appearances with her father before his death in 2015, alternating acoustic versions of her songs with Miller Williams's poetry readings.

In 2006, Lucinda Williams announced her engagement to music executive Tom Overby, who became her manager in 2007 and co-produced the *Little Honey* album. On September 18, 2009, Williams performed at the First Avenue nightclub in Minneapolis, Minnesota, and she and Overby were married onstage before her encore.

In *TIME* magazine's issue of July 9, 2001, a feature titled "America's Best" named Lucinda Williams as Best Songwriter. The accompanying piece by musician Emmylou Harris said, "She comes up with extraordinary words for that voice to sing—deceptively simple words like back steps or hairdo. How do you use the word hairdo in a song and make it so poignant that it almost breaks your heart?"

For more information:

Buford, Bill. "Delta Nights." *New Yorker* (June 5, 2000). Online at http://www.newyorker.com/magazine/2000/06/05/delta-nights (accessed December 8, 2015).

Lucinda Williams. http://www.lucindawilliams.com (accessed December 8, 2015).

Susan Webber Wright (1948–)

AS A U.S. DISTRICT JUDGE, SUSAN WEBBER WRIGHT received international attention during the sexual harassment lawsuit brought by Paula Jones against U.S. president Bill Clinton. Wright later made global headlines in a landmark decision when she found President Clinton to be in civil contempt of court.

Susan Webber was born in Texarkana, Arkansas, in 1948. With a younger sister, Missy, she was the first child born to Betty Webber and attorney Thomas E. Webber III. When Susan Webber was sixteen years old, her father died and her mother went to work at a bank to provide for the family. Susan was an excellent student who won a scholarship to Randolph-Macon Woman's College in Lynchburg, Virginia, from which she graduated with a bachelor's degree in 1970.

Susan Webber then received a scholarship that enabled her to return to Arkansas, receiving a master's degree in public administration from the University of Arkansas in Fayetteville (UA) in 1973. With earnings from summer and part-time jobs, Susan Webber enrolled in the UA School of Law, from which she would receive a juris doctor degree in 1975. In addition to being the first woman to edit the school's *Arkansas Law Review*, Susan Webber was a leading candidate to be class valedictorian. It was at this point that Webber had her first encounter with Bill Clinton and his then-fiancée Hillary Rodham [SEE ENTRY].

Bill Clinton was teaching admiralty law at the UA Law School when Susan Webber took his course. At that time, Clinton began his first political campaign, running in 1974 against popular Republican incumbent Congressman John Paul Hammerschmidt. Amid distractions, Clinton lost a batch of final exams, including Webber's. Clinton offered to give his students all a "B+" for the course in lieu of re-taking the exam. As potential valedictorian, Susan Webber needed a better grade. After meeting with Rodham, who also taught at the UA School of Law, Webber took the exam again and received an "A." Webber ultimately was not named valedictorian. She volunteered for Hammerschmidt's successful re-election campaign.

After graduation, Webber clerked in the office of J. Smith Henley of the U.S. Court of Appeals for the Eighth Circuit from 1975 to 1976. In 1976, Webber joined the faculty of the newly formed University of Arkansas at Little Rock (UALR) School of Law, where she taught and served as assistant dean until 1990. She earned a strong reputation as a scholar in oil, gas, and mineral rights law.

During that period, she also served as a research assistant for the Arkansas Constitutional Convention in 1979, and was a visiting professor at the UA School of Law, the Ohio State University College of Law, and Louisiana State University's Law Center. In 1983, she married Robert R. Wright III, a distinguished law professor who had been one of the founders of the UALR law school. The couple had a daughter, Robin.

Although she was not very active politically, Susan Webber Wright headed a local group of lawyers supporting George H. W. Bush in 1988. Recommended by the state's ranking Republican, John Paul Hammerschmidt, in 1989, Wright was appointed to a federal judgeship by President Bush. She was commissioned to serve as U.S. district judge for the Eastern District of Arkansas beginning in 1990.

In 1998, Wright traveled from Little Rock to Washington DC, where she would preside at the deposition of her former law professor, Bill Clinton. With the world awaiting the outcome, President Clinton testified under oath for Wright in the Paula Jones sexual harassment case. The allegations were based on claims regarding events that were said to have taken place when Clinton was governor of Arkansas. Wright issued a protective order, cautioning the parties not to reveal details about the deposition.

Wright declined to grant Clinton presidential immunity against the lawsuit, but she did rule that a sitting president could not be sued, thus deferring a trial until after the end of his presidential term. The latter ruling was later overturned by the Eighth Circuit Court of Appeals. Clinton petitioned the U.S. Supreme Court to affirm Wright's ruling, but the Supreme Court unanimously upheld the decision of the Eighth Circuit, allowing a trial in the Jones lawsuit while Clinton was still in office. Wright granted summary judgment to Clinton in a ruling stating that she believed the Jones case to be without legal merit. Clinton and Jones settled out of court.

In 1999, amid the Monica Lewinsky sexual harassment allegations, Wright cited Clinton for contempt of court, fining him for lying under oath. It was the first time a sitting president was sanctioned for disobeying a court order. In a thirty-two-page ruling, Wright said, "The court takes no pleasure whatsoever in imposing contempt sanctions against this nation's President and, no doubt like many others, grows weary of this matter."

Wright was also involved with the Whitewater investigation, issuing rulings that were both favorable and unfavorable to Clinton. Wright imprisoned Susan McDougal [SEE ENTRY] for the maximum eighteen months for civil contempt of court for refusing to answer questions about Clinton.

In 2006, her husband died. She later remarried and became known as Susan Webber Carter. In 2009, she was appointed to a seven-year term on the U.S. Foreign Intelligence Surveillance Court by Chief Justice John Roberts of the U.S. Supreme Court. In 2012, she announced her judicial retirement effective in August of 2013.

For more information:

"Judge Susan Webber Wright Commencement Address to the 2015 University of Arkansas School of Law." http://www.c-span.org/video/?325460-1/judge-susan-webber-wright-commencement-address-university-arkansas-school-law (accessed December 8, 2015).

"Profile: Susan Webber Wright." *CBS News*, April 1, 1998. http://www.cbsnews.com/news/profile-susan-webber-wright (accessed December 8, 2015).

Toobin, Jeffrey. *A Vast Conspiracy: The Real Story of the Sex Scandal That Nearly Brought Down a President*. New York: Random House, 1999.

ABOUT THE AUTHOR

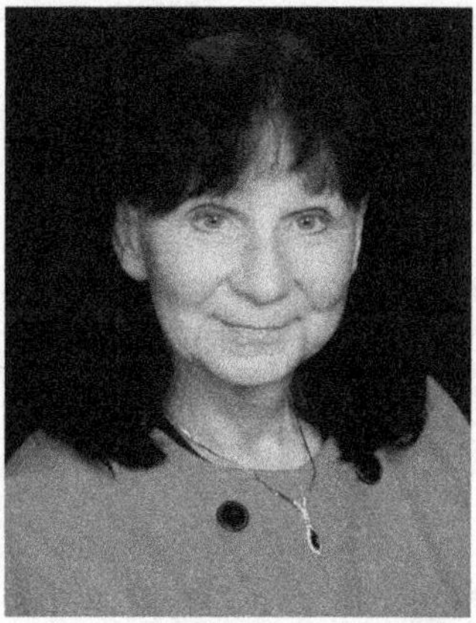

NANCY HENDRICKS HOLDS A DOCTORATE IN EDUCATION along with degrees in English and theater. Before becoming a full-time professional writer, she was director of alumni communications at Arkansas State University, where she also taught English.

Dr. Hendricks is an award-winning author whose book *Senator Hattie Caraway: An Arkansas Legacy* takes a fresh look at Hattie Caraway of Arkansas, the first woman elected to the U.S. Senate, through previously unseen letters and photographs as well as newspaper accounts from the 1930s and '40s. In 2015, it was named by *Cosmopolitan* magazine as one of the "Twenty Political Books All Women Should Read." Her historical novel *Terrible Swift Sword: Long Road to the Sultana* tells little-known stories of the Civil War and was published in the spring of 2015 to the mark the commemoration of 150 years since the end of the war.

Hendricks is also the author of *America's First Ladies: The Remarkable Women of the White House*, published in 2015. Its unique format, featuring letters, notes, and speeches, allows the first ladies to speak for themselves. Lively, informative sidebars place the first ladies in the cultural context of their times. Her next book will be the two-volume *"Tremendous Trivialities": Fads and Crazes through American History*, to be published by Greenwood Press in 2018.

Hendricks wrote and acted in the play *Miz Caraway and the Kingfish*, which portrays the colorful story of Hattie Caraway's 1932 campaign with Huey Long. Its New Orleans production was held over for an extended run and nominated by the American Critics Association for "Best Play Produced Outside New York." In her signature role as Caraway, she can also be seen in the film *Hattie Caraway: The Silent Woman*, which has been shown on public television. Hendricks performs nationwide in her one-person program, *Hattie to Hillary: Women in Politics.* She wrote and performed in the play *Dear Mrs. Caraway, Dear Mr. Kays* and authored a book of the same name.

A member of the Dramatists Guild of America, she has chaired a national playwriting competition. She has written and performed in professional productions of her plays *Second to None* and *Boy Hero: The Story of David O. Dodd.* She is also author of the children's books *Hello Howl* and *Howl's Journey*.

She has been a columnist for the *Northwest Arkansas Times*, *Jonesboro Sun*, and *Citiscapes* magazine, and is a major contributing author for the online Encyclopedia of Arkansas History & Culture. Her writing can also been seen in *American Historic Sites and Landmarks*; *Music around the World*; *Women in American History*; and *Disasters and Tragic Events: An Encyclopedia of Catastrophes in American History*, all published by ABC-CLIO, and *To Can the Kaiser: Arkansas and the Great War* published in 2015 by Butler Center Books.

Hendricks worked in public relations for Texas governor Ann Richards. She is a founding member of the proposed National Women's History Museum in Washington DC. She also belongs to the Southern Association of Women Historians and the Queen Elizabeth I Society. She is the recipient of a Pryor Award for Arkansas Women's History, the Arkansas Governor's Arts Award, the National Society Daughters of the American Revolution "Women in American History" Award, and the White House Millennium Award.

APPENDIX A: Note about Photos

Many people believe pictures are easily available on the Internet. However, most are not of sufficient quality to be published. More importantly, ethical authors and publishers request permission to use photos. In this case, that meant attempting to contact 100 individuals, families, and/or rights-holders.

Pictures were requested from all honorees or their representatives where contact information could be found. If a picture isn't there, it means a photo and/or permission was not forthcoming for one reason or another. For the curious, pictures of the honorees can be seen online at sources such as Google Images.

A number of very kind people have provided and/or granted permission to use photos of the notable women in this book.

Special thanks for the gracious assistance of:
Debbye Turner Bell
Beth Brickell
Rhonda Coullet
Crescent Dragonwagon
Joycelyn Elders
Mary Good
Kay Goss
Mary Cal Hollis
Deena Kastor
Carlotta Walls LaNier
Susan McDougal
Lee Williams-Purcell
Mitch Danton for his mother, Julie Adams
Terrie Davis for her mother, Gail Davis
Richard Reeves for his mother, Mary Medearis

Many thanks to Bob Abbott/Martha Beall Mitchell Home & Museum (Martha Mitchell); Arkansas Public Policy Panel (Brownie Ledbetter); David Bowden/Kelcey Wixstrom (Twila Paris); Claude Bryan/On Track Management (Veronica Campbell-Brown); Marcia Camp (Lucille Babcock); Edmond Davis/Aviate Through Knowledge, LLC (Mary Frances Silitch); Encyclopedia of Arkansas (Iris DeMent); Erika Gudmudson/Clinton Foundation (Chelsea Clinton); Hemingway-Pfeiffer Museum (Pauline Pfeiffer Hemingway); *Hot Springs Sentinel-Record* (Edith Irby Jones); Laura Jacobs/University of Arkansas University Relations (Diane Blair); Michael Keckhaver (Annie Abrams); Library of Congress (Hillary Clinton); Methodist News Services (Theressa Hoover); Tom Overby (Lucinda Williams); Dori Shaffer (Dorothy Shaver); U.S. Food & Drug Administration (Margaret Pittman); Steve Voorhies/University of Arkansas (Donna Axum Whitworth); Danna Woldan (Charlaine Harris); Susan Williams/Highlander Center (Zilphia Horton).

Special thanks to the Butler Center's Brian Robertson (Diane Blair, Hattie Caraway, Elizabeth Ward Gracen, Barbara Hendricks, Elizabeth Huckaby, Raye Montague, Charlie May Simon, Louise Thaden, Jamie Vogel); Cabot Public Schools' Museum of American History's Mike Polston (Helen Gurley Brown, Betty Bumpers, Irene Castle, Blanch Lincoln, K. T. Oslin); Garland County Historical Society's Liz Robbins (Marjorie Lawrence, Edith Irby Jones, Mary Sybil Kidd Lewis, Regina Kaplan, Mamie Phipps Clark); and the UALR Center for Arkansas History and Culture (Bernie Babcock, Daisy Bates, Roberta Fulbright, Deborah Mathis, Patsy Montana, Florence Price, Lottie Shackelford, Mary Steenburgen).

APPENDIX B: Questions for Discussion

1. Were there any Arkansas women with whom you were not familiar before reading this book? If so, who?

2. Was there a particular Arkansas woman who left an impression on you, good or bad? If so, why?

3. How did your opinions about Arkansas women change after reading this book?

4. Did you become interested in learning more about any of the Arkansas women in this book? If so, who?

5. How did some of the women profiled in the book change their particular field?

6. Was there something especially surprising about any of the Arkansas women in the book? What was it and why did it surprise you?

7. What new facts did you learn from reading this book?

8. Are there any of the Arkansas women you especially admire, and, if so, who?

9. What life lessons might be learned from the stories of the Arkansas women in this book?

10. Which of the Arkansas women do you feel had the most challenging life?

11. Were there any of the women you especially liked or disliked? Who and why?

12. Are there any of the women in this book with whom you especially identify, and, if so, who and why?

13. Which Arkansas woman in this book would you most like to have as a close friend, and why?

14. Which of the women in the book best personifies the concept of "Rags to Riches"?

15. Why do you feel it is significant to profile each of the women of the Little Rock Nine individually?

16. If you were to prepare a Living History presentation by one of the women in this book, who would you choose and why?

17. Which of the women in the book do you feel had to overcome the greatest obstacles?

18. Which of the women born in the nineteenth century or early twentieth century might have had different lives if they had been born later?

19. Which of the women made achievements that are still felt today?

20. What major emotion did the book evoke in you as a reader?

APPENDIX C: Test Your Knowledge

WHICH ARKANSAS WOMAN ...

1) … became the first African American surgeon general of the United States, although she had never seen a doctor until she went to college?

2) … was a world-renowned opera star whose fame was increased by her heroic comeback after being struck by polio at the height of her career?

3) … is the award-winning author of dozens of books and helped establish the famed Writers Colony at Dairy Hollow in Eureka Springs?

4) … was a philanthropist in education, the arts, and for families and children, and was the first woman to chair the Presbyterian Church Foundation?

5) ... was nominated for a Grammy as Best Female Pop Vocalist, and was also a regular on Michael Landon's beloved TV series *Little House on the Prairie*?

6) ... was the first African American to be named Miss Arkansas, and the first African American to rank in the top five as a Miss America finalist?

7) ... conducted landmark research that played a central role in the civil rights movement?

8) ... was called "probably the most widely known high school student in the whole United States"?

9) ... did the *New Yorker* magazine call "the single best thing about opera in America"?

10) ... was a nationally known civic leader, the first political action chair of the National Women's Political Caucus, and executive board member of the Women's Environmental Development Organization, working with the United Nations?

11) ... made country music history when her album rose higher and faster on the charts than the debut work of any previous woman?

12) ... was expelled from Central High School for reacting to the harassment of the Little Rock Nine and became so well known around the world that she once received a letter addressed simply with her first name and "USA"?

13) ... is the writer who won a National Book Award for her collection of short stories *Victory Over Japan*?

14) ... was known for her impact on the gospel music industry and her musical compositions, as well as her business sense and flair for innovation?

15) ... has been called the "Rosa Parks of Arkansas"?

16) ... was a pioneering country music singer and the first female country artist to sell a million records?

17) ... became the most decorated Olympic athlete connected with Arkansas?

18) ... was a nationally known journalist and newspaper editor who is often best known for her connection to spiritualism?

19) ... went to a high school that did not offer chemistry, yet went on to become a renowned chemist, industrial innovator, and government leader?

20) ... was the classical cellist who founded the Avant Garde Festival in New York?

21) ... inspired Broadway producers to restore a song to the classic play *Show Boat* especially for her, and became the first person from Arkansas to win the Tony Award?

22) ... was associate director of the Federal Emergency Management Agency (FEMA) from 1994 to 2001?

23) ... suffered from a heart ailment since infancy and faced harassment as one of the Little Rock Nine but received a diploma from Central and had a distinguished career in education?

24) ... was the first female artist from Arkansas to rise to international fame as a painter?

25) ... won an Academy Award nomination for her very first movie role, in *Tender Mercies*?

26) ... was said by *TIME* magazine to be "America's best songwriter"?

27) ... is known for Peace Links, the international organization she helped create, as well as working with First Lady Rosalynn Carter to promote childhood immunization?

28) ... became the first Miss Arkansas to win the title of Miss America, remaining the only Miss Arkansas to do so for two decades?

29) ... is the actress, producer, and writer known for her leading role on the television series *Gentle Ben* and for writing the book *The Disappearance of Maud Crawford*?

30) ... was called America's "Queen of the West" and composed about 200 songs, including "The Bible Tells Me So" as well as "Happy Trails"?

31) ... taught and preserved valuable artwork by Japanese American people held in camps in Arkansas during World War II?

32) ... is an actress, playwright, singer, and songwriter who has appeared on Broadway, performed on *Saturday Night Live*, and was the only Miss Arkansas to relinquish the crown?

33) ... made global headlines in a landmark legal decision regarding the president of the United States being in civil contempt of court?

34) ... was a pioneering aviator during the 1920s and '30s who rivaled Amelia Earhart as one of America's most famous female pilots?

35) ... wrote a book based on her Arkansas childhood, *Summer of My German Soldier*, which was made into an award-winning TV movie?

36) ... was named the Gospel Music Association's Female Vocalist of the Year three years in a row, and whose songs are often sung in churches nationwide?

37) ... is a singer-songwriter whose songs have led to comparisons with Bruce Springsteen?

38) ... wrote the book *Warriors Don't Cry: A Searing Memoir of the Battle to Desegregate Little Rock's Central High School*?

39) ... made headlines after her death with the release of notes about the Clinton-Gore campaign that national commentators called a "treasure trove"?

40) ... is a nationally syndicated newspaper columnist who was a White House correspondent and the only Arkansas reporter to cover the Gulf War?

41) ... was a pioneering researcher in microbiology and the first woman to head a major laboratory at the National Institutes of Health?

42) ... was the acclaimed author whose novel *Big Doc's Girl* is said to have stayed in print longer than any other work of fiction by an Arkansan?

43) ... performed gospel music that was a mix of spiritual lyrics combined with what was later called rock and roll?

44) ... was one of the few people who served prison time as a result of the so-called

Whitewater investigation, and was later found not guilty?

45) ... played Sheriff Andy's love interest on the *Andy Griffith Show*, as well as playing the only one of TV lawyer Perry Mason's clients ever to be convicted?

46) ... was the first woman to become editor-in-chief of a national aviation magazine, and has been inducted into two aviation halls of fame?

47) ... was a candidate for president of the United States in the 1996 election and was a vice-presidential candidate in 2000?

48) ... portrayed a legendary historical figure, was a role model for girls, and was called "the perfect Western actress"?

49) ... is considered the state's most prolific literary author, with almost thirty published works?

50) ... was the first African American woman to become a top executive for the United Methodist Church and promoted the leadership of laywomen in the church?

51) ... received nominations for a Pulitzer Prize, Tony Award, and Emmy Award along with winning several Grammys?

52) ... is the bestselling fantasy/mystery writer whose work was the basis for the HBO television series *True Blood*?

53) ... became the only female member of the Little Rock Nine to participate in Central High School's graduation exercises and the first black woman to graduate from Central?

54) ... was an influential bank president and newspaper publisher whose son went on to a distinguished career in the U.S. Senate?

55) ... starred with Adam Sandler in the hit movie *Big Daddy*, as well as appearing on the TV shows *United States of Tara* and *Switched at Birth*?

56) ... was the first African American woman signed to a contract with a national television network and helped pave the way for African American women in "glamour" roles?

57) ... said she felt it was her duty to tell the truth about the government, and of whom Richard Nixon said if it had not been for her, "there'd have been no Watergate"?

58) ... is the Academy Award–winning star who was spotted by Jack Nicholson in a waiting room with dozens of better-known actresses?

59) ... was a television and Broadway actress who gained national recognition for her heroism when she was sixty-five years old and disabled?

60) ... is an internationally renowned opera and concert singer who is also a leader in efforts toward peace and human rights?

61) ... was a trailblazer in advertising, business, and publishing, as well as being an internationally known voice for women's liberation and the "sexual revolution"?

62) ... is known for her memorable portrayals in the films *Absence of Malice*, *Close Encounters of the Third Kind*, and *A Christmas Story*?

63) ... was the only woman known to own, manage, and star on her own professional basketball team?

64) ... is the longest-serving national vice chair in the history of the Democratic Party, and a delegate to every Democratic National Convention since 1980?

65) ... adapted songs such as "Keep Your Eyes on the Prize," "We Shall Not Be Moved," and, especially, "We Shall Overcome" from traditional hymns into globally

recognized anthems?

66) ... was an international star and fashion trendsetter from World War I through the 1930s, had a movie made about her life, and influenced a style worn by Princess Diana?

67) ... became a nationally known physician after being the first African American to attend and graduate from the University of Arkansas Medical School?

68) ... was the first Arkansas woman listed in *Who's Who of North American Authors* and who established the Arkansas Museum of Natural History and Antiquities?

69)... is a singer-songwriter of country and gospel music who is best known for her hit "The Teddy Bear Song"?

70) ... was the first African American to hold the Miss America crown for an entire year?

71) ... became known for her role in the 1957 Little Rock Central High School desegregation crisis and was portrayed in a movie by Academy Award–winning actress Joanne Woodward?

72) ... was selected to travel to Switzerland as a delegate to a United Nations conference on institutional racism and discrimination?

73) ... broke through gender and racial barriers to be credited with designing the first computer-generated draft of a U.S. naval ship?

74) ... was the nationally prominent religious and cultural leader who wrote, produced, and directed the *Chicago Passion Play*?

75) ... is the art patron, businesswoman, and philanthropist who established Arkansas's Crystal Bridges Museum of American Art?

76) ... became Miss America in 1982 and is known for playing Amanda in the series *Highlander* and its spin-off, *Highlander: The Raven*?

77) ... was the first student to give the Wellesley College commencement address, which was featured in *Life* magazine?

78) ... had six-foot-long hair, spent more than twenty years singing with New York's Metropolitan Opera, and appeared in Hollywood movies?

79) ... was the first woman elected to the U.S. Senate?

80) ... is an Olympic medalist for the marathon and eight-time national cross-country champion who was named the top women's marathoner in the world by *Track and Field News* magazine?

81) ... was the female outlaw called "The Bandit Queen"?

82) ... won a Golden Globe for her role in the hit movie *An Officer and a Gentleman* and also became an Oscar-winning producer?

83) ... was the first African American woman to be nationally recognized for her symphonic works, and the most widely known African American woman composer from the 1930s to the 1950s?

84) ... is an award-winning opera singer who specializes in Verdi's heroines and also supports up-and-coming musicians through her charitable foundation?

85) ... was at the center of a national scandal when she married a Cherokee leader and later became instrumental in establishing Fayetteville's reputation as an educational center?

86) ... wrote books about Arkansas children such as *Cotton in My Sack*, *Houseboat Girl*, and *We Live by the River*?

87) ... was the member of the Little Rock Nine who became an internationally renowned computer analyst, mathematician, patent attorney, teacher, and writer?

88) ... wrote biographies of notable women, often written from a psychological point of view?

89) ... became the first woman in the United States to head a multi-million-dollar firm and is known as the "First Lady of Retailing"?

90) ... was the youngest woman ever elected to the U.S. Senate?

91) ... is an author, lecturer, and publisher who served as presidential diarist to President Bill Clinton, the first such appointment in presidential history?

92) ... was a celebrated opera singer and *Ziegfeld Follies* star who was probably doomed to an early death by a radium-laced costume?

93) ... is host of *Tales from the South*, an internationally broadcast radio show recorded live in Arkansas?

94) ... wrote *It's Your World: Get Informed, Get Inspired & Get Going*!, which was published in 2015 to inspire young people to help make a difference in the world?

95) ... did Ernest Hemingway credit with being the best editor with whom he ever worked?

96) ... has been called Arkansas's "Lady with the Lamp," was honored by First Lady Eleanor Roosevelt at the White House, and gave a speech before Congress?

97) ... is the actress who was discovered and mentored by screen icon Steve McQueen?

98) ... was a movie actress and pioneering female screenwriter best remembered for her work on *The Blob*, a movie title she suggested?

99) ... violently opposed the sale of alcohol by destroying taverns?

100) ... is honored at the Baseball Hall of Fame for her work with the All-American Girls Professional Baseball League, and had a role in the hit movie *A League of Their Own*?

ANSWER KEY: 1) Joycelyn Elders 2) Marjorie Lawrence 3) Crescent Dragonwagon 4) Helen Walton 5) Ketty Lester 6) Lencola Sullivan 7) Mamie Phipps Clark 8) Elizabeth Eckford 9) Sarah Caldwell 10) Brownie Ledbetter 11) K. T. Oslin 12) Minnijean Brown Trickey 13) Ellen Gilchrist 14) Roberta Martin 15) Daisy Bates 16) Patsy Montana 17) Veronica Campbell-Brown 18) Lessie Stringfellow Read 19) Mary Lowe Good 20) Charlotte Moorman 21) Gretha Boston 22) Kay Goss 23) Thelma Mothershed Wair 24) Jenny Delony Rice 25) Tess Harper 26) Lucinda Williams 27) Betty Bumpers 28) Donna Axum Whitworth 29) Beth Brickell 30) Dale Evans 31) Jamie Vogel 32) Rhonda Coullet 33) Susan Webber Wright 34) Louise Thaden 35) Bette Evensky Greene 36) Twila Paris 37) Iris DeMent 38) Melba Pattillo Beals 40) Deborah Mathis 41) Margaret Pittman 42) Mary Medearis 43) "Sister Rosetta" Tharpe 44) Susan McDougal 45) Julie Adams 46) Mary Silitch 47) Mary Cal Hollis 48) Gail Davis 49) Charlie May Simon 50) Theressa Hoover 51) May Angelou 52) Charlaine Harris 53) Carlotta Walls LaNier 54) Roberta Fulbright 55) Joey Lauren Adams 56) Ena Hartman 57) Martha Mitchell 58) Mary Steenburgen 59) Lucille Babcock 60) Barbara Hendricks 61) Helen Gurley Brown 62) Melinda Dillon 63) Hazel Walker Crutcher 64) Lottie Holt Shackelford 65) Zilphia Horton 66) Irene Castle 67) Edith Irby Jones 68) Julia "Bernie" Babcock 69) Barbara Fairchild 70) Debbye Turner Bell 71) Elizabeth Huckaby 72) Annie Abrams 73) Raye Jordan Montague 74) Willa Saunders Jones 75) Alice Walton 76) Elizabeth Ward Gracen 77) Hillary Rodham Clinton 78) Blanche Thebom 79) Hattie Caraway 80) Deena Kastor 81) Belle Starr 82) Lisa Blount 83) Florence Smith Price 84) Kristin Lewis 85) Sarah Ridge 86) Lois Lenski 87) Gloria Ray Karlmark 88) Katharine Susan Anthony 89) Dorothy Shaver 90) Blanche Lincoln 91) Janis Kearney 92) Mary Lewis 93) Paula Morell 94) Chelsea Clinton 95) Pauline Pfeiffer 96) Regina Kaplan 97) Lee Purcell 98) Kay Linaker (aka Kate Phillips) 99) Carry Nation 100) Sue Kidd

APPENDIX D: Suggested Lesson Plan/Activities

After students read the book, suggested activities include the following:

Students will research primary documents to present a short "Living History" presentation of one of the women based on the woman's own words.

Students will write a hypothetical journal as written by one of the women at a significant time in her life.

Students will choose a prop or costume piece that best signifies one of the women in the book.

Students will write two simulated journal entries by one of the Little Rock Nine students, the first describing her feelings the night before her first day of school and the second describing her feelings after she returns home that day.

Students will present a hypothetical "talk show" that might have existed in 1957. Students will portray the Little Rock Nine and assorted white students, with each expressing their feelings before a national audience. Then, "fast-forward" to a current-day talk show with the same characters as adults looking back and exploring how their attitudes may have changed.

Students will research the work of the scientists profiled here and present a detailed report on the scientific/technological contributions the women made to their fields.

Students will present a panel discussion, portraying male and female political candidates discussing how things differ for men and women both in the campaign and after election.

Students will research and bring samples of the music created by Arkansas women to play for the class.

Students will read passages of literature produced by Arkansas women.

Students will discuss athletic achievements by the women in the book and explain why these achievements were important in the sports world.

Students will investigate contributions to national defense by the women in the book.

Students will research and share with the class images of the women in the book whose photos were not available for publication.

Students will seek historical photographs of the women and present a "read-this-photo" activity for the class to discuss.

Students will seek out the final resting places of women from their area, and produce a photographic essay of their headstones.

Students will seek out commemorative sites dedicated to the women in their area, and they will then produce a photographic essay of the sites.

Students will compose a poem, short story, or song based on the life of one of the women.

Students will create an extensive bibliography and/or "webliography" for the women in the book.

Students will create a crossword puzzle and/or a quiz based on the women in the book.

A

B

C

D

E

F

G

H

I

J

K

L

M

N

O

P

Q

R

S

T

U

V

W

Y

Z

CPSIA information can be obtained
at www.ICGtesting.com
Printed in the USA
BVHW081914240120
570269BV00001B/33

9 781935 106951